An Imaginative Glimpse

Princeton Theological Monograph Series

K. C. Hanson, Charles M. Collier, D. Christopher Spinks,
and Robin Parry, Series Editors

Recent volumes in the series:

Koo Dong Yun
*The Holy Spirit and Ch'i (Qi):
A Chiological Approach to Pneumatology*

Stanley S. MacLean
*Resurrection, Apocalypse, and the Kingdom of Christ:
The Eschatology of Thomas F. Torrance*

Brian Neil Peterson
*Ezekiel in Context: Ezekiel's Message Understood in Its Historical
Setting of Covenant Curses and Ancient Near
Eastern Mythological Motifs*

Amy E. Richter
Enoch and the Gospel of Matthew

Maeve Louise Heaney
Music as Theology: What Music Says about the Word

Eric M. Vail
Creation and Chaos Talk: Charting a Way Forward

David L. Reinhart
*Prayer as Memory: Toward the Comparative Study of Prayer
as Apocalyptic Language and Thought*

Peter D. Neumann
Pentecostal Experience: An Ecumenical Encounter

Ashish J. Naidu
*Transformed in Christ:
Christology and the Christian Life in John Chrysostom*

An Imaginative Glimpse

The Trinity and Multiple Religious Participations

JOAS ADIPRASETYA

☙PICKWICK *Publications* • Eugene, Oregon

AN IMAGINATIVE GLIMPSE
The Trinity and Multiple Religious Participations

Princeton Theological Monograph Series 198

Copyright © 2013 Joas Adiprasetya. All rights reserved. Except for brief quotations in critical publications or reviews, no part of this book may be reproduced in any manner without prior written permission from the publisher. Write: Permissions, Wipf and Stock Publishers, 199 W. 8th Ave., Suite 3, Eugene, OR 97401.

Pickwick Publications
An Imprint of Wipf and Stock Publishers
199 W. 8th Ave., Suite 3
Eugene, OR 97401

www.wipfandstock.com

ISBN 13: 978-1-62032-699-2

Cataloging-in-Publication data:

Adiprasetya, Joas

    An imaginative glimpse : the Trinity and multiple religious participations / Joas Adiprasetya, with a foreword by Amos Yong.

    xiv + 202 pp. ; 23 cm—Includes bibliographical references and index.

    Princeton Theological Monograph Series 198

    ISBN 13: 978-1-62032-699-2

    1. Trinity. 2. Theology of Religions (Christian theology). 3. Religions—Relations. I. Yong, Amos. II. Series. III. Title.

BT111.3 A246 2013

Manufactured in the USA

To

my teacher Robert C. Neville,

and

my students at Jakarta Theological Seminary

Contents

Foreword by Amos Yong   ix

Preface   xiii

1   Introduction   1
2   The Trinity and Religions: Three Models   12
3   Comparative Analyses   58
4   Perichoretic Indwelling of and in the Triune God   104
5   A Perichoretic Theology of Religions   152

   Embracing, Rather than Including, Others: Toward an Interreligious Ethics of Perichoresis—An Epilogue   183

Bibliography   187

Index   197

Foreword

It is encouraging for me as a Malaysian-born theologian to see Joas Adiprasetya's book in print. It is not surprising that both of us, born and raised in the pluralistic milieus of our native countries, come to the Christian theological task exercised by a need to rethink the theology of religions question. For various reasons, Adiprasetya's first book shows that Indonesians no longer need to take a back seat to these discussions.

First, there is immensity to the scope of his project. Not only is Adiprasetya taking on one of the most challenging of questions confronting Christian faith in the present time—that related to theology of religions—he is doing so by going to the heart of the Christian tradition and engaging what some believe is its most abstruse and others are convinced its most fecund idea: that regarding the Trinity. By doing so, some might think he is compounding one difficult problem (that of theology of religions) with another incomprehensible one (that regarding the trinitarian mystery). Yet it is also possible that their mutual consideration will be dialogically illuminative. Adiprasetya does not shy away from the most complex of issues. His dialogue partners range from the breadth of the patristic tradition, in particular their legacy of thinking about the doctrine of *perichoresis* (the interpenetration of divine persons and attending ideas), to major contemporary theologians of the religions: Raimon Panikkar, one of the most visionary and hence non-conventional theologians of our time; Gavin D'Costa, one of the most well-respected Roman Catholic theologians at work today; S. Mark Heim, a brilliant, bold, and constructive Protestant theologian; and Jürgen Moltmann, perhaps still the most important Protestant theologian alive. Lesser thinkers or novice theologians starting out in the guild will focus their initial gaze usually on one major figure but Adiprasetya deftly handles the Panikkarian *oeuvre*, responsibly and respectfully engages with the shifts in D'Costa's thinking, admirably builds on the openings afforded by Heim's work while avoiding the major pitfall identified by his critics, and creatively draws into the mix the robustly trinitarian theology (robust precisely because of the developed pneumatology) of Moltmann. In addition, he does all this by crossing back and forth over the centuries with ease. As such, the following pages reflect a mastery of the tradition's literature that few theologians display, even into their second or later books.

Second, there is an imaginativeness at work at various levels in this book. The overall intuition is itself stunning both in its simplicity and in its complexity. Adiprasetya documents the various alternatives well but shows why the various exclusivisms, inclusivisms, and pluralisms nevertheless are straining to give way to what is now only dimly yet discerned, which he simply calls a post-pluralist perspective. More technically, of course, he presents a trinitarian and perichoretic theology of religions that imaginatively navigates the epistemological, ontological, and theological issues intertwined in this field of inquiry. Yet this is a disciplined imagination. Our theologian of the religions does not stray onto the many tangents that open up because he works intentionally and consistently at articulating a theological view of religious pluralism that remains committed to Christian faith while yet open to other religious self-understanding. This means that the critical and dialectical analysis that occurs at each turn—whether when interacting with his primary or secondary interlocutors, or of assessing the viability of the theological model being deployed, or of anticipating the reception and application of the overall proposal—is constantly interrogated according to these two criteria. Hence the argumentation itself respectfully but not uncritically engages the work that has gone before while boldly charting a constructive path forward—all with a profound humility reflecting awareness of our present post-metaphysical, post-Enlightenment, and post-modern climate. All of this to say that on all of these convoluted fronts Adiprasetya models what it means to think creatively and constructively within the Christian theological tradition in ways that are relevant to and engaging of the contemporary challenges in a global context.

Third, then, *An Imaginative Glimpse* ought to be variously inspirational. Biblical, philosophical, historical, and systematic theologians will want to weigh in on the proposal. Adiprasetya's thesis is innovative but yet sufficiently plausible to command such attention. If it is to fulfill its promise, it will need to run the gauntlet of theological criticism, especially from those who are best equipped to evaluate the degree to which what is suggested conforms to the criterion of Christian faithfulness, in all of its many dimensions, that is at the heart of this book. Beyond this, those involved in the interreligious dialogue and engaged in the interfaith encounter in its various venues and forums will also need to weigh on in the helpfulness of

Foreword

the basic ideas. Along these same lines, missiologists, theologians of mission, and those engaged in interfaith mission will want to consider if and how this proposal empowers appropriate Christian witness in a pluralistic world. Last but certainly not least, comparative theologians ought to assess the dialogical potential of *An Imaginative Glimpse*, whether it enables that authentic interaction with those in other faiths that is centrally motivating its author. The point is that Adiprasetya's work ought to inspire responses at many levels.

The Christian center of gravity is shifting from the Euro-American West to the global South. Christian theology is itself gradually also evidencing similar shifts. The emergence of theologians in the majority world is one sign of how globalizing forces and factors are shaping a different type of Christianity as a third millennium world religion. Joas Adiprasetya shows in this volume that a new generation of theologians is emerging in Southeast Asia and Oceania who will be able to provide capable leadership for the global theological conversation into the middle of the twenty-first century. What he brings is not only for Indonesian theologians—although they will certainly gain much from it—but also for all who are concerned about Christian faith in a pluralistic world, as well as the ongoing work of Christian theology in general. Take up and read, and may the conversation continue . . .

Amos Yong
Dean of the School of Divinity and
J. Rodman Williams Professor of Theology
Regent University, Virginia Beach

Preface

FOR SOME TIME NOW, the central issue engaged in this book has been widely addressed by theologians of religions who struggle with the impasse of the classical typology of exclusivism, inclusivism and pluralism. Following the trails left by Raimundo Panikkar, Gavin D'Costa, and S. Mark Heim, I try to answer the following question: how can we employ the Christian doctrine of the Trinity as a creative tool in dealing with the fact of religious diversity? Emerging from this research is an imaginative construction of a perichoretic theology of religion, through which we are able to respect diverse religious traditions on their own terms, while at the same time still remaining faithful to the Christian belief rooted in the Trinity. What I offer in this book is an imaginative glimpse that sees all religious tradition, each in its unique and different way, participating in the multidimensional Trinitarian perichoresis. In proposing my idea, therefore, I am very much indebted to Panikkar, D'Costa, and Heim—my three conversation partners in this book. On the one hand, I have learnt from each of these theologians and, on the other hand, this book is my attempt to extend the conversation to a point they have not yet reached.

This book can also be imagined as a junction of two major highways in Christian theology—theology of religions and Trinitarian theology. Yet, there are small roads around the junction: church fathers, Jürgen Moltmann's theology, Richard Kearney's philosophy of the God who may be, and many others. I have taken all those to the place where the readers can, hopefully, if I have done my job well, glimpse the beauty of diverse religions in the embrace of the Triune God. The readers might also sense my passion for such an imaginative glimpse, particularly if they understand the depth of my sadness over the interreligious situation in my own country, Indonesia. Such a feeling is so profound that I have not even discussed it theoretically. Yet, it was *always* there, behind every word I have written.

In the long process of development from theoretical thinking to a dissertation, and from a dissertation to a book, I'd like to express my gratitude to my *doktorvater*, Professor Robert C. Neville, for his fatherly friendship

Preface

and scholarly guidance during my doctoral study at the School of Theology, Boston University. Since I met him for the first time, he has never ceased to amaze me with his philosophical clarity and theological creativity. I was also privileged to work as assistant to Dr. Kirk Wegter-McNelly and Dr. Shelly Rambo. From all three teachers I have learnt very much how to teach and how to theologize creatively and imaginatively.

It was also a privilege to have my early thoughts challenged by several other theologians at the 2007 Asian Theological Summer Institute, namely: Eleazar Fernandez, Kwok Pui Lan, Andrew Sung Park, J. Paul Rajashekar and R. S. Sugirtharajah. Special thanks go to Professor Amos Yong, who encouraged me to publish my dissertation. He was also so kind as to write the Foreword.

My enormous debt of gratitude to Catherine Hudak can hardly be repaid. She helped me with the proofreading of the manuscript as well as providing me with many substantive challenges which helped clarify my arguments. Krishana Ann Suckau and Rebecca Young have also helped me with proofreading some parts of this dissertation. My thanks go out to them. My heartfelt appreciation also to my colleagues and students at Jakarta Theological Seminary, with whom I have been experiencing the beauty of doing theology in a lovely, communal environment.

I'd like also to express my sincere thanks to the publisher, Pickwick Publications, an imprint of Wipf & Stock Publishers, for their wonderful cooperation and meticulous processing of the manuscript. I want to thank my editor, Robin Parry, for his expert guidance and shared interest in the Trinitarian theology.

Finally, none of this could have been accomplished without the encouragement, joy, and patience of my beloved family: Lito, Dio, Dillion, and my lifelong companion, Sofie. *Aku menyayangi kalian semua!*

1

Introduction

THIS BOOK CRITICALLY APPLIES THE COMPLEX TRINITARIAN DOCTRINE OF *perichoresis* to the issue of religious plurality. The Greek word *perichoresis* refers to the mutual indwelling or coinherence of two or more persons (in the Trinity) or natures (in the person of Christ) or beings (in the case of God-world relationship), where each interpenetrates the others without confusion, separation, or division.[1] The classical understanding of the doctrine, as it appears in the Eastern Orthodox tradition, emphasizes the perichoretic relation in the hypostatic union of Christ's two natures in the incarnation (*nature-perichoresis*) and the perichoretic relations between the persons of the Trinity (*person-perichoresis*).[2] There is another type of perichoretic relation, which I call *reality-perichoresis*, referring to God's cosmological embrace of the world that makes it possible for the world to participate in the inner life of God. Although the third perichoretic relation has not received as much attention as the other two, it nonetheless appeared consistently in the writings of the Orthodox church fathers.

Since the focus of the book is on the issue of religious plurality, it needs to be clearly understood from the beginning that any Christian theology of religions should maintain dialectically the commitment to Christian truth and openness to the truths of other religious traditions. Based on this

---

1. The word is derived from the Greek, *perichoreo* ("to encompass") and not from the word *perichoreuo* ("to dance around"), although the latter illustrates well the dynamic sense of perichoresis. The Greek word is later translated into Latin as *circumincessio* (from *circum-incedere*: to permeate or interpenetrate) and *circuminsessio* (from *circum-in-sedere*: to be seated); the former expresses a more dynamic and active indwelling. LaCugna, *God for Us*, 272; Hunt, *Trinity*, 244.

2. I borrow the distinction between the terms nature-perichoresis and person-perichoresis from Oliver D. Crisp, *Divinity and Humanity*.

conviction, my thesis is that, within a creative appropriation of the doctrine of the Trinity, the concept of perichoresis can function as the fundamental principle of the plurality of the world's religions, such that they can be reconciled as different dimensions of one complex perichoretic reality.

In my attempt to prove my thesis, I will demonstrate the plausibility of my model of perichoretic theology of religions in comparison with other Trinitarian theologies of religions. To do so, a critical analysis of three other models, proposed by Raimundo Panikkar, Gavin D'Costa, and S. Mark Heim, will be in order. I will demonstrate that all employ the Trinity as the central category for theology of religions, yet each of them arrives at a very different explanatory model of how the Trinity relates to the multiple religious traditions and how the doctrine becomes the principle of differentiation among those multiple religious traditions.

Significance of the Study

This study is significant in furthering the conversation within the contemporary Trinitarian theology of religions. The term "Trinitarian theology of religions" points to one of the most recent trends in Christian theology merging two significant developments in the twentieth century, namely, the discipline of theology of religions and the revival of the doctrine of the Trinity.[3] Thus, it is indispensable to demonstrate in brief the recent developments in both fields and how they become the proper contexts of this study.

For a long period of time, theology of religions has been dominated by the typology of exclusivism, inclusivism, and pluralism.[4] Recently, however, this way of positing various attitudes toward other religions from within Christianity has become the target of strong criticisms. Perry

---

3. Veli-Matti Kärkkäinen, *Religious Pluralism*, is the first scholar to survey several theologians who employ the Trinity in their works on theology of religions.

4. Alan Race is the originator of this typology; see Race, *Religious Pluralism*. In 1986, D'Costa follows Race's typology although in different order; see D'Costa, *Religious Pluralism*. Since then, the typology has become a standard in academic discourse. In the Christian context, the *exclusivist* is one who believes that the ultimately saving truth can only be found in and through Jesus Christ, while the other religions cannot provide valid ways to salvation. Someone is an *inclusivist* if she believes that Jesus Christ is the normative savior, although people from other religious traditions could also be saved by Jesus Christ through their own religious traditions. In the other words, other religious paths are considered valid insofar as they are fulfilled by Christ's saving work. The *pluralist* is one who believes that each religious tradition is an equally valid, effective, and final vehicle of salvation.

Introduction

Schmidt-Leukel has surveyed the various criticisms and mapped them into eight major categories.

> 1. The typology has an inconsistent structure, "because the positions are not of the same genre and do not address the same question." 2. The typology is misleading, because it obscures or misses the real issues of a theology of religions. 3. The typology is too narrow. There are more than three options . . . 4. The typology is too broad. There are not really three options but only one . . . 5. The typology is too coarse or abstract. It does not do justice to the more complex and nuanced reality of real theologies . . . 6. The typology is misleading, because it does not do justice to the radical diversity of the religions . . . 7. The typology is offensive. 8. The typology is pointless, because we are not in a position to choose any of these options and therefore have to refrain from all of them.[5]

Although particular rebuttals may be developed in response to any of the objections, it is clear that together they help us to see fundamental flaws in the classical typology as a whole. In addition to the discontent with the classical typology, the contemporary discourse in theology of religions is marked by the emergence of theologians who take a critical stance toward pluralistic theology.[6] The proponents of the position that is often called "post-pluralism" have at least two things in common.[7] First, "they defend the rights of religions to hold on their own, mutually inconsistent truth claims," and second, "they can evaluate and encounter other faiths only from a Christian perspective."[8]

These two commonalities can be seen in the models proposed by Panikkar, D'Costa, and Heim. On the one hand, each argues that all religions are mutually incommensurable. This attitude certainly shows their willingness to accept other religions in their own terms. On the other hand, however,

---

5. Schmidt-Leukel, "Tripolar Typology," 14–18.

6. It is not coincidental that, generally speaking, critiques of the classical typology have been made by people who are also critical of the pluralistic model expounded in the typology. Alan Race proposes the typology in order to show the superiority of pluralistic model over the two others; see Race, *Religious Pluralism*.

7. Heim, *Salvations*, 225; Komulainen, *Emerging*, 10–17.

8. Komulainen, *Emerging*, 12. Komulainen also argues that post-pluralism can be viewed as "an application of so-called post-liberalist theology in the field of the theology of religion." Komulainen, *Emerging*, 13. Knitter, *Introducing*, 178–90, comes to the same observation. Moreover, he tries to replace the classical typology by proposing a new one consisting of Replacement, Fulfillment, Mutuality, and Acceptance models. It is clear that Komulainen's post-pluralism is a different name for the Knitter's Acceptance Model.

An Imaginative Glimpse

each believes that there is no non-tradition-specific or neutral approach toward the plurality of religions. It is precisely for this reason that they all employ the Christian Trinity as their starting point for theology of religions.[9]

Looking at the second field, Trinitarian theology, we can find that after the so-called "rediscovery" of the doctrine of the Trinity in the twentieth century, commonly credited to Karl Barth and Karl Rahner, Trinitarian theology in the twentieth and twenty-first centuries has developed in various directions and has become the central category not only in systematic theology, but also in other fields, such as ecological theology,[10] liberation theology,[11] feminist theology,[12] pastoral theology,[13] ecclesiology,[14] and many others.[15] The linkage of the Trinitarian theology to theology of religions, which is the focus of the book, is also a part of this new development.

Many of those who attempt to perform a mutual and creative conversation between the doctrine of the Trinity and other fields of theology have taken Social Trinitarianism as their basic model. This has led Leonardo Boff, for example, to employ the communal-relational characteristic of the Trinity expressed by the term perichoresis as a basis on which to perfect human community; or in Boff's words, following Nicholas Fedorov, "The holy Trinity is our social program."[16] Others who adopt this approach are Jürgen Moltmann, Elizabeth Johnson, and Catherine LaCugna.

However, from the Western point of view—often called Latin Trinitarianism—the primacy of God's inner relationality sounds suspiciously tritheistic.[17] This approach is also criticized as having destroyed the radical

---

9. There are of course other post-pluralist theologians who employ different categories. John B. Cobb, Jr., for instance, uses the Whiteheadian philosophical thinking that results in an understanding of three different ultimates: God, creativity, and the cosmos; Cobb, "Whiteheadian Assumptions." Cobb calls his model the complementary pluralism as opposed to the identist pluralist promoted by Hick, Knitter, and others. A similar argument made by Stephen Kaplan, *Different Paths*, who borrows Bohm's holographic model to argue that three different ultimate realities can simultaneously exist, equally real, and equally interpenetrating.

10. Edwards, *Jesus*. Edwards' other book employs the Trinity as the central category for discussing evolution; see Edwards, *God of Evolution*.

11. Boff, *Trinity and Society*.

12. Johnson, *She Who Is*.

13. Buxton, *Trinity*; Fiddes, *Participating*.

14. Volf, *After Our Likeness*.

15. For good resources on this development, see for example, Grenz, *Rediscovering*; Hunt, *Trinity*; Kärkkäinen, *Trinity*; Peters, *God as Trinity*.

16. Boff, "Trinity," 78.

17. Some writers try to make a distinction between Social Trinitarianism and the

distinction between God and human being.[18] While the debate still continues, the most important question at hand concerns how to arrive at an appropriate understanding of the reality-perichoresis without eradicating the fundamental difference between God and creation. This question needs to be asked repeatedly of Panikkar, Heim, D'Costa, and myself.

The discussion of these three theologians is important in creating a discursive context for my study. Each of them represents a different model of Trinitarian theology of religions. The first model, proposed by Raimundo Panikkar, construes the Trinity as the structure of reality. Panikkar views the Trinity through the notion of *cosmotheandrism*, which he understands as the complete unity between the divine, the cosmos, and the human, and which becomes the ultimate goal of all reality. The second model, which is the most popular, and of which D'Costa is a representative, employs the dynamic relationship between the Word and the Spirit as one between the particularity and universality of God's salvific works in Christianity and in other religions.[19] The third model, proposed by Heim, employs the notion of multiple religious ends rooted in the plenitude of the Trinity.

Each model clearly offers a very different, and yet plausible, explanation of how the Trinity relates to the multiple religious traditions, and how it becomes the principle of differentiation among religious traditions. They all maintain, however, that any *Christian* theology of religions cannot claim a neutral universality and should rather be based on the symbol of the Trinity as the central category in the Christian faith. By analyzing each model critically and comparing them I will try to find their similarities and, more importantly, their dissimilarities.

I will pay special attention to how each model deals with the notion of perichoresis. Among the three thinkers, D'Costa shows the least interest in linking the perichoretic idea to other religions. He does not, however, entirely want to abandon the idea of perichoresis. He accepts perichoresis only within the inner life of God, which is applicable to the Christian ecclesial

---

Orthodox view of the Trinity, despite their greater commonalities. See Butin, *Trinity*, 63–64. The debate between Latin Trinitarianism and Social Trinitarianism is best demonstrated by Brian Leftow, "Anti Social Trinitarianism," as the proponent of the former and Stephen T. Davis, "Perichoretic Monotheism," from the latter side.

18. Tanner, *Jesus*, 81–88.

19. This model occurs in two variants: Christocentric Trinitarianism and Pneumatocentric Trinitarianism. While both emphasize the importance of the Trinity for doing theology of religions, the former uses Christ as the starting point and the latter begins with the Spirit. While the first variant is represented by Jacques Dupuis, the second is represented by Amos Yong.

An Imaginative Glimpse

community yet experienced in a fragmented way through interreligious prayer. Unlike D'Costa, Panikkar makes use of perichoresis optimally as the principle of the unity of reality, while Heim takes the idea only as one among three types of relation with God.

Panikkar and Heim have their own ways of "linking" the multidimensionality of the Trinity to different religious traditions. While Panikkar links each person in the Trinity to different religious traditions, Heim tries not to separate the Triune persons but links different "types of relation" with the Triune God to different traditions. In this context, my proposal will take a different path than ones taken by Panikkar and Heim.

After discussing the three thinkers, I will argue that only by putting the dissimilarities among the models within a notion of perichoresis can they be reconciled. To do so, a precise understanding of the three perichoretic relations (person-, nature-, and reality-perichoresis) is necessary. In this regard, Moltmann's idea of "open Trinity" is expected to contribute a deep insight for my task, since it provides a theological basis for connecting intra-Trinitarian perichoresis to the possibility of all creation to participate in God's perichoretic relationality.

Also, drawing from Richard Kearney's philosophical perspective, I will argue that this linkage will be helpful only if we do not do this with each person in the Trinity, as Panikkar has done, but rather focus on different dimensions of perichoresis—unity of reality, *khora*, personal relation, and God who may be (or "the possible God")[20]—and link each of these to different religious traditions. Thus, while my method is similar to Heim's, my work is original in its attempt to find the principle of multiplicity in a different place, that is, in the concept of perichoresis. It must be noted, however, that my attempt to link different dimensions of perichoresis to different religious traditions can be plausible insofar as it is seen as a second order approximation, that is, that it is theologically constructed as what I call an "imaginative glimpse." Hence, the title of the book. The first order of perichoretic theology of religions, furthermore, is based on the conviction that reality-perichoresis is an indispensable implication of person-perichoresis.

---

20. Kearney's phenomenological understanding of God as "the God who may be" offers a very different image of God than that of the classical idea of God, which focuses on being and actuality. His understanding of the possible God provides a promising basis for a non-absolutist theology of religions. Moreover, the possible God can be a third alternative between the God-as-being of the classical philosophy and theology and khora, which he understands as "neither identical with God nor incompatible with God but marks an open site where the divine may dwell and heal"; Kearney, *Strangers*, 194. I will argue that Kearney's khora can rightly be interpreted as God's nonbeing.

Introduction

The decision to draw from Moltmann's "open Trinity" and Kearney's "God who may be" also has value in giving an eschatological dimension to my proposal. I will argue that the perichoretic communion among religions *within* the Trinity will be perfected and fulfilled only in an eschatological sense. Thus, my perichoretic theology of religions could have a significant value in its criticism of any inclination to make absolute religious claims at the cost of religious "others."

Method of Investigation

The general strategy of the book is to employ some sort of theological *bricolage*,[21] by using several sources available at hand (see the "Sources of the Study" section below). In order for this bricolage to be successful, I will have to analyze critically what my sources say (e.g., about the Trinity, perichoresis, or religious plurality) and retrieve some elements from them.

However, it needs to be acknowledged that the method of bricolage will serve only as a starting point. The final purpose of this study is to construct a more coherent and comprehensive Christian theology of religions. To do so, I will also employ a comparative analysis of different models of Trinitarian theology of religions. Key ideas such as commitment versus openness, dialectic between the Word and the Spirit, God-world perichoretic relation, etc. will serve as lenses through which these models will be compared. Furthermore, while the method of bricolage is useful in gathering resources from different perspectives, and comparative analysis is useful for setting up the discursive context within which my own model will be constructed, I will need to deal throughout the study with various philosophical and theological dialectics, such as ones between commitment to one's truth and openness to others, otherness and sameness, economic and immanent Trinity, etc. In this context, I will employ a reconstruction of the notion of perichoresis, which becomes the basis for an imaginative appropriation of the Trinity to diverse religious traditions.

---

21. I borrow the bricolage model from Jeffrey Stout borrowing from Claude Lévi-Strauss. Although Stout uses the term in the field of moral philosophy, the image of bricolage can be useful for my purpose here. By bricolage Stout means the "selective and retrieval and eclectic reconfiguration of traditional . . . elements in hope of solving problems at hand." Stout, *Ethics after Babel*, 293.

An Imaginative Glimpse

Structure of the Book

This book is organized in five chapters. The introductory chapter will provide an overview of the project. Included in this chapter are the larger contexts within which it will be developed and its importance to contemporary theological discourse.

Chapters 2 and 3 will be focused on three Trinitarian theologies of religions proposed by Panikkar, D'Costa, and Heim. Chapter 2 will explore, in a more descriptive mode, different models of Trinitarian theology of religions suggested by Panikkar, D'Costa, and Heim. I will demonstrate that the three theologians under discussion signify the emergence of the Trinitarian model in field of theology of religions. With the exception of Panikkar's, all models of Trinitarian theology of religions have emerged recently.[22] Thus, to some extent, the Trinitarian theology of religion can be considered as a post-pluralistic critique of pluralism.[23] In this chapter, each theologian will be examined critically by asking whether they are successful in employing the Trinity as their central category in theology of religions, especially in moving beyond the impasse left by pluralism. It will also be important to see whether or not the notion of perichoresis is central in the models under discussion.

Chapter 3 presents a critical comparison of the three models. In the first section, I will examine critically how each model deals with the theoretical issues such as the dialectic between the commitment to Christian truth and openness to the truths of other religious traditions. A special attention will be paid to the idea of transversality as a complementary element to Heim's orientational pluralism. My suggestion is that the combination of transversality and orientational pluralism can best serve the theoretically most satisfactory theology of religions based on the idea of the Trinity. The second section will investigate in their theologies the understanding of the Trinity

---

22. Beside their recent appearance, the thinkers also share a critical position against pluralism. Again, Panikkar should be analyzed separately due to his participation in the publication of the 1988 *The Myth of Christian Uniqueness*, which is published as a collective declaration of the pluralist position; see Knitter and Hick, *Christian Uniqueness*.

23. In keeping with the complexity of Panikkar's theological position, Komulainen's response to Panikkar, *vis-à-vis* post-pluralism, is complicated. On one hand, he is convinced that the "post-pluralistic critique should be applied to Panikkar's theology of religions." Komulainen, *Emerging*, 19. On the other hand, he realizes that many have characterized Panikkar as "the one who has established the foundations of the post-pluralistic way of thinking." Komulainen, *Emerging*, 19. Based on this difficulty, he suggests locating Panikkar in the middle of the pluralistic and post-pluralistic position. See also Komulainen, *Emerging*, 10–21.

Introduction

in general and perichoresis in specific. This chapter will be concluded with my proposal of a modest approach, which seeks to transcend the limitations shown in Panikkar's, Heim's, and D'Costa's models while embracing their valuable insights.

In the chapter 4 I will investigate how perichoresis became a valuable concept in the Christian theology. Special attention will be paid to the writings of the Eastern church fathers, Jürgen Moltmann, and Richard Kearney. I will argue that the church fathers have provided comprehensive images of the Trinitarian perichoresis, which is further developed and enriched by later theologians. This chapter will also deal with contemporary contributions to the Trinity and perichoresis, i.e., Moltmann's idea of "open Trinity" and Kearney's theory of the possible God and its implication to the Trinitarian discourse. The basic theological significance of this chapter is in its proposal that the Trinitarian perichoresis is neither exclusive to divine reality, without any possibility for creation to participate in it, nor so inclusive that the distinction between the divine and creation is diminished. Rather, the Trinitarian perichoresis can be understood as an open and dynamic communion of both intra-divine life and between the divine and creation, yet still maintaining a radical difference between the divine and creation, as well as among different facets of creation.

Kearney's groundbreaking proposal of the possible God as the third alternative to the classical distinction between God and *khora* (being and non-being) is of importance for my entire project. Instead of using the notion of the possible God and discarding God-as-being and khora, I will put these three together as the trialectic-perichoretic basis for theology of religions.

In chapter 5 I will develop my constructive model of perichoretic theology of religions. I will argue that perichoresis can become a sufficient basis for a theology of religions that maintains dialectically the commitment to Christian truth and openness to the truths of other religious traditions. However, I will also suggest that the radicalness of perichoresis to embrace the diversity of all reality can still allow us to imagine different dimensions of perichoresis, each of which corresponding to different religious traditions. I will conclude this chapter with an epilogue that contains the ethical implication of my proposal. By using the image of embrace I will argue for an interreligious ethics based on the idea of perichoresis.

Sources of the Study

The second and third chapters, dealing with three different models of Trinitarian theology of religions, will take as its primary sources the writings from theologians whose models I will compare and analyze (Panikkar, D'Costa, and Heim). Although each theologian has published many writings in this field, certain writings should be mentioned here as the most important ones for my study: Panikkar's *The Trinity and the Religious Experience of Man*, D'Costa's *The Meeting of Religions and the Trinity*, and Heim's *Salvations: Truth and Difference in Religion* and *The Depth of the Riches: A Trinitarian Theology of Religious Ends*.

The sources for chapter 4 will be diverse, yet the focus on the issue of the Trinitarian perichoresis will serve to narrow my choice of material. I use the classical writings from the church fathers,[24] Moltmann's writings on the Trinity, as well texts from Kearney. Among Moltmann's numerous writings in books and articles, his most important work on this issue is *The Trinity and the Kingdom: the Doctrine of God*. He also writes specifically about the idea of perichoresis, in an essay entitled, "Perichoresis: New Theological Wine in an Old Theological Wineskin."

Kearney's writings will be chosen selectively: only those that focus on the idea of the possible God, and specifically Kearney's interpretation of perichoresis. His two books that are of central importance here are *The God Who May Be: A Hermeneutics of Religion* and *Strangers, Gods, and Monsters: Interpreting Otherness*.

Limitations

The first major limitation of the study is that it does not offer a full-fledged account either of Trinitarian theology or of theology of religions or of the history of the notion of perichoresis. The focus on the Trinitarian notion of perichoresis and its implication for constructing a more plausible theology of religions makes this study limited in dealing with many issues in both fields. However, those who have delved more deeply in each field may find my study helpful in investigating the importance of perichoresis for their more systematic projects.

The second limitation of the study is its lack of engagement with comparative theology. As described before, one of the most recent developments

---

24. This will include, but not limited to, Gregory Nazianzus, Maximus the Confessor, Pseudo-Cyril of Alexandria, and John of Damascus.

Introduction

in theology of religions is the emergence of post-pluralism, into which this study fits. Comparative theology is another significant development, without which any theoretical analysis of religions will be in danger of reductionism.[25] Nevertheless, due to the scope of the study, I will not engage with religious comparative studies or comparative theology. Such studies are needed in the future.

Finally, the lack of a more contextual—Third-World countries, Asian or even Indonesian—element, which readers might expect coming from an Asian theologian, is another limitation of the study. The choice of Panikkar and D'Costa as two of the theologians that I will analyze may nevertheless be seen as my attempt to give space to the representatives of Asian voices in the present study.[26] Moreover, of course, I am doing this research with my personal background in my mind as an Indonesian person, even though it is not reflected explicitly. A more contextual perichoretic (or Trinitarian) theology of religions surely deserves further investigation.

---

25. Paul F. Knitter mentions both post-pluralist theology of religions and comparative theology as the two most important developments in the *Acceptance Model*; Knitter, *Introducing*, 192–215. For the critique of reductionism in theology and the argument for comparative theology, see Neville, "Toward."

26. Beside Panikkar, there are several Asian theologians who deal with the relation between the Trinity and religious pluralism; e.g. Lee, *Trinity*; Miyahira, *Towards*.

2

The Trinity and Religions
Three Models

TRINITARIAN THEOLOGY OF RELIGIONS AS A PARTICULAR DISCIPLINE HAS now come to the point where one can neither talk satisfyingly about Christian theology of religions without touching the issue of Trinity nor discuss the meaning of the doctrine of Trinity without looking for its relevance in the context of religious plurality. Some theologians have made serious attempts to relate the two disciplines—Trinitarian theology and theology of religions—more closely to each other. Three theologians, each of whom has proposed a very different model of Trinitarian theology of religions, are Raimundo Panikkar, S. Mark Heim, and Gavin D'Costa.

The objective of this chapter is to discuss the three models of Trinitarian theology of religions proposed by these three theologians. I examine these three models by treating each of them separately. The critical position against pluralistic theology of religions taken by each scholar, his key theoretical concept, and his Trinitarian view of religious diversity will be addressed. Discussion of the first issue is important in situating each theologian within the discursive context of theology of religions traditionally dominated by the classical typology of exclusivism, inclusivism, and pluralism. The second sections—concerning the key theoretical concepts of each theologian—deals with the basic principle upon which each constructs his theological model. Finally, the third sections focus on the models themselves.

Raimundo Panikkar: Trinity and Cosmotheandric Reality

Raimundo Panikkar is a theologian who has been exposed to diverse religions and cultures from the beginning of his life. Describing his spiritual pilgrimage in crossing over multiple religious traditions, he writes: "I 'left' as a Christian, I 'found' myself a Hindu and I 'return' a Buddhist, without having ceased to be a Christian."[1] This rich and complex background is obvious in all his works. With respect to the voluminous nature of his works, however, I limit my review of Panikkar's thought by focusing on three aspects: his ambiguous place within the pluralist camp, the cosmotheandric principle underlying all of his theological works, and his Trinitarian theology of religions.

A Maverick Pluralist

Panikkar is often grouped into the pluralist camp, especially after his contribution to *The Myth of Christian Uniqueness*. While it is true that in the article, titled "The Jordan, the Tiber, and the Ganges,"[2] Panikkar makes arguments in support of pluralistic theology, we must also aware that his position radically differs from other pluralists in the book. His more radically pluralistic position is acknowledged even by some authors in *Christian Uniqueness Reconsidered*, another collection whose purpose is to criticize *The Myth of Christian Uniqueness*. Panikkar has also tried to clarify his public image by distancing himself from other pluralists. In his letter to the editor of *International Bulletin of Missionary Research*, he clarifies his position, "It seems that I am thrown into the same bag with all those who defend a certain eclecticism and undermine the centrality of the Christian mystery, as if I were espousing relativism, when—in fact—I am propounding relativity."[3]

The distinction between relativity and relativism is for Panikkar very significant. Relativism is a pessimistic attitude toward any possible criteria of truth. It is "a mere agnosticism, a premature renunciation of any attempt to make valid assertions."[4] On the contrary, the concept of relativity that he employs avoids both relativism and absolutism. It is against relativism in the sense that relativity affirms "the constitutive relationship of everything with everything else."[5] It is also against absolutism in its assertion that "any human affirmation, and thus any truth, is relative to its very own parameters and that there can be no absolute truth, for truth is essentially relational."[6]

1. Panikkar, *Intrareligious*, 2.
2. Panikkar, "Jordan."
3. Panikkar, "Reader's Response," 80.
4. Panikkar, *Silence of God*, 134; Panikkar, *Invisible Harmony*, 156.
5. Panikkar, *Silence of God*, 134.
6. Panikkar, *Invisible Harmony*, 156.

An Imaginative Glimpse

Moreover, Panikkar believes that the relativity of all reality is radical not only in the sense that it refers to the whole of the real, but also in sense that it is rooted in God's relativity, both *ad extra* and *ad intra*. Thus, the horizontal dimension of relativity mirrors the vertical dimension of relativity, and both reflect the Trinitarian character of radical relativity. In his own words, "to the intratrinitarian *circumincessio* corresponds an extratrinitarian *perichoresis*."[7]

To the notion of radical relativity, Panikkar adds the notion of *perspectivism*, through which he argues that there are radically different perspectives on reality. To explain this notion, Panikkar uses the windows metaphor. It will be helpful to quote what he says at length,

> We should . . . be aware that we see the *totum per partem*, the whole through a part. We will have to concede that the other, the non-Christian, for instance, may have a similar experience and that the non-Christian will have to say that the Christian takes the *pars pro toto*, for from the outside one only sees the *pars*, not the *totum*—the window, not the panorama. How to combine these apparently contradictory statements? We will have to say that the other is right in discovering that we take the *pars pro toto* (because the outsider sees the window), but that we are also right in seeing the *totum per partem* (because we see the panorama). It is a *totum* for us, but *per partem*, limited to our vision through the one window. We see the *totum*, but not *totaliter* one may say (because we do not see through other windows). We see all that we can see. The other may see equally the *totum* through another window, and thus describe it differently, but both see the *totum*, although not *in toto*, but *per partem*.[8]

The principles—or "the twofold awareness," as Panikkar calls it[9]—of relativity and perspectivism are essential elements for Panikkar's version of pluralism. Both imply the importance of mutual relationship and intersubjective dialogue. Also, the consequence of having these two principles is obvious. There cannot be a universal theory of reality. After depicting the principles of relativity and perspectivism through the windows metaphor, he says,

> This means that we do not need a universal theory as if we could enjoy a global perspective—which is a contradiction in terms. It means that each one of us may be aware of the whole under one

---

7. Panikkar, *Silence of God*, 142.
8. Panikkar, *Invisible Harmony*, 171–72.
9. Panikkar, "Self-Critical Dialogue," 253.

particular aspect—and not just that we see only a part of it. Both the subjective and objective models break down. There is neither subjective nor objective universality. We see all that we can see—one may grant—but only *all* that *we* can see, our *totum*. The whole is what is wholesome for us. . . . Something is complete when it has an inner harmony—as we shall still emphasize.[10]

Panikkar's rejection of any universal theory, thus, distinguishes him from other pluralists, who assume that there should be an overarching theory that is universal enough to include any particularities. Unavoidably, these indifferent versions of pluralism deny the centrality of Christian faith, that is, Jesus Christ. In the letter to the editor of *International Bulletin of Missionary Research* that I quote above, Panikkar continues his "distancing" attempt from the other pluralists by saying, "The pluralism I defend is in no way a negation of the centrality of Christ when we speak Christian language, or when we think or write about the Christian economy of salvation."[11] The clause "when we speak Christian language" precisely refers to the perspectivist position that he holds. Again, he argues for his perspectivist point of view, "Now, the context in which the Christian text is meaningful—and for a Christian, true—is not a universal context. Only within one particular context can Christian affirmations make sense, and be believed or disbelieved."[12]

If Panikkar rejects the notion of universal theory held by his pluralist colleagues, what kind of pluralism does he suggest? It is obvious that his position of perspectivism and relativity is only a stepping-stone to his broader idea of pluralism, which has both epistemological and ontological dimensions. Pluralism, on the one hand, is epistemologically related to human attitudes: ". . . I understand by pluralism that *fundamental human attitude* which is critically aware both of the factual irreducibility (thus incompatibility) of different human systems purporting to render reality intelligible, and of the radical non-necessity of reducing reality to one single center of intelligibility, making thus unnecessary and *absolute* decision in favor of a particular human system with universal validity—or even one Supreme Being."[13]

---

10. Panikkar, "Self-Critical Dialogue," 140.
11. Panikkar, "Reader's Response," 80.
12. Ibid.
13. Panikkar, "Self-Critical Dialogue," 252–53, italics his. By defining pluralism, first of all, as an open, human attitude, Panikkar stands against the idea of pluralism as a system, or even a supersystem. He says, "A pluralistic system would be an ideology in the pejorative sense of the word, a procrustean bed into which we fit contradictory diversities just to serve our purposes, a supersystem artificially concocted to dominate a given situation. In this sense, I am 'contra pluralism.'" Panikkar, "Self-Critical Dialogue," 257.

An Imaginative Glimpse

It is in the above quotation that we find not only Panikkar's idea of pluralism as human attitude, but also the fact that such human attitude is directed toward the ontological irreducibility of reality. Reality itself is thus pluralistic. Jyri Komulainen succinctly summarizes Panikkar's twofold pluralism by saying that Panikkar "indeed rejects the age-old differentiation between being and knowing. . . . It cannot be denied that both aspects—pluralism as attitude and pluralism as metaphysics—belong to Panikkar's thinking. It is true that pluralism is an attitude of human consciousness. For Panikkar, however, human consciousness does not stand, so to say, outside the realm of reality. Instead, it participates authentically in the pluralistic reality and its processes."[14]

We have seen the radicality of Panikkar's version of pluralism, which makes him different from other pluralists. Even more, he is critical of those pluralists who try to construct certain universal theories that can be used to frame religious particularities within their own supersystems. It is not mistaken, therefore, when Knitter calls him "a maverick or gadfly pluralist."[15]

In the following section I discuss Panikkar's idea of cosmotheandrism that becomes his core principle in dealing with the issue of the Trinity and religious plurality.

Cosmotheandrism as the Structure of Reality

Panikkar defines cosmotheandrism in many different ways.[16] One formulation depends upon the theory that "the divine, the human and the earthly—however we may prefer to call them—are the three irreducible dimensions which constitute the real, i.e., any reality inasmuch as it is real."[17] These three dimensions thus constitute the radical structure that underlies all reality. Panikkar observes that, for the past three millennia, people have tried to grasp such a reality not by putting it together, but by separating it. In contrast to such failed attempts, cosmotheandrism tries to put together "the fractured pieces of these partial insights."[18] More simply, Panikkar explain

---

14. Komulainen, *Emerging*, 81.
15. Knitter, "Cosmic Confidence," 178.
16. Francis X. D'Sa summarizes several in his article, "Notion of God," 34–35.
17. Panikkar, *Cosmotheandric Experience*, 60.
18. Panikkar, *Dwelling Place*, 97. Although Panikkar envisions a non-fractured view of reality, it is also true that he still allows us to see reality through the dialectic between part and whole. In this sense, his cosmotheandric vision can be explained imaginatively through the geometric concept of a fractal, in which parts have a shape similar to the

his cosmotheandric vision by emphasizing that "There is no God without Man and the World. There is no Man without God and the World. There is no World without God and Man."[19]

Since the three elements are so deeply interrelated and interdependent, Panikkar allows himself to employ the term *perichoresis*, which has traditionally been used for referring to immanent Trinity or the inner self of the Triune God. Now, he uses it for his cosmotheandric vision, in which the triadic or threefold *cosmos-theos-aner* constitutes the whole structure of reality. He believes that "the Trinity . . . is neither a monopoly of Christianity nor . . . of the Divinity. Every bit of reality has this trinitarian imprint."[20] He reinterprets and transcends the traditional language of the Trinitarian perichoresis, in which he is greatly interested, through his cosmotheandric lens. So much is obvious when he writes, "I am within tradition, although transcending it (as any *traditio* demands), when I apply this notion [perichoresis] to the radical Trinity, i.e. to reality. . . . This is the *circumincessio* between the Divine, the Human and the Cosmic."[21]

Interestingly, Panikkar here proposes the term "radical Trinity," which refers not to the traditional doctrines of immanent and economic Trinity but to the triadic cosmotheandrism.[22] I will discuss the relation between Panikkar's radical Trinity and the Christian idea of Trinity in chapter 3. For now, suffice it to say that, through his idea of cosmotheandrism, Panikkar has enlarged the scope of the Trinitarian notion and its perichoretic characteristic, from one that constitutes the divine life as witnessed by Christian tradition to the radical Trinity that focuses on the whole reality of the Divine, the Human, and the Cosmic. His employing of perichoresis shows a significant refocusing, from person-perichoresis to reality-perichoresis. While the former

---

whole in some way; cf. Feder, *Fractals*. Panikkar also indicates this idea when he says, for instance, "There are not three separate histories or realms; instead, each realm penetrates the other two; *each of these dimensions is present even in the smallest piece of reality*." Panikkar, *Dwelling Place*, 97, italic mine. I am indebted to Dr. Wesley Wildman for helping me make the connection between Panikkar's cosmotheandrism and the fractal concept.

19. Quoted in Raj, *New Hermeneutic*, 86; cf. Panikkar, *Dwelling Place*, 72.

20. Panikkar, *Blessed Simplicity*, 128.

21. Panikkar, "Self-Critical Dialogue," 276.

22. Ibid., 273. The notion of radical Trinity appears in his latest publications, especially after his Gifford Lecture in 1988–89. In our personal correspondence, he shared with me his plan to publish the revision of the lecture, which focuses on the idea of radical Trinity. He finally published it in 2009, *Rhythm of Being*, which seems to be his last book before he passed away in August 2010. A short preview, however, is available in his personal response to the collection of some critiques of and commentaries on his work; Panikkar, "Self-Critical Dialogue," 272–76; cf. MacPherson, *Critical Reading*, 67–71.

refers to the perichoretic relation among the three persons of the Triune God, the latter points to the triadic relationship among the three dimensions of Reality: *cosmos-theos-aner*.

Our analysis would be misleading if we miss another aspect of Panikkar's cosmotheandrism: *advaita*. For him, "*advaita* and Trinity are two homeomorphic equivalents for the ultimate structure of reality. . . . And the cosmotheandric or theanthropocosmic intuition would like to be a qualified version of those ultimate insights."[23] Ewert H. Cousins thus rightly combines both by calling Panikkar's idea the "advaitic Trinitarianism."[24] By describing advaita and trinity as homeomorphic, Panikkar tries to say that each of them comes from a different religious system, yet having equivalent function. Whereas the Trinitarian language that he uses is Christian, the advaitic language is typically Hinduistic.

The word *advaita* consists of two Sanskrit words: *a* (not) and *dvaita* (two). Thus, etymologically, it simply means "not-two." Generally used by Advaita Vedanta, one of the six orthodox schools of Indian philosophy, the term refers to the monistic understanding that all reality is undifferentiated and one. However, Panikkar frequently expresses his irritation at the western scholars who identify advaita with monism and at those who accuse him as promoting monism.[25] Even more, his entire philosophical and theological journey is dedicated to overcoming the dilemma of monism and dualism, and he believes that the notion of advaita can best serve such an aim. He maintains, "By [advaita] I mean the immediate experience which opens up to us a reality where differences are not absolutized (dualism: God—world; matter—spirit), not ignored (monism: pure materialism, pure spiritualism), not idolized (pantheism: everything is divine and solely that), not reduced to mere shadows (monotheism: one single principle, one ruler, many subjects). A *polarity able to endure tension* is the ultimate characteristic of what is real."[26]

Thus, through the notion of advaita Panikkar tries to situate himself at a certain point that does not belong to one of those rejected positions (dualism, monism, pantheism, or monotheism, but especially the first two).

---

23. By homeomorphic equivalence, or simply homeomorphism, he means "a functional equivalence discovered through a topological transformation . . . [two things] are homeomorphic in the sense that each of them stands for something that performs an equivalent function within their respective systems." Panikkar, *Intrareligious*, xxii.

24. Cousins, "Panikkar's."

25. Panikkar, "Self-Critical Dialogue," 273.

26. Panikkar, *Dwelling Place*, 94, italics his.

We have seen above that his position is best described as Trinitarianism, and the advaitic notion helps him secure this position. "Reality is trinitarian, non-dualist, neither one nor two. Only by denying duality (*advaita*), without reducing everything to unity, are we able consciously to approach it."[27]

I have discussed in general Panikkar's ideas of pluralism as well as his cosmotheandrism which focuses on two homeomorphic notions, Trinity and advaita. In the next part, I discuss his attempt to implement those ideas to the problem of religious diversity.

Trinity and Diverse Forms of Spirituality

Panikkar's clearest and most direct account of his theology of religions from the Trinitarian perspective can be found in *The Trinity and the Religious Experience of Man*.[28] In this concise book he acknowledges that he begins from a Christian perspective, and insists that this perspective does not result in a sectarian mentality. Rather, he claims, "Christianity is especially called to 'suffer' this purifying transformation."[29] Clearly, by employing a Christian point of view, Panikkar has consistently held to the principle of perspectivism in his theology.[30]

His main intention in this book is to show "how in the light of the Trinity the three forms of spirituality . . . can be reconciled."[31] We can see clearly through the structure of the book how he tries to fulfill his intention. After discussing three forms of spirituality in Part I, Panikkar moves to the discussion of the Trinity itself in Part II. Part III summarizes his Trinitarian theology of religions from the perspective of his (cosmo-)theandrism.

---

27. Panikkar, *Experience of God*, 66.

28. This book is a revision of his previous work, Panikkar, *The Trinity and World Religions: Icon-Person-Mystery*. Panikkar also wrote a lengthy article in the *Journal of Ecumenical Studies*, under the title "Toward an Ecumenical Theandric Spirituality," which seems to contain the basis for the ideas that he develops later.

29. Panikkar, *Religious Experience*, 6.

30. Panikkar provides four reasons for why Christianity is the starting point of his Trinitarian idea. First, there is a continuity between his Trinitarian idea and the Christian doctrine of the Trinity; second, he believes that one cannot have a neutral position; third, he expresses his willingness, in a dialogical spirit, to begin from a different point of departure; fourth, it is in Christianity that we find Trinitarian terminology, although this terminology may also be found in other religious traditions; see Panikkar, *Religious Experience*, 43.

31. Panikkar, *Religious Experience*, 41.

An Imaginative Glimpse

Three Forms of Spirituality

In Part I of the book Panikkar identifies three basic forms of spirituality (iconolatry, personalism, and mysticism or advaita), which are parallel with three ways of life in Hinduism: action (*karmamārga*), devotion (*bhaktimārga*), and knowledge (*jñānamārga*). Before discussing those three forms of spirituality, it is important to remember the distinction that Panikkar makes between spirituality and religion. Where spirituality is more flexible than religion in its tendency to detach itself from "the mass of rites, structures, etc.," a single religion may comprise several spiritualities at the same time. Michael Barnes correctly summarizes Panikkar's idea by saying, "[W]hile it can never be separated from particular religious phenomena, such as ritual and myth and dogmatic beliefs, spirituality somehow manages to transcend them. Where the term religion is largely conterminous with the belief system of a group or community, spirituality crosses cultural and religious boundaries . . . a spirituality is almost by definition cross-religious."[32]

The first form of spirituality, iconolatry or *karmamārga*, is characteristically cosmo-anthropomorphistic, in the sense that it entails "the projection of God under some *form*, his objectivation, his personification *in an object*, which may be mental or material, visible or invisible, but always reducible to our human 'representation.'"[33] Based on this definition, iconolatry is for Panikkar merely a euphemism for idolatry, since both represent "the homogeneity which subsists between God and his creature. . . . There is a mutuality between idol and worshipper."[34] However, if we still want to make a distinction between idolatry and iconolatry, the most important question is whether the adoration of one image "stops short at the object, without going beyond it in an ongoing movement towards the Creator, the Transcendent" (idolatry) or "takes this object as a point of departure for a slow and arduous ascent towards God" (iconolatry).[35] Thus, the problem of idolatry is not that it is a false *latria* (worship), but that "it is false *qua* objectification of this adoration."[36]

---

32. Barnes, "Theology of Religions," 411.
33. Panikkar, *Religious Experience*, 15.
34. Ibid. In his previous article, Panikkar calls the first form of spirituality "idolatry," which makes it clear that, for him, idolatry can be generally identified with iconolatry; see Panikkar, "Toward," 509.
35. Panikkar, *Religious Experience*, 16.
36. Ibid., 17.

The Trinity and Religions

Panikkar concludes his discussion of iconolatry by emphasizing that the fundamental attitude of this form of spirituality is "the cultic *act* of adoration of an 'image' of God, believed to represent each time the true God."[37] As such, it is parallel to the Indian spirituality of *karmamārga*, which he understands as the practice to reach salvation.

A second form of spirituality is personalism. Focusing on the concept of person, Christian personalism results from the transformation of the ancient Hebrew cosmo-anthropomorphism. What is of importance here is the human-divine relationship that comes out of the conviction that God is a personal being. Panikkar maintains, "We call God a personal being *because* we ourselves are persons. We consider God a Being because ourselves are beings."[38] This personalist tradition is parallel with the Indian *bhaktimārga*, the way of devotion and love. In short, what we have in this form of spirituality is "the gift of oneself to the Lord, love of God, [which] necessarily demands a meeting of persons, a mutual acceptance and a communication between persons."[39]

A third form of spirituality is advaita or mysticism. Panikkar asks, "Is there such a thing as an experience of God that does not lead to interpersonal dialogue? Can one conceive an authentic spirituality in which God is not a 'thou' for man nor his commandment the 'ultimate' of all perfection?"[40] He needs to ask these questions due to the limitations that he sees in the previous forms of spirituality. For example, the issue of theodicy is very problematic in the personalist model.[41] The personal God appears as a sadist or indifferent God when suffering occurs. In short, he concludes, "If God is a person he corresponds very poorly to man's own ideal of a person."[42] Panikkar believes that it is in other religious traditions, especially in Hinduism, that we can find an alternative to the notions of God as iconic or personal. In the Upanisads, for instance, what we have is "the supra-rational experience of a 'Reality' which in some way 'inhales' us into himself. The God of the Upanisads does not speak; he is not Word. He 'inspires'; he is *Spirit*."[43]

This idea of the divine is fundamentally different from how the modern West understands the transcendent and immanent God. In the latter,

37. Ibid., 18.
38. Ibid., 22.
39. Ibid., 23.
40. Ibid., 29.
41. Ibid., 28.
42. Ibid., 27.
43. Ibid., 29.

An Imaginative Glimpse

transcendence is perceived in terms of "pure exteriority" and immanence is viewed in terms of "pure interiority."[44] In result, speaking in a more spatial terms, human beings become the centre, against which we situate God, be it above (transcendent) or within (immanent) us. In contrast to such a limitedly anthropocentric view, Panikkar suggests his advaitic notion of transcendence and immanence. An authentic transcendence, he argues, implies the divine inaccessibility that is "beyond any 'real relationship' [since] transcendence implies heterogeneity between God and man, and rejects any relatedness which is at root of all religious anthropomorphism whether iconolatrous or personalist."[45] As to divine immanence, he maintains, "An immanent God cannot be a God-person, 'someone' with whom I could have 'personal' relationship, a God-Other. I cannot *speak* to an immanent God. If I attempt to do so I cause this immanence to vanish because I am rendering it *other* and *exterior*. I cannot *think* of God-immanent for, if I try, I make him the *object* of my thought and project him before and outside me."[46]

Despite the impossibility of a real relationship, Panikkar's advaitic spirituality allows us to use some "names," such as Brahman, *ātman*, ultimate ground of everything, Supreme Reality, and others, just in order to signify the dimension of immanence. Both God and Brahman are the same reality, but they should be viewed from two opposed perspectives. Where God is "the summit," Brahman is "the base of the triangle representing the Divinity."[47] He also explains that Brahman, or the dimension of immanence, is "like the horizon from which the God of the 'religions', the living and true God himself, emerges."[48]

Panikkar devotes more discussion to this form of spirituality than to the other two, since it is more compatible with his cosmotheandric project. Although I do not need to repeat what he means by advaita here, it is important to note that for Panikkar this form of spirituality is parallel to the Indian way of knowledge or *jñānamārga*.

Three "Persons" of the Trinity

In Part II of his book, Panikkar moves to a discussion of the Trinity. His primary purpose is to "show how in the light of the Trinity the three forms of

44. Ibid., 30.
45. Ibid., 30–31.
46. Ibid., 31
47. Ibid., 32.
48. Ibid., 33.

spirituality described above can be reconciled."⁴⁹ The Trinitarian concept, he believes, possibly becomes a synthesis between and a junction point for the three spiritual dimensions. On the one hand, he argues that his interpretation of the Trinity is "authentically *orthodox*"—in the sense that it "gives to God a truly right (*orthos*) honour and glory (*doxa*)—as well as "fully ecclesial"; on the other hand, his Trinitarian idea "goes beyond the traditional idea given by Christianity."⁵⁰ Even more, he warns his readers of the danger of "unwarranted overstatement to affirm that the Trinitarian conception of the Ultimate, and with it of the whole reality, is an exclusive Christian insight or revelation."⁵¹ In the following section, I discuss Panikkar's ideas concerning each "person" of the Trinity. However, I need to postpone until the last section the more direct relations between his Trinitarian ideas and other religious traditions.

The Father, for Panikkar, is the Absolute One, who has no name. All religious traditions recognize the unnamability of the divine under different "names"—brahman, tao, the Father, etc. But, he argues, they are only how we designate the Absolute One. Even more, Panikkar can go further by saying that the Absolute *is* not, in the sense that the Absolute has no *ex-sistence*. Thus, "In the Father the apophatism (the *kenosis* or emptying) of Being is real and total."⁵²

How should then the spirituality of the Father be understood or attained? Since the Father or the Absolute *is* not, there is no such thing as the spirituality of the Father, properly speaking. However, it still allows him to say that, "[the spirituality of the Father is] a movement towards . . . no place, a prayer which is always open towards . . . the infinite horizon which, like a mirage, always appears in the distance because it is no-where. . . . It is like the invisible bedrock, the gentle inspirer, the unnoticed force which sustains, draws and pushes us. God is truly transcendent, infinite. The moment that one stops, takes a stand, objectivises and 'manipulates' religion, faith, and God, one destroys, so to speak, this ultimate ground of all things, which in itself is quite 'ungraspable.'"⁵³

Interestingly, even in the section where he discusses the Father, Panikkar cannot stop speaking of the Son and the Spirit. Not only does this prove the interrelatedness of the three, but also it reflects Panikkar's idea that the

49. Ibid., 41.
50. Ibid., 6, 43.
51. Ibid., viii.
52. Ibid., 46.
53. Ibid., 48, 50.

An Imaginative Glimpse

Father is "Silence total and absolute, the silence of Being—and not only the being of silence. His word who completely expresses and consumes him, is the Son."[54]

With regards to the Son, properly speaking, we can say that it is only the Son who is person and, therefore, it is only with the Son we can have interpersonal relationships with the divine.[55] Panikkar, furthermore, employs a perspective particularly significant within the Christian tradition, that is, the cosmic-Christ tradition. According to this tradition, as Panikkar also maintains, everything exists in the Son. "It is the Son who acts, who creates. Through Him everything was made."[56] The role of Christ as mediator is significantly important here. The Son is the High Priest (*summus pontifex*) not only for creation but also for redemption and glorification. It is "*from, with* and *through* him" that "Beings are [and] participate in the Son."[57] In other words, Panikkar boldly claims that every being is a Christophany—a showing forth of Christ.[58]

Unlike the revelation of the Father, which is the revelation of God transcendent, Panikkar maintains that the revelation of the Spirit is the revelation of God immanent.[59] The immanence of the Spirit that we are talking about

---

54. Ibid., 47–48.

55. According to Panikkar, since "Person . . . is an equivocal term which has a different meaning in each case," we cannot say that God is three Persons; see Panikkar, *Religious Experience*, 51–52. To use Person in a univocal sense would be to imply a *quaternitas*, that is, the Father, Son, and Spirit plus "a God-divine nature, outside, inside, above, or beside" the three; Panikkar, *Religious Experience*, 52. However, Panikkar still allows for the use of the term person for the Father and Spirit as long as "they are real relative oppositions at the heart of the divine mystery." Panikkar, *Religious Experience*, 52. The problem is nevertheless still present, since whenever we use the term Person, it is always a constitutive relation.

56. Panikkar, *Religious Experience*, 51.

57. Ibid., 54.

58. Ibid., 54, 68. To support this notion, Panikkar maintains the necessity of seeing incarnation as a continuous event. Learning from Maximus of Confessor and Meister Eckhart, Panikkar argues for the extending of the classical notion of *creatio continua* to *incarnatio continua*, "the continuous incarnation of the Son in every creature." Panikkar, *Christophany*, 179. It is in the book that I just quote that Panikkar explore more deeply his understanding of Christ the Son.

59. Of course, properly speaking, Panikkar only allows us to talk about the revelation of the Son. Neither transcendence nor immanence can be revealed. "Transcendence ceases to be when it reveals itself; immanence is incapable of revealing itself." Panikkar, *Religious Experience*, 59. But, he says, we can still talk about the revelations of the God transcendent (the Father) and God immanent (the Spirit), if only through meditative language.

The Trinity and Religions

is the immanence *within* the divine life, in the sense that God is immanent *to* Godself. In keeping with the understanding of the Spirit traditional since Augustine, Panikkar says, "The Spirit is the communion between the Father and the Son. The Spirit is immanent to Father and Son jointly. In some manner the Spirit 'passes' from Father to Son and from Son to Father in the same process."[60] Thus, the Spirit is the *we* of the *I*-and-*Thou* of the Father and Son. Since the Spirit constitutes the divine immanence, we can say that the Spirit makes it possible for us to employ the notion of *perichoresis* or *circumincessio*, "the dynamic inner circularity of the Trinity."[61] The spirituality of the Spirit, therefore, is not interpersonal. What we can have is "a non-relational union with him" signified with a "total passivity."[62]

At the end of his discussion of the Trinity, Panikkar also offers an alternative to the more anthropocentric Augustinian model of the Trinity: Father-Being, Son-Intellect, Spirit-Love. Conversely, Panikkar's Trinitarian model can be summarized as follows: "the Father, Source, the Son, being, the *Thou*; and the Spirit, return to being (or Ocean of Being), the *we*."[63] Panikkar concludes his book with a suggestion that the term "theandrism" (later on he uses the term cosmotheandrism) is a better alternative than the term "trinity."[64] Once again, here, his advaitic perspective comes to the fore, when he maintains, "There are not two realities: God *and* man (or the world); but neither is there one: God *or* man (or the world) . . . reality itself is theandric."[65]

Trinity and World Religions

It should be clear from the previous section that Panikkar's project in *The Trinity and The Religious Experience of Man* is to explicate different forms of spirituality and to see them through the Trinitarian or cosmotheandric lens. To put it another way: Panikkar tries to appropriate each "person" of the Trinity to one of three forms of spirituality emerging in diverse religious

---

60. Panikkar, *Religious Experience*, 60.
61. Ibid.
62. Ibid., 63–64.
63. Ibid., 68.
64. He argues that the term "trinity" can limit the mystery only to the divine realm, without conceding the importance of humanity and creation. He also wants to avoid a direct connotation of the Christian terminology.
65. Panikkar, *Religious Experience*, 75.

An Imaginative Glimpse

traditions.⁶⁶ Ewert H. Cousins neatly summarizes Panikkar's project, based on his personal conversation with Panikkar, which is worth quoting at length.

> From Panikkar's perspective, then, one could in a most general fashion designate Buddhism as the religion of the Father, since the Buddhist moves to the experience of apophatic silence by negating the way of the word, of thought, of logos. . . . On the other hand, Judaism, Islam, and Christianity are religions of the Word, since they claim to have received a personal revelation from the divinity in words, images, and concepts. The Jew and Muslim see ultimate reality expressed in the word of God; and the Christian in the person of Christ, who is the personal Word of the Father. . . . In contrast, the advaitic Hindu seeks undifferentiated union with the Absolute; in this he or she reflects the spirituality of the Spirit since the Spirit's work is primarily that of union.⁶⁷

While I believe Cousins' summary of Panikkar's idea is accurate, it is interesting to see Panikkar's own attempt to make his argument. Regarding the spirituality of the Father, he sees in the Buddhist experience of *nirvāna* and *śūnyatā* the greatest possibility of accepting the apophatism of the divine.⁶⁸ He further says, "One is led onwards towards the 'absolute goal' and at the end one finds nothing, because there is nothing, not even Being. 'God created out of nothing' (*ex nihilo*), certainly, i.e. out of himself (*a Deo*)—a Buddhist will say."⁶⁹

In the section where he discusses the Son, the basic principle that he holds is that Christ signifies the mediatory role between divine and human, infinite and finite. He writes, "I would propose using the Lord for that Principle, Being, Logos or Christ that other religious traditions call by a variety of names and to which they attach a wide variety of ideas. . . . Each time that I speak of Christ I am referring (unless it is explicitly stated otherwise) to the Lord of whom Christians can lay claim to no monopoly. It is Christ, then, known or unknown—who makes religion possible."⁷⁰

---

66. Interestingly, there is in Panikkar's model an unmatched correspondence between the set of spiritualities (iconolatry, personalism, and mysticism) and the set of the Trinity (Father-apophatism, Son-theism, and Spirit-monism); cf. Heim, *Depth of the Riches*, 156.

67. Cousins, *Christ*, 81–82.

68. Panikkar, *Religious Experience*, 46–47.

69. Ibid., 47.

70. Ibid., 53.

The Trinity and Religions

Thus, for Panikkar, Christ is present not only in Christianity but also in every religion with different names and manifestations. The last statement in the above quotation is of importance with regard to one of Panikkar's most important works, *The Unknown Christ of Hinduism*. Originally published in 1964, the book was revised in 1981 with some significant changes. Although it is beyond the scope of my study to explore this book in detail, it is important to note that in the 1981 edition Panikkar makes a significant move from inclusivism to pluralism.[71] This shift is joined with his severing the universal-cosmic Christ from the particular-historical Jesus.

How about the Spirit? As Cousins mentions, the spirituality of the Spirit is evident in Hinduism. Panikkar himself affirms it by saying, "It is to this Spirit that most of the upanisadic assertions about the Absolute point, when seen in their own deepest light. One could cite almost every page of the Upanisads for examples. Indeed what is the Spirit but the *ātman* of the Upanisads, which is said to be identical with *brahman*, although this identity can only be existentially recognized and affirmed once 'realisation' has been attained?"[72]

In the 1981 edition of *The Unknown Christ of Hinduism*, Panikkar explicitly identifies the Spirit with the Divine *śakti* in Hinduism, which is described as "penetrating everything and manifesting God, disclosing him in his immanence and being present in all his manifestations."[73]

In this section, I have demonstrated Panikkar's approach to a theology of religions. His contribution to the broader conversation on this topic is substantial; he has taken the relation between Christianity and other religions in a new direction through his understanding of the Trinity. Moreover, his personal and deep engagement with Christian, Hindu, and Buddhist traditions contributes to his radical idea of cosmotheandrism, which becomes an all-encompassing principle for grasping all of reality: the divine, the human, and the cosmic. When applied to the issue of religious diversity, cosmotheandrism or "radical Trinity" enables Panikkar to say that every religious tradition demonstrates a different kind of spirituality; each corresponds to a different person of the Trinity. Through such an approach to religious diversity, Panikkar pushes pluralism to its outer limits. Yet, he is also aware that his highly abstract approach of religious pluralism must not become

---

71. About the analysis of Panikkar's shift, see Kärkkäinen, *Religious Pluralism*, 120–21. A more detailed comparison between both editions is provided by MacPherson, *Critical Reading*, 85–87, 101–2.

72. Panikkar, *Religious Experience*, 64–65.

73. Panikkar, *Unknown Christ*, 57.

just another theoretical supersystem. Rather, it must continually reflect both the human attitude toward reality as well as the ontological irreducibility of reality. In other words, pluralism must be lived rather than theorized. This position, of course, raises a number of issues that I will address in chapter 3. I will concentrate on three important issues. First, is Panikkar's non-theoretical pluralism plausible? Is it really possible to envision the structure of reality without having some theoretical basis? Second, is Panikkar's radical Trinity faithful to the Christian idea of the Trinity? To be more specific, has radical Trinity or cosmotheandrism made God dependent on non-divine (human and cosmic) beings? Finally, does Panikkar's appropriation method violate the classical Trinitarian principle: *opera trinitatis ad extra sunt indivisa* ("the external work of Trinity is undivided")?

In the following section, I discuss Gavin D'Costa's approach to the issue of religious diversity. Like Panikkar, D'Costa employs the Trinity as the central category for theology of religions, although he approaches the issue differently, using the Irenaean notion of "two hands of God." Unlike Panikkar, however, he rejects radical pluralism. D'Costa's own writings reveal an interesting shift from inclusivism to exclusivism, especially after his decision to return to the Catholic tradition.

Gavin D'Costa: The Christo-Pneumatological Dialectic and Dialogical Invitation

Gavin D'Costa's Trinitarian theology of religions, in Veli-Matti Kärkkäinen's words, "represents the most nuanced response to other religions from the perspective of classical Christian Trinitarian faith."[74] His approach, with the focus on the dialectic relation between the distinct yet complementary roles of Son and Spirit, undoubtedly resonates the Irenaean idea of Son and Spirit as the "two hands of God."[75] In this sense, therefore, D'Costa can be grouped with those who employ the similar approach, such as Amos Yong, Jacques Dupuis and others. My choice of D'Costa is primarily based on the fact that he has shown very long and intense conversations with pluralistic theologies of religions, as I will demonstrate below. His personal intercultural background, as an Afro-Indian Catholic theologian receiving education in England, also becomes an important factor to consider in his theology.

---

74. Kärkkäinen, *Religious Pluralism*, 76.
75. Irenaeus, *Against Heresies* IV.20.1.

The Trinity and Religions

My discussion of D'Costa's theology falls into two major sections. First, I examine his criticism of pluralistic theologies of religions as appearing not only in the Christian circle but also in other religions (Jewish, neo-Hindu and Buddhist). Second, I analyze his proposal of Trinitarian theology of religion. We also need to examine the sources of his ideas, which stem from the Catholic tradition (especially Vatican II and post-Vatican II) and contemporary philosophers (John Milbank, Alasdair MacIntyre, and Roland Barthes).

Pluralism and Modernity's Hidden God

Throughout his theological career, D'Costa has consistently demonstrated his rejection of pluralistic theologies. Already in his *Theology and Religious Pluralism* and *John Hick's Theology of Religions*, D'Costa harshly criticizes John Hick's pluralism. In his later writings he critiques other pluralists, both Christian and non-Christian. We can find D'Costa's most mature position against pluralism in his *The Meeting of Religions and the Trinity*, which provides the primary source for my analysis of his theological position. In this book, D'Costa provides critical evaluation of not only of the pluralistic theologies of Christian writers (John Hick and Paul F. Knitter), but also of Jewish, neo-Hindu, and Buddhist thinkers (Dan Cohn-Sherbok, Radhakrishnan, and Dalai Lama, respectively).

According to D'Costa, pluralism is doomed to fail. The reason is because the non-specific-tradition approach that the pluralists try to hold turns out, in fact, to be a traditional approach in itself. "Despite their intention to encourage openness, tolerance, and equality," D'Costa argues, "they fail to attain these goals . . . because of the tradition-specific nature of their positions. Their particular shaping tradition is the Enlightenment."[76] There are three consequences following this accusation. First, pluralists' attempts to present themselves as "brokers to disputing parties" end with invitations to the disputing parties to leave their initial positions and join the pluralists' specific tradition, namely, liberal modernity. Thus, the principle of neutrality that pluralists hold is basically a myth. Second, the failure to avoid their own tradition-specific standpoint makes it clear that pluralists' gods are modern gods: Unitarian, deistic, or agnostic. Third, if both consequences above are correct, D'Costa argues, it is undeniably that pluralism is in fact exclusivism. In short, pluralists fail to fulfill their own goals: to promote better

---

76. D'Costa, *Meeting of Religions*, 2.

interreligious dialogue. D'Costa tries to prove this through his analyses of three pluralists: Hick, Knitter, and Cohn-Sherbok.

D'Costa's long-standing adversary is John Hick, whose theology is a proof *par excellence* of the failure of pluralism in engaging with religious diversity. Hick's failure is multifaceted. First, he gradually yet consistently removes any connection between human language and divine reality, not only in Christian tradition but also in other religions. After suggesting that the incarnation of Christ is mythological, Hick applies the same way of thinking to the notion of God. He shifts the term God to "Real" that can express better personal and impersonal ideas of the Divine.[77] D'Costa concludes, "The notion of myth is utilized . . . [and] applied not only to the incarnation, but to the very idea of God; and is further extended to the ultimate realities designated by the various religions, such as the Hindu Brahman, or Allāh in Islam, Yahweh in Judaism, and so on."[78]

D'Costa blames this reductionism and essentialism to the typically Kantian distinction between the noumenal and the phenomenal. The result is as follows: "This privileging of the particular is a major theme within modernity's interpretation of Christianity. If the adherents of world religions are not allowed to make fundamental ontological claims with their full force and implications, then harmony is arrived at through destruction and neutralizing of the Other."[79]

In short, neutralization of Otherness undermines historical particularities. D'Costa sees the failure of Hick's pluralism as so severe that it touches all aspects of religion: ontological, epistemological, and ethical. Ontologically, any particularity of the divine in religions is undermined and viewed as merely phenomenal and mythical. Epistemologically, Hick's rejection of any real access to "the Real" leads his pluralism to agnosticism. Ethically, the universal ethic that Hick espouses is too formal and vague because it is not rooted in any religious tradition.

Where Hick's approach is more philosophical, Knitter's is more ethical. However, D'Costa's critique of Knitter's pluralist version is as strong as his critique of Hick's. He argues that Knitter has prioritized the Kantian type of a universal ethical imperative over metaphysics and religion. Through his eco-liberation theology of religions, Knitter maintains that the "basis of a common commitment to human and ecological well-being" is to be established

---

77. Hick, *Interpretation of Religion*.
78. D'Costa, *Meeting of Religions*, 26.
79. Ibid., 27.

The Trinity and Religions

by firstly understanding that suffering has "universality and immediacy."[80] D'Costa says that the universality and immediacy of ethical common ground that Knitter discusses are nothing but reminders that they belong to the "Encyclopedic genealogy"[81]—a term that he borrows from Alasdair MacIntyre, which is intended to name the tradition-specific starting point of liberal modernity.[82] The story of the universe becomes the "mastercode within which religions find themselves interpreted" and such a story provides all religions "a common creation myth" generating "a common ethical story."[83] D'Costa's criticism of Knitter concludes at the same point as his criticism of Hick: "Knitter propounds a fundamentally non-religious form of exclusivism. In fact, as with Hick's project, [Knitter's project] is unwittingly unhelpful in addressing the ecological, political, and interreligious tensions it tries to diffuse, for it excludes those very groups (the religions) in the process of reconciliation and peace making, by demanding that they be baptized in modernity before coming to the dialogue."[84]

Before analyzing three non-Christian thinkers, D'Costa summarizes his critiques of the Christian pluralistic theologies of Hick and Knitter, in a passage worth quoting at length:

> First, [both] have assimilated themselves to modernity rather than the triune God, they end up representing modernity's god: agnosticism (in the case of Hick) and a form of neo-pagan-unitarianism (Knitter). Second . . . they deny or obliterate difference and Otherness. In Hick's case, he mythologizes the differences away so that the religions can be fitted into his system. In Knitter's case, the religions are all judged by allegedly self-evident criteria that are found in the eco-system. Both Hick and Knitter know the full truth and what is ethically required of the religions independently of any of the religions. Third, and as a consequence, their pluralism turns out to be a strong form of Kantian exclusivist modernity. It cannot succeed in its claims to be more tolerant and open that forms of Christian Trinitarian theology.[85]

I will not discuss in detail D'Costa's critiques of the non-Christian pluralists, but only to give several important points briefly. First, he discusses

---

80. Knitter, *One Earth*, 15, 89.
81. D'Costa, *Meeting of Religions*, 31.
82. MacIntyre, *Three Rival Versions*.
83. D'Costa, *Meeting of Religions*, 32; Knitter, *One Earth*, 119, 23.
84. D'Costa, *Meeting of Religions*, 37.
85. Ibid., 39.

An Imaginative Glimpse

Dan Cohn-Sherbok in the same chapter as Hick and Knitter (chapter 1) for the very clear reason that "Hick's pluralism is thoroughly modernist and not Christian in so much as it is transferable and can be defended" by anyone from different religion.[86] Thus, in Cohn-Sherbok we find the Jewish version of the Encyclopedic tradition. Second, as to the neo-Hindu pluralism of Radhakrishnan and the Tibetan Buddhist pluralism of the Dalai Lama, which are discussed in two different chapters, D'Costa argues strongly that, even though both thinkers are not modernist pluralists, receiving only a "secondary influence" from modernism, their pluralisms also fail. In the final analysis, their basic attitude is exclusivistic.

Theoretical Approaches to Theology of Religions

Before discussing D'Costa's Trinitarian theology of religions, it is important to see his theoretical approach to the whole issue of religious plurality. I discuss in this section three aspects of D'Costa's standpoint that will be helpful in understanding his theological position. First, I analyze the development of his position regarding the classical typology of exclusivism, inclusivism, and pluralism. Second, his philosophical-theological debts to several contemporary thinkers need special investigation. Third, I examine his ecclesial starting-point, grounded in the Catholic tradition.

After the publication of Alan Race's *Christians and Religious Pluralism*, the typology of exclusivism, inclusivism, and pluralism became standard in the discourse of religious plurality. Three years after Race's book, D'Costa published his book using the same typology.[87] However, how D'Costa employs the threefold typology is fundamentally different from Race in some respects.[88] First, where Race employs the typology in a more epistemological way, according to criteria for assessing truth, D'Costa's focus is more soteriological, in which the two axioms of God's universal salvific will and Christ's decisiveness for salvation are addressed. Second, Race defends pluralism as the most justifiable theological position, whereas D'Costa believes that inclusivism is the best option in avoiding the two extremes of pluralism and exclusivism, in which it "tries to do full justice to those two most important Christian axioms: that salvation comes through God in Christ alone, and that God's salvific will is truly universal. By maintaining these two axioms in

---

86. D'Costa, *Meeting of Religions*, 39.
87. D'Costa, *Religious Pluralism*.
88. Perry, *Radical Difference*, 12.

fruitful tension, the inclusivist paradigm can be characterized by an openness and commitment."[89]

D'Costa's hero in this book is Karl Rahner, because of the latter's theory of "anonymous Christians." D'Costa attempts to prove to liberals and conservatives that Rahner's thought neither represents a Christian triumphalism nor is anthropocentric, relativist, or historically reductive.

Later on, however, D'Costa takes a critical stance toward Rahnerian inclusivism, which results from his deeper discontent with the classical typology of exclusivism, inclusivism, and pluralism. He says, "My own position has changed over the years. Once a convinced Rahnerian, I now find myself both troubled by the threefold paradigm and the theological construal of the problem. . . . The typology is constantly inadequate. . . . I think it is the case that in using the depictions (pluralism, inclusivism, and exclusivism) we disguise the fact that what we are really dealing with are different forms of *exclusivism*."[90]

He argues that Rahner's thought has the same exclusivistic logic as any other theology of religions. When it comes to the question of the final destiny, D'Costa maintains, "Rahner cannot depart from the necessity of the beatific vision, the trinitarian glory of God, which thereby requires that all non-Christians will only be finally and fully saved through participation in the beatific vision . . . it does finally require what exclusivists require, explicit confession to the triune God. In this sense, inclusivists are ontologically no different from exclusivists, although they sometimes have different epistemological assumptions."[91]

Nevertheless, it must be clear that his finding of the Trinitarian paradigm for doing theology of religions comes first before his final position, that all theologies are just different forms of exclusivism. In 1990, for the first time, he employs the Trinity as the central idea for his theology.[92] In these texts, he maintains his "inclusivist" position.[93] In the 1990 article he proposes five hypotheses, but only the first two appear in the second article. First, "A Trinitarian Christocentrism guards against exclusivism and pluralism by dialectically relating the universal to the particular"; second: "The

---

89. D'Costa, *Religious Pluralism*, 136.
90. D'Costa, "Theology of Religions," 637–38.
91. Ibid., 638.
92. D'Costa, 1990 article, "Christ," appears in the multi-authored book edited by himself, *Christian Uniqueness*, which criticizes another collection published by the pluralist camp, edited by Knitter and Hick, *Christian Uniqueness*.
93. D'Costa, "Christ," 16, 26; D'Costa, "Trinitarian Theology," 146–47.

Holy Spirit allows the particularity of Christ to be related to the universal activity of God in human history."[94] These points merit discussion. First, the dialectic between particularity and universality employed by D'Costa is solidly grounded in the Irenaean image of the two hands of God—the Son and the Spirit—and in the way that the Spirit makes it possible for the particularity of the Son to relate to the universal salvific will of God.

Second, D'Costa believes that this dialectic cannot lead to the idea that there is another salvific agent beside the Son, namely, the Spirit. Jesus is still and always normative, in the sense that nothing that we know through Jesus can contradict that which is of God. Jesus, in short, is the decisive and irreversible self-utterance of God. On the one hand, this is D'Costa's consistent position against pluralistic theologies which, in his view, have divorced the understanding of God from the story of Jesus and, consequently, the universal from the particular.[95] On the other hand, his position toward exclusivism and inclusivism is rather ambiguous. In these two articles, D'Costa clearly defends the inclusivist model, in opposition to exclusivist and pluralist models. In this phase, D'Costa still employs the typology in a more soteriological way, in which the key question is how to harmonize the two axioms of God's universal salvific will and Christ's decisiveness for salvation. In this sense, exclusivism fails to engage with the former, precisely because it overemphasizes the latter. He writes, "Against exclusivists, it must be stressed that the 'Son is not the Father' . . . we cannot turn Jesus into an idol and claim that the Father is exclusively known through him."[96]

Third, the second hand of God, the Spirit, makes it possible for D'Costa to affirm God's universal salvific will and God's ongoing self-revelation beyond Christianity. Consequently, he argues, "the story of Jesus is incomplete until the end of history and through the Spirit, is constantly unfolded."[97] Thus, it is within the work of the Spirit that the eschatological meaning of the Son's works is established. Nevertheless, while he maintains this pneuma-eschatological aspect, D'Costa continuously warns his readers that God's continuing self-disclosure "is authorized and measured insomuch as it is in conformity to Christ."[98] The question is why the particularity of the Son becomes so normative that other particularities, if any, needs to be in conformity to Christ. Obviously, the answer to this question is that there is

94. D'Costa, "Trinitarian Theology," 18–19; cf. D'Costa, "Christ," 147, 50.
95. D'Costa, "Trinitarian Theology," 148.
96. D'Costa, "Christ," 18; D'Costa, "Trinitarian Theology," 148.
97. D'Costa, "Trinitarian Theology," 148.
98. Ibid., 152.

another universal aspect of God's revelation, but this time it is found not in the Spirit, but "Christ, the universal Logos [that is] the normative criteria for God."[99] In short, one particularity cannot be used as a judge or norm of other particularities unless in itself it also has universal dimension.[100]

D'Costa seems to realize the problem of his approach. The inclusivist mode that he promotes fails if he holds to a purely and symmetrically dialectical relation between the Son and the Spirit. The universality of Spirit is not universal enough, since it is subordinated to the universality of the Son. I believe this is one among many reasons why D'Costa revises his position from inclusivism to exclusivism. Another reason is that he finds in the writings of Alasdair MacIntyre and John Milbank more solid bases, on which he can repudiate more severely the gods of modernity hidden in pluralistic theologies.

D'Costa owes to MacIntyre the uncovering of the impact of modernity on Christian theology, which is also reflected in pluralistic theologies. According to MacIntyre, not only is the Enlightenment project responsible for the demise of Trinitarian theology, but it also diminishes the Christian *telos*. What is offered by the Enlightenment project is a reconstruction of the world within some grand-narratives. D'Costa then follows the development of MacIntyre's thinking from *After Virtue* to *Whose Justice? Whose Rationality?* In this latter work, MacIntyre answers his critics who accuse him as promoting relativism. MacIntyre argues that it is not the case, since he believes in the importance of rational discourse and its possible outcomes. What is missing in MacIntyre, according to D'Costa, however, is that "his virtue ethics lacks substantial teleological specification to provide a credible social alternative."[101]

D'Costa's discussion of John Milbank's critique of MacIntyre is also of importance, although I will not discuss it in detail here. It is enough to mention some important points. First, D'Costa disagrees with Milbank in criticizing MacIntyre's hidden foundationalism through the emphasis on rational dialectics as the means to truth. On the contrary, Milbank argues for the rhetorical out-narration to replace MacIntyre's dialectics. What D'Costa suggests is that we should employ both rhetoric and dialectics, along with

---

99. Ibid.

100. I would argue that D'Costa offers an asymmetrical idea of two hands of God, in which the Spirit has universal value, while the Son has both universal and particular value. In this sense, D'Costa stands firmly in the Western *filioque* tradition. Thus, the seeming dialectic between the Son and the Spirit is not exactly dialectical.

101. D'Costa, *Meeting of Religions*, 6.

the apologetic method. He tries to present these three in his book, *The Meeting of Religions and the Trinity*. While the apologetic element is shown in his rejection of pluralistic theologies in four religious traditions, as we have already seen, the rhetoric and dialectic elements manifest in his attempt to "show that the most important aspirations of pluralists (openness, tolerance, and equality toward other religions) are actually better embodied, more coherently justified, and fully articulated within modern Roman Catholic trinitarianism."[102]

Second, in contrast to MacIntyre and Milbank, D'Costa attempts to propose a different theological reflection of the religious other, one that does not construe the other as a "rival" (MacIntyre) or an object of "out-narration" (Milbank). He believes that in this case, the Roman Catholic Trinitarianism provides a more friendly way of dealing with the other, in which "the other is always interesting in their difference and may be the possible face of God, or the face of violence, greed, and death."[103] Even more, in open engagement with the other, Christians may learn from them certain aspects to understand and worship the Trinitarian God more deeply.

Third, it is central in D'Costa's view that any theology of religion should begin with a certain non-neutral position or a tradition-specific perspective. This view is deeply indebted to MacIntyre and Milbank, but especially the former. This view is part of the reason of why he changes his position from Trinitarian inclusivism to Trinitarian exclusivism. This change, however, does not happen from one theoretical model to another within the same category. In his earlier phase of inclusivism, D'Costa argues for inclusivism and against pluralism and exclusivism by using a more soteriological category. However, his move to exclusivism is no longer based on the same category. It is not a soteriological perspective that D'Costa uses here as it is an epistemological one.[104]

102. Ibid., 9. D'Costa proposes to replace terms valued as ultimate goals by pluralists: openness, tolerance, and equality. Openness becomes "taking history seriously," tolerance becomes the "qualified establishment of civic religious freedom for all on the basis of revelation and natural law," and equality becomes the "equal and inviolable dignity of all persons." D'Costa, *Meeting of Religions*, 32–38, 101.

103. D'Costa, *Meeting of Religions*, 9.

104. In 1998, D'Costa still defends his inclusivism, while distinguishing his open version of inclusivism from more closed versions. While closed inclusivists insist that we possess the truth and recognize the same truth in other religions, D'Costa argues that "open inclusivists like myself can be depicted as saying that in Christ or/and Christian church we have the truth of God. *But* this truth is never our possession but, rather, we are possessed by it." D'Costa, "Trinitarian Différance," 37–38. This open version of inclusivism, D'Costa maintains, can prevent us from the possibilities of projecting Otherness as

D'Costa believes that inclusivism, in the final analysis, collapses into exclusivism and therefore his shift to exclusivism is reasonably justified. He gives several reasons for this shift.[105] First, both inclusivists and exclusivists believe that "their tradition finally contains the truth regarding ontological, epistemological, and ethical claims" that helps them narrate all creation. This leads to the second reason: that such inseparability of ontology, epistemology and ethics cannot separated from the mediator (Christ or the church). These two reasons, thirdly, result in the affirmation of the tradition-specific nature of their position.[106] D'Costa provides another significant argument regarding his identification of inclusivism and exclusivism. When inclusivists try to "include" other religious traditions into their system, what they include is not their totality but rather certain parts of the traditions. The selective part is "not the religion *per se*, but a reinterpretation of that tradition in so much as that which is included in now included within a different paradigm."[107] Again, D'Costa says, "In affirming something from another tradition, the significance of this affirmation for the affirmer might well be quite different from that given in its original home. . . . This cannot be said really to affirm, both because it is a part and not the whole, and because what is being affirmed is not that tradition as it understands itself, but what the alien theologian chooses to prioritize and select."[108]

This is a very serious observation that holds weight for my project as well. The importance of tradition-specific approach is paramount in D'Costa's last position, so that he has to specify his own tradition as the starting point for his proposal. This leads us to the third aspect of our theoretical analysis of D'Costa's theology, that is, his ecclesial perspective. Since the Trinity is a "community-forming doctrine," D'Costa argues, it is unavoidable "to use the community's own authoritative documentary sources."[109] D'Costa explicitly declares his Roman Catholic tradition, especially Vatican II and post-Conciliar documents, as the point of departure of his theology of religions. He

---

negative mirror-opposite (exclusivism) or total assimilation of Otherness to Sameness (pluralism and closed inclusivism). Nevertheless, this article operates neither in soteriological nor epistemological category.

105. D'Costa, *Meeting of Religions*, 22.

106. D'Costa, however, permits one significant difference between inclusivism and exclusivism. While both agree on the possibility that *non-Christians* can be saved, inclusivism move farther by seeking to affirm *non-Christian religions* as the means to salvation. The distinction is of importance in D'Costa, as further discussed below.

107. D'Costa, *Meeting of Religions*, 23.

108. Ibid.

109. Ibid., 12.

admits that his approach may have no authority for those outside the Roman Catholic tradition. To address this limitation D'Costa undertakes an analysis of the Johannine understanding of the Holy Spirit functioning in the formation of the body of Christ and in the leading of the church to greater truth. This, he hopes, can provide persuasive arguments based on what is shared by larger Christian tradition. But, we will see later that his dependence on the Roman Catholic texts is much more fundamental; in fact, his biblical account cannot function optimally without them.

The Trinity, the Holy Spirit, and the Church

Do Other Religions Save?

That non-Christians can be saved is not debatable within the Catholic tradition. *Lumen Gentium*, for instance, clearly states that salvation can be attained by Jews, "to whom the testament and the promises were given and from whom Christ was born according to the flesh," Muslims, "who acknowledge the Creator . . . [and] who, professing to hold the faith of Abraham, along with us adore the one and merciful God, who on the last day will judge mankind," and other religious people.[110] Regarding the last category, religious people from non-Abrahamic traditions, "those who in shadows and images seek the unknown God," the document also declares that salvation is available to them under three conditions: "[1] through no fault of their own do not know the Gospel of Christ or His Church, yet sincerely seek God and moved by grace strive by their deeds to do His will as it is known to them through the dictates of conscience . . . [2] without blame on their part, have not yet arrived at an explicit knowledge of God and with His grace strive to live a good life . . . [3] Whatever good or truth is found amongst them is looked upon by the Church as a preparation for the Gospel."[111]

D'Costa gives three notes on this issue.[112] First, the "good life" used in the second condition refers to conscience and natural law. Second, the idea of "preparation for the Gospel" (*preparatio evangelica*) resounds a classical Thomistic dictum: *gratia non tollit naturam, sed perficit* (grace does not destroy but perfects nature). Third, this statement is consistent with what is said in *Nostra Aetate*, that all religions "reflect a ray of that Truth which en-

---

110. *Lumen Gentium* 16.
111. Ibid.
112. D'Costa, *Meeting of Religions*, 104.

lightens all men."[113] This statement, D'Costa argues, simply emphasizes the fact that "truths found in non-Christian religions . . . are never more nor can they be, than the Truth found in Christ."[114] Thus, it is Christ who saves them.

While it is clear for the Catholic thinking that *non-Christians* can attain salvation through Christ, there remains the question of whether non-Christian *religions, per se,* can be supernatural means of salvation. The answer, for D'Costa, is clear: silence! And this silence is obviously intentional. This silence, he argues, can be and has been interpreted in two ways by two different groups of theologians. First, those who emphasize a very close relationship between grace and nature tend to understand this silence as the affirmation that other religions are indeed salvific. Second, those who hold the sharp distinction between grace and nature tend to interpret the silence as a "no" answer. John Paul II, and D'Costa himself following the Pope, agree with the latter. Moreover, D'Costa suggests that this intentional silence, with its seemingly negative answer, does not prohibit the Christian church to proclaim that "supernatural saving grace is operative in other religions and that in those other religions there is much that is true, good, and holy, and much to be admired and learned by the church."[115]

How can this be understood theologically? How can we affirm both the normativity of Jesus Christ, resulting in the fact that other religions *per se* are not salvific, and the operation of supernatural saving grace in other religions? For D'Costa, the answer is to be found in the proper understanding of the Spirit framed within its Trinitarian context. I now want to turn to this subject.

The Spirit and Relational Engagement

In discussing Pope John Paul II's magisterial works, D'Costa sees the similar silence that he finds in the Vatican II Council regarding non-Christian religions as salvific structures *per se*. Similarly, an emphasis on the works of the Spirit is predominant in the Pope's theology. In *Redemptoris Missio*, for example, the Pope writes,

> This is the same Spirit who was at work in the Incarnation and in the life, death and resurrection of Jesus, and who is at work in the Church. He is therefore not an alternative to Christ, nor does he

---

113. *Nostra Aetate* 2.
114. D'Costa, *Meeting of Religions*, 104.
115. Ibid., 105.

An Imaginative Glimpse

> fill a sort of void which is sometimes suggested as existing between Christ and the Logos. Whatever the Spirit brings about in human hearts and in the history of peoples, in cultures and religions serves as a preparation for the Gospel and can only be understood in reference to Christ, the Word who took flesh by the power of the Spirit "so that as perfectly human he would save all human beings and sum up all things."[116]

Two important things appear in the quoted text. First, the Spirit who works in other religions is the same Spirit who at work in Jesus' incarnation. Thus, we cannot talk about two forms of grace, but one grace of both the Son and the Spirit. Second, the Pope anchors his theology of Spirit within the classical doctrine of *preparatio evangelica*. A third important aspect needs to be mentioned, that is, that the dialectic between universality and particularity is now understood no longer precisely in terms of the two hands of God (the Son and the Spirit), but in terms of the Spirit (the universal) and the church (the particular). This is obvious in the next sentence, "Moreover, the *universal* activity of the Spirit is not to be separated from his *particular* activity within the body of Christ, which is the Church."[117] The church, however, is understood as both the body of Christ and the particular activity of the Spirit. In short, the church is the locus where the universality of the Spirit and the particularity of the Son meet. The universality of the Spirit is particularized within the church, and thus it must be seen as concurrent with the particular activity of Jesus Christ.

The dialectical relation between the Spirit and the church is also evident in the conciliar documents. On the one hand, in *Gaudium et Spes*, we find a statement that "the Holy Spirit in a manner known only to God offers to every man the possibility of being associated with this paschal mystery."[118] On the other hand, *Lumen Gentium* clearly maintains that the church is "necessary for salvation."[119] D'Costa indicates a clue concerning how to reconcile this tension:

> The main route for reconciling these tension lies within the Conciliar teaching that whenever God is present, this is the present of triune God; and it is this triune God who is the foundation of the church. Hence, one very important point follows from these Conciliar statements: the Holy Spirit's presence within other religions

116. *Redemptoris Missio* 29.
117. Ibid.; italics mine.
118. *Gaudium et Spes* 22.
119. *Lumen Gentium* 14.

The Trinity and Religions

is both intrinsically trinitarian and ecclesiological. It is trinitarian in referring the Holy Spirit's activity to the paschal mystery of Christ, and ecclesial in referring the paschal event to the constitutive community-creating force it has, under the guidance of the Spirit.[120]

The Trinitarian aspect D'Costa offers, in which the activity of the Spirit is closely related to the paschal mystery of Christ, is relatively unproblematic.[121] It is his ecclesial aspect that needs a critical examination, which I will undertake in chapter 3. For now, suffice it to say that, despite the fact that he makes a bold and innovative proposal in making the church an asset for his theology of religions,[122] D'Costa's notion of the ecclesial position is problematic from the intra-Christian or ecumenical point of view.[123] The question of whether the church that D'Costa means includes all other Christian churches outside the Roman Catholic Church shadows him every time he discusses the ecclesiological aspects of his theology.

How do the Conciliar and post-Conciliar documents understand the presence of the Spirit in other religions? As D'Costa has shown, *Redemptoris Missio* 29 argues that the Spirit is present in relating the paschal mystery to all people, and that she also constitutes a *preparatio evangelica*. Moreover, the same magisterial document acknowledges "the inchoate reality of the Kingdom" present within other religions, yet argues that such "remains incomplete unless it is related to the Kingdom of Christ in the Church and straining toward eschatological fullness."[124] D'Costa also joins this aspect with an admission to the fact that, through "many voices of our age . . . revealed truth can always be more deeply penetrated, better understood,

---

120. D'Costa, *Meeting of Religions*, 110.

121. Of course, there is still an ongoing issue of *filioque* that, surprisingly, is not discussed by D'Costa. I will return to this issue in chapter 3.

122. Kärkkäinen, *Religious Pluralism*, 76.

123. The necessary and intrinsic relations between the Trinitarian persons, the church, and the economy of the Trinity are the parameters through which D'Costa criticizes several Catholic theologians who deal with the same issue. He criticizes Knitter as the theologian who has moved farthest beyond the parameter by disassociating the Spirit's activity from its Christological link. In Panikkar he sees an attempt to rehabilitate a Logos Christology, but his universalizing of the Logos makes the particularity of Jesus Christ only one among many expressions of the Logos. As for Dupuis, D'Costa agrees with his idea of connecting Christ and the Spirit, yet rejects his removal of the church as the necessary parameter for salvation. D'Costa's position is closest to Rahner's in providing a balanced view of the relations between the economic activity of the Trinity, the kingdom, and the church. See D'Costa, *Meeting of Religions*, 110–11.

124. *Redemptoris Missio* 20.

An Imaginative Glimpse

and set forth to greater advantage."[125] Putting these two together, D'Costa concludes boldly,

> That is, if the church is not attentive to the possibility of the Spirit within other religions, it will fail to be attentive to the Word of God that has been entrusted to it. In this sense, if one were to retain and utilize the category of fulfillment in a very careful sense, then it is *not only the other religions that are fulfilled* in (an in one sense, radically transformed) their *preparatio* being completed through Christianity, but *also Christianity itself that is fulfilled in receiving the gift of the God that the Other might bear, self consciously or not*.[126]

Thus, on the one hand, the conviction of the activity of the Spirit in other religions leads to another conviction that Christianity can have an inner transformation after implanting and developing the gifts of the Spirit coming from other religions "through dialogue."[127] The possible transformation in the church, because of the affirmation that the Spirit works in other religions, "might always call the church into question in a way that cannot be predicted a priori."[128]

On the other hand, what should the church do as to the presence of the Spirit in other religions? D'Costa here explicates certain principles. First, the Christian church needs to give "painstaking attention to the inner logic and intrasystematic richness within another religion (i.e. auto-interpretation) prior to being able to affirm, critique, and engage with that tradition."[129] Otherwise, the Other will be approached not as genuinely Other but as something that to be domesticated and negated. Second, the respectiveness of the church to what the Spirit might do in other religions also means that

---

125. *Gaudium et Spes* 44. The original context of this statement is the Western secular culture, but D'Costa extends it to other religions by saying, "It is perhaps a matter of time before similar acknowledgments regarding other religions enter into post-Conciliar documentation, but will do so only, and should do so only, on the basis of the historical experience of the local churches." D'Costa, *Meeting of Religions*, 112.

126. D'Costa, *Meeting of Religions*, 114, italics mine.

127. *Redemptoris Missio* 29. Again, however, D'Costa reminds his readers that this dialogical imperative is a community-based or church-based activity, not merely individual activity.

128. D'Costa, *Meeting of Religions*, 117.

129. D'Costa distinguishes between auto-interpretation and hetero-interpretation. The former refers to self-understanding of a religion on its own terms, whereas the latter is a theological evaluation of a religious from outside that religion. He argues that both auto-interpretation and hetero-interpretation may coincide, but the latter is always reliant on the former. D'Costa, *Meeting of Religions*, 100.

The Trinity and Religions

the church should be open to the possibility of non-Christians to be more Christ-like.[130] Such circumstances, however, will still require serious discernment by the church.

Furthermore, the place of the Johannine texts of the Paraclete (John 14–16) within D'Costa's whole system cannot be underestimated. Veli-Matti Kärkkäinen provides a very good summary:

> After and by virtue of the crucifixion, resurrection, and ascension of Jesus Christ, the Holy Spirit perichoretically indwells the disciples of Jesus, predicated upon the indwelling of the Son and the Father, calling the church, the body of Christ, "to be Christ to the world" in mutual love and sharing, as well as in sharing love with the world, even (as in John's case) over against the hostile "world." . . . The Spirit, facilitating the church's participation in God's trinitarian love, thus brings to focus the trinitarian foundations of the church and thus the integral connection between ecclesiology, pneumatology and the Trinity.[131]

What is relevant to my own project is that this is the first time that D'Costa employs the term "perichoresis" in his book. Interestingly, D'Costa relates two different images of perichoresis: person-perichoresis and ecclesial-perichoresis. The mutual-indwelling of the Triune persons now includes the potential of the disciples of Jesus to participate in God's inner life and love. As such, the intrinsic connection between trinity and ecclesiology, and between doctrine and practice, is settled. Also, it is the Spirit who facilitates such a connection.

D'Costa moves further by saying that "perichoretic relations do not stop at the boundaries of the church."[132] He explores this possibility in the context of conversations on interreligious prayer.[133] The fullness of this perichoretic embracing of other religious others, however, is "fragmented relationality and perichoresis" and will only be enjoyed "eschatologically when together, all creation, transformed and redeemed, gives praise to God."[134] Also, another theological consequence of using perichoretic language needs to be taken seriously: the presence of the Spirit, who facilitates the peri-

---

130. D'Costa, *Meeting of Religions*, 115, 29.

131. Kärkkäinen, *Religious Pluralism*, 73.

132. D'Costa, *Meeting of Religions*, 143.

133. Due to space limitation, I do not discuss D'Costa's exploration of interreligious prayer, a special case that he uses to test his overall theology; see D'Costa, *Meeting of Religions*, ch. 5.

134. D'Costa, *Meeting of Religions*, 154.

choretic relations among religions, is at the same time the presence of two other Triune persons, the Father and the Son, as well as the church and the kingdom of God.

To conclude, D'Costa demonstrates a totally different approach to the relation between the Trinity and religious diversity. While Panikkar embraces pluralism as the most desirable position and pushes it in a non-theoretical and ontological direction, D'Costa rejects pluralism and embraces exclusivism as his final position. He justifies this approach on the grounds that any theology of religions must be tradition-based. Arguing against those who attempt to find universal salvation "leaking" out of Christianity through works of the Spirit, he insists that the universality of the Spirit is inseparable from the particularity of the Son and the universality of the church. Still, for D'Costa this by no means limits the "inchoate" works of the Spirit in other religions. Since the Spirit works outside the Christian tradition, we can and should learn from certain aspects of other religions in order to understand and worship the Triune God more deeply. In chapter 3, I will address some important issues in D'Costa's model, especially his ambiguous exclusivism and the strictness of his tradition-based approach. In spite of my concern about these issues, D'Costa's "silence" regarding other religions' destinies will end up playing a surprisingly significant role in my own approach.

Panikkar and D'Costa have demonstrated two radically different approaches to the issue of religious diversity, although they start from the same Trinitarian notion. S. Mark Heim, whose approach will be discussed in the following section, suggests a third alternative to the two previous views. Heim's theology of multiple religious ends offers something of a "middle way" between Panikkar and D'Costa.

S. Mark Heim: The Trinity and Multiple Religious Ends

In his *Introducing Theologies of Religions*, Paul F. Knitter praises S. Mark Heim as the "strongest and clearest voice among advocates of the Acceptance Model in stressing the real and abiding differences of the religions."[135]

---

135. Knitter, *Introducing*, 135. Knitter offers an alternative to Alan Race's typology of exclusivism, inclusivism, and pluralism, by expanding the range of Christian attitudes toward other religions into four models: Replacement, Fulfillment, Mutuality, and Acceptance models. While the first three models are similar to Race's three types, the last model refers to the most recent development represented by theologians like S. Mark Heim, George Lindbeck, and Joseph A. DiNoia and comparativists such as Francis X. Clooney and James Fredericks.

Knitter's description of Heim is accurate for two reasons, which I need to emphasize before exploring them more deeply.

First, the real differences of the religions, for Heim, refer not only to multiple ways of salvation, but also to multiple salvations. Each religion offers its own unique ultimate aim that is totally different from that of the others. In his aptly titled book, *Salvations: Truth and Difference in Religion*, Heim makes his critical argument in conversation with pluralistic theologies of religions. He maintains that, while offering a radical alternative to the Christocentrism of exclusivism and inclusivism, the advocates of pluralistic theology add nothing distinctive in terms of religious ends. All three models dispute over the question of one way or many ways of salvation, but they also share the same assumption that there is only one unequivocal salvation. In contrast to the classical models, Heim suggests that his hypothesis of multiple religious ends makes the question of one or many ways no longer relevant.

The second reason is that Heim bases his hypothesis of multiple religious ends on a theological idea that the real differences between religions are authentically rooted in the differences within God. In *Salvations*, Heim offers a general interpretive perspective in conversation with pluralistic theology. In his second book, *The Depth of the Riches: A Trinitarian Theology of Religious Ends*, attempts to address some questions left unanswered in the first book, and "to map a Christian theology that has place for distinct religious ends."[136] It is through the classical notion of the Trinity that Heim tries to secure the reality of religious diversity. To him, the multiplicity of salvations offered by different religious traditions replicates a variety of relations to God, which is possible only because there is an array of relations within the Trinitarian God.

In the following pages I critically explore Heim's Trinitarian theology of religions by focusing on these two aspects. First, I examine Heim's critique of pluralistic theologies and his epistemological solution to the issue of the incommensurability of different religious traditions. Second, I investigate his Trinitarian theology of religions in general.

Against the Pluralistic Meta-Theology

Heim's target of critique in *Salvations* is the pluralistic theology of religions that appears in three dominant streams, each of which ends up in affirming

---

136. Heim, *Depth of the Riches*, 12.

An Imaginative Glimpse

what they intentionally deny, that is, the imperialistic tendency in Christian attitudes toward other religions. The three streams discussed in Part One of the book are John Hick's philosophical pluralism, Wilfred C. Smith's historical pluralism, and Paul F. Knitter's ethical pluralism. Here, I will not repeat Heim's extensive criticisms of each of these pluralistic theologians (presented in chapters 1 [Hick], 2 [Smith], and 3 [Knitter] of *Salvations*). Rather, I will summarize his general criticism of pluralistic theology and discuss how he tries to avoid the mistakes of the pluralists by adopting Nicholas Rescher's "orientational pluralism" for his theology.[137]

Heim begins with the doubt that the pluralist proposal is truly novel. He refers to four already-present types of Christian-Hindu dialogues, three of which are similar to ones suggested by Hick, Smith, and Knitter: dialogue of doctrine (corresponding to Hindu's *jnana* or knowledge), of spiritualities (similar to Hindu's *bhakti* or devotions), of reformation (analogous to the Indian path of *karma*), and of popular culture. Based on this fact, Heim maintains that the pluralistic doctrines "add nothing distinctive to these existing dialogues."[138]

However, the more serious failure of the pluralistic theologies is to be found in the way their *statuses* as theories of religion are positioned among other alternatives.[139] Heim maintains that in the final analysis they fall short of the principles they try to defend and end up with what they want to reject: inclusivism, if not exclusivism. The reason of this is because they are unable to resolve the paradox in their central principles. While acknowledging the possibility of many faiths to save through their different paths, the pluralists insist that it is possible only within the conceptual framework they have already constructed. Those who do not agree with the plan of the pluralists are in need of enlightenment and fulfillment. In Heim's words:

> Given the apparent insistence on the validity of many ways, we might expect pluralists to affirm the full and equal value of religious paths that are inclusivist or exclusivist in character. But they seem very hesitant to do so. In fact they themselves adopt a classically inclusivist posture. Unenlightened, sincere devotees of

---

137. While my summary of Heim's criticism of pluralistic theologies is primarily dependent on chapter 4 of his *Salvations*, the description of his orientational pluralism appears in chapter 5 of the same book. See Heim, "Pluralistic Hypothesis"; Heim, "Orientational Pluralism."

138. Heim, *Salvations*, 101.

139. Heim believes that the unmasking of the *status* of pluralistic theories of religion is the first and most important task in attaining a more adequate view of religious diversity; see Heim, *Salvations*, 124, 31.

various faiths may be saved both historically and cosmically. But *not on the basis they imagine*. It is the Real [Hick], of faith [Smith], or justice [Knitter] as the pluralists know them that redeem. Ignorance and error need not bar others from salvation. Yet, only the priests of world theology can lead us to its full realization.[140]

In other words, the acceptance of religious diversity by the pluralists is not as radical as they claim it to be. Religions are not accepted as they are, in their own terms, but as already framed within the conceptual understanding of the pluralists. In this sense, Heim's identification of the "inclusivist posture" of pluralistic theologies is inescapably correct.

Even more, the pluralists' insistence to use a particular framework beyond all particular traditions implies an exclusivist attitude, in which those who do not agree with such a framework are in need of conversion into their "structure of plausibility."[141] Heim uses the term "exclusivism in the mirror" as one of the sub-titles of chapter 4.[142] Although he does not explain this term, I believe he is drawing attention to the tendency common to both pluralist and exclusivist theologians to exclude those who are not in agreement with their conceptual frameworks.

The conceptual frameworks predominant in pluralistic theologies are thus ambiguous. On the one hand, by focusing on an idea of the Real, or faith, or justice, the pluralists attempt to acknowledge as many ways of salvation as possible. On the other hand, these frameworks are so remote and abstract that they are positioned above or beyond any particular idea of salvation provided by religions. In short, they function as meta-theologies pretending to provide a "God's-eye view" of all religious traditions.

Heim gives a harsh criticism of this kind of meta-theology.[143] He argues that the pluralistic meta-theology fails, because the pluralists do not admit the fact that in fact it works from within a particular tradition or a "framework of commitment." On the contrary, they tend to mask this tradition-based position by offering some universal principles applied to all traditions and by using them as a view "on a different level and in some qualitative way beyond such particularity."[144] What is exactly the tradition on which the pluralists base their theories? Heim shows that the pluralistic meta-theology expresses "cultural structures of plausibility against which modern Western

140. Heim, *Salvations*, 102, italics mine.
141. Ibid., 103.
142. Ibid., 101.
143. Ibid., 104–7.
144. Ibid., 105.

An Imaginative Glimpse

Christianity has been defined."[145] It therefore is not universal at all; rather, it is a universalizing of a particular tradition imposed on others. In this sense, as Heim strongly argues, "the old lamented triumphalist attitudes of Christians remain in vigorous health, if in different forms."[146]

It is key to Heim's overall project to unmask the universalizing tendency in the pluralistic theologies. As he writes, "The primary challenge to pluralist theories is to make explicit their case for the global normativity of the Western critical principles that determine their univocal definitions of religions." Having learned from the failure of pluralistic theologies, Heim stresses the necessity to construct a new theory of religious diversity that overcomes the failures of the pluralistic theologies. Such a theory has to fulfill certain criteria, through which we are able to "[1] recognize the integrity of the religious traditions in their own terms . . . [2] intrinsically acknowledge its own lack of neutrality, [3] recognize that it exists on the same plane with alternatives, and [4] yet have the universal scope pluralistic theories claim."[147]

Heim elaborates further these four criteria by setting up eight points of a "Job Description" for the new theory he is proposing.[148] However, those criteria, as well as the Job Description itself, may be recapitulated in the twofold dialectical principle expressed in the subtitle of his book: *Truth and Difference*. The theory of religious diversity he is proposing must maintain, on the one hand, the possibility for one to affirm one's commitment to *ultimate truth*, and, on the other hand, the invitation to celebrate *radical religious otherness or difference*. The plausibility of this theory, however, depends heavily on its success in maintaining this dialectic, and Heim find in Rescher's orientational pluralism a great assistance in undertaking this task.[149]

Orientational Pluralism and Inclusivist Pluralism

Orientational Pluralism as a Solution

Rescher defines "orientational pluralism" as "a position that maintains that philosophical positions hinge on diverse views regarding matters of

---

145. Ibid., 103.
146. Ibid., 109.
147. Ibid., 131.
148. Ibid., 124–26.
149. Heim is not the only one who makes use of Rescher's orientational pluralism, although he employs it most extensively; cf. James, *Tillich*, 71–72; Kiblinger, *Buddhist Inclusivism*; Saarinen, "After Rescher," 209–13; Thomas, "Religious Plurality," 197–213.

cognitive-value, so that philosophical disagreement becomes inevitable."[150] He begins with the fact that there is continuing pervasive disagreement among philosophers. The disagreement, argues Rescher, is in the very nature of philosophy and cannot be eliminated, because "different philosophers are bound to adopt different cognitive-value orientations,"[151] and it is impossible for one person to occupy several orientations at once. Also, Rescher's orientational pluralism allows for neither the sublimation of two or more cognitive-value orientations to a higher level nor the possibility of a "neutral 'God's-eye point of view' from which philosophical positions can be criticized or evaluated."[152]

What is the difference between Rescher's and Heim's orientational pluralism and the conventional pluralism held by Hick, Smith, and Knitter? Apparently, while conventional pluralism argues for the possibility to have a "God's-eye perspective" or meta-theology beyond all particular traditions and to see from above the "rough parity" among those traditions, orientational pluralism rejects this idea by saying that "one and only one position is rationally appropriate from a given perspective, but we must recognize that there is a diversity of perspectives."[153] The two pluralisms also offer different views on the status of theories of religions. Orientational pluralism allows us to make an evaluative claim about the universal scope of one's particular orientation while thinking the others who hold different perspectives as wrong, whereas conventional pluralism believes that all views are equally valid, but merely as expressions of the same principle. Orientational pluralists would be willing to admit that their claim is characteristically doctrinal so that it should be put on the same plane as other theories, while conventional pluralists reject other theories as alternatives to their own.

It is obvious, therefore, that Rescher's orientational pluralism is of significant help to Heim, not only in his rejection of pluralistic meta-theology, but also in constructing his own theology of religions. Rescher's perspectival idea is compatible with most, if not all, of Heim's Job Description. However, while Rescher's view provides an epistemologically solid basis for Heim's theory, it does not help him discuss the content of that theory. This is consistent with what Rescher argues, "It should be stressed, accordingly, that this stance [orientational pluralism] represents a particular position regarding the *methodology* of philosophy. At the level of substantive *ontology*,

150. Rescher, *Strife of Systems*, 125.
151. Ibid.
152. Ibid., 188.
153. Heim, *Salvations*, 134.

An Imaginative Glimpse

where what concerns us is the nature of the things rather than the nature of philosophy, orientational pluralism as such is altogether neutral. On the question of ontological monism or dualism or pluralism, of idealism vs. materialism vs. monism, and so on, orientational pluralism as such has nothing to say. It is a theory about the nature of philosophy and not about the nature of the world."[154]

Heim agrees with Rescher about the impossibility of having a God's-view perspective above all traditions. One should begin from a certain orientation, which in Heim's case is the Christian perspective. But, this is not as much an ontological claim as it is an epistemological one. Therefore, Heim still needs to take his own road in constructing his Christian understanding of religious diversity. Moreover, not only should such an understanding recognize the particularity of each religious tradition, but it must also create an inclusive and universal framework, grounded in Christian faith, that affirms all other traditions. As Heim maintains, "It is appropriate then for each to argue for and from its own universal view, so long as the diversity and actuality of religious ends are recognized."[155] What is required in the new framework, therefore, is that adherents of each religious tradition can still find their belief-system unmodified or recognized on their own terms. Hence, Christian *truth* and religious *difference* are simultaneously avowed.

Inclusivist Pluralism

Heim's strategy to maintain both aspects—truth and difference—of his new theory of religious diversity is expressed under the term of "inclusivist pluralism."[156] On the one hand, he offers a new idea of multiple religious ends as an alternative to the three classical types of exclusivism, inclusivism, and pluralism. All of these three types, despite their disagreements in many aspects, share the same presupposition that the religious end or salvation is singular. The debate among them is merely centered on the question of whether there is one way or many ways toward the one salvation or religious end. While exclusivists and inclusivists believe that there is only one valid way, which is in and through Jesus Christ, pluralists argue that there are many valid ways toward the Ultimate One. In this case, pluralistic theologies seem to be the only position that respects religious diversity. However, Heim

---

154. Rescher, *Strife of Systems*, 177–78, 88, 95.

155. Heim, *Salvations*, 215.

156. For Heim, "inclusivist pluralism" and "pluralistic inclusivism" are interchangeable; see Heim, *Salvations*, 152, 219.

The Trinity and Religions

argues vividly that this is not the case at all. Not only are pluralistic theologies in fact another form of exclusivism (through their meta-theological position), but they also commit the same error that exclusivist and inclusivist theologies make; that is, they rule out the possibility that there are many religious ends or salvations. The idea of multiple religious ends, therefore, enables Heim to say that his view is more pluralistic in nature than the pluralistic visions of Hick, Smith, and Knitter.[157]

Moreover, Heim not only pushes the pluralistic idea much farther than the classical pluralists, but he also reinterprets in a more radical way the meaning of "including others" within classical inclusivism. His critique of inclusivism seems to be much less harsh than that of pluralism, mainly because he believes that ultimately, "all theories of religions are either exclusivist or inclusivist in nature," and that "orientational pluralism is consistent with advocacy of virtually all varieties of inclusivism."[158] Compared to the exclusivist position, inclusivism is more favorable in its readiness to recognize other orientations. However, argues Heim, the problem of this view is its assumption that "other defensible views will ultimately dissolve into recognition and realization of the religious end of the inclusivist's 'home.'"[159] In short, there is only one religious end found in the Christian faith and all other religions are considered valid insofar as they are directed to and fulfilled by the Christian end. Heim then suggests his own version of inclusivism, by saying, "It is just at this point I propose a change. I suggest that Christians can consistently recognize that some traditions encompass religious ends which are real states of human transformation, distinct from that Christians seek. There are paths in varying religious traditions which is consistently followed prove effective in bringing adherents to alternative fulfillments. The crucial question among the faiths is *not* 'Which one saves?' but 'What counts as salvation?'"[160]

In conclusion, Heim tries to combine the two previously competing types (inclusivism and pluralism) by reinterpreting and radicalizing each of them, through the lens of Rescher's orientational pluralism. The term "inclusivist pluralism" or "pluralistic inclusivism," therefore, expresses Heim's twofold idea. It is a pluralistic theology in the sense that it celebrates the diversity of religious tradition through its recognition of the particularity of

---

157. Heim uses the term "a more pluralistic hypothesis" to distinguish his view from Hick's "pluralistic hypothesis." See Heim, *Salvations*, 129–57.
158. Heim, *Salvations*, 152.
159. Ibid.
160. Ibid., 160.

each religious end. As such, it differs from the classical pluralistic theologies in its openness to acknowledge its status as one among many theories of religions and its readiness to respect all religious traditions on their own terms. It is an inclusivist theology in the sense that it argues for a particularly Christian ultimate end that includes all other religious ends as penultimate. As such, it differs from the classical inclusivism in its refusal to dissolve other traditions within the category of a "home" religion.

Multiple Religious Ends and the Trinity

The idea of multiple religious ends empowers Heim to criticize the classical models of exclusivism, inclusivism, and pluralism and to offer his own inclusivist-pluralistic model. But how does he explain such diversity of religious ends with a theologically plausible framework? Here we come to the very center of his proposal: the Trinity. His basic principle is, "If Trinity is real, then many of *these* religious claims and ends must be real also. If they were all false, then Christianity could not be true."[161] This means, the religious multiplicity must be generated from God's reality as Trinity. Furthermore, Heim draws an analogy between three human interpersonal relations with three aspects of the shared Triune life as a whole: *impersonal relations with each other, personal relations with each other as agents,* and *communion*.[162] These dimensions exist because of the complexity of the Trinitarian life, in which each belongs to all the persons together, not to anyone.[163] Since it is the central point of Heim's proposal, a more detailed analysis is necessarily in order.

---

161. Heim, *Depth of the Riches*, 167.

162. Heim is cautious of the danger of analogical language by saying that he is not trying to analogize "this relation between two people with the relation of one human or community to one of the Triune persons." Heim, *Depth of the Riches*, 184. This type of analogy performed by Panikkar, in Heim's analysis, violates Augustine's oft-repeated doctrine: *opera trinitatis ad extra sunt indivisa* (the external operations of the Trinity are undivided). D'Costa, therefore, is wrong in suggesting that at this point Heim "relies heavily on Raimundo Panikkar's *Trinity*." D'Costa, "Review," 137. Heim frequently mentions that his thinking at this point is parallel with that which is suggested by Ninian Smart and Steven Konstantine; see Heim, *Depth of the Riches*, 156–64, 85; Smart and Konstantine, *Systematic Theology*.

163. Heim, *Depth of the Riches*, 183; Heim, "Trinity and Religious Ends," 390.

The Trinity and Religions

The First Dimension: Impersonal

The impersonal dimension of the Triune life, in Heim's model, is similar to what Smart and Konstantine call the "infinity of the divine life."[164] This dimension refers to "the flux of relation among the [Triune] persons."[165] In such a shared life, the divine persons mutually indwell one another. Heim writes, "This is the radical immanence and the radical emptiness, by which the divine persons indwell each other and make way for others to indwell them."[166] The mutual indwelling of the Triune persons is thus manifest in two ways: the radical emptiness and the radical immanence, each of which can be found in some particular religions.

The first way, the radical emptiness, is best seen in the Buddhist idea of emptiness and *nirvana*. For Buddhists, all positive representations of God in Christianity are considered "passing, instrumental representations, suitable to the spiritually underdeveloped," while emptiness belongs to "a different and more ultimate plane of reality."[167] Heim tries to recognize emptiness as the ultimate end for Buddhists. However, consistent with his inclusivist position, he also argues from the Christian perspective that emptiness is only one, not the entire, feature of inner relations of the Trinitarian persons. He also finds in Christian tradition a similar emphasis on emptiness in apophatic theology. Apophatism focuses on one of three sides of God's negativity: the idea of contingency, the idea of reservation in which God is revealed yet never fully revealed, and the notion of God's self-contraction. All of these sides of negativity refers to "a fundamental dimension of *distance* given in the creative act itself."[168]

The second aspect of the impersonal dimension of the Trinity is radical immanence. The whole reality is perceived as identical with a single and absolute self without relation, a matrix that anonymously sustains the totality of all beings. The Advaita Vedanta tradition of Hinduism, Heim argues, is the best representation of this notion, in which "Brahman, the one unshakable reality, sustains all things by pervading all things, by identity with all things."[169] Moreover, from the Christian perspective, Heim maintains, this

---

164. Smart and Konstantine, *Systematic Theology*, 168, 174, 290.
165. Heim, *Depth of the Riches*, 186.
166. Ibid., 185.
167. Ibid., 188.
168. Ibid., 197.
169. Ibid., 190.

idea may be interpreted as the immanent activity of God on which all realities are dependent.

Heim concludes that both radical emptiness and the radical immanence are two sides of the same coin of divine contraction, in which there is an ontological distance established by divine "making space" among Triune persons. Therefore, while each of these apprehensions points to two uniquely different yet equally viable religious aims, both have a root in the inner-Trinitarian relationship.[170]

The Second Dimension: Personal or Iconic

The second dimension involves an approach to God as an agent. Theologically speaking, the doctrine of Trinity provides the idea that the three persons constitute "one will, one purpose, one love toward creation."[171] This is summarized beautifully in the Augustinian formula *opera trinitatis ad extra sunt indivisa* ("the external work of Trinity is undivided"). Therefore, God encounters creation as a free individual or, in Smart and Konstantine's words, as the common divine "I" of the Trinity.[172]

Heim also describes this second dimension as "the iconic dimension," following Panikkar's idea of iconolatry that refers to the relation with the divine through the Word. Even though he disagrees with Panikkar's way of appropriating each person of the Trinity to different religious traditions, Heim find it helpful to use Panikkar's general insight of iconolatry to express his own idea of personal dimension of God's relation to the world. What is of importance here is that the relationship between God and the world exists through mediating forms. Heim, moreover, demonstrates the rich possibilities of this "mediating form" (or icon) that can occur in events, a personal deity of "God," the Tao of Taoism, the Kantian law, the Buddhist *dharma*, etc. Thus, the iconic encounter could occur via an impersonal rule, like that of the Tao, or the personal God of monotheism. Heim indicates the distinctive nature of this dimension by arguing,

> The key point that distinguishes this dimension as a whole from the impersonal one we discussed first, is not personality in the

---

170. It is important to note that Heim also describes some "less traditionally religious forms" of this impersonal dimension of the Trinity, such as that of a spiritualized form of reductionistic science and ecological science, and even in the modern atheism and in the death-of-God movement. See Heim, *Depth of the Riches*, 191–92.

171. Heim, "Trinity and Religious Ends," 394.

172. Smart and Konstantine, *Systematic Theology*, 290.

The Trinity and Religions

divine . . . [but] that an iconic view of the divine allows for contrast and tension. The icon points to the fact that the divine is not empty nor is all being already in perfect identity with it. There is a distance between us and the divine, between us and our religious end, which must be traveled. Iconolatry typically manifests an ethical or moral emphasis, a drive toward transformation. Icons lie between us and the transcendent, pointing the way for change. It is not an existing condition that must be recognized (though that step is a valuable one), but a new condition or transformation that must be attained.[173]

Although this iconic encounter is present in many religious as well as non-religious traditions, Heim finds it existing most clearly in Islam, in which God is perceived as a personal and transcendent creator who encounters humans as individuals, and in which the Quran becomes the icon existing between God and humans.

Before moving to the third dimension, it is worth noting the importance of understanding this iconic or personal dimension in relation to the impersonal dimension. Heim argues that it is the impersonal relation that makes the personal relation possible. He maintains, "It is God's 'absence' and background immanence which allow for a free and historical encounter of humans with God as a single 'Thou' on the stage of creation."[174]

THE THIRD DIMENSION: COMMUNION

Communion is the third dimension of Heim's Trinitarian theology, since it signifies the Christian end, that is, the "relation of communion with God and other creatures in Christ."[175] Heim provides a fuller understanding of communion as the third dimension in the chapter 2 of his *The Depth of the Riches*. It is worth noting that in this book Heim no longer uses the term Salvation in the plural sense as he does in his 1995 book, *Salvations*. He accepts Grace Jantzen's critique of transporting the term "salvation" into interreligious discussion.[176] Thus, instead of using the plural word "salvations," Heim now employs the more vague term "religious ends" for all religious ultimate aims and refers the term "salvation" exclusively to the Christian end.

---

173. Heim, *Depth of the Riches*, 194.
174. Ibid., 192.
175. Ibid., 49.
176. Ibid., 20; Jantzen, "Human Diversity," 579–80.

An Imaginative Glimpse

Salvation, as the Christian end, is a complex reality, precisely because of its relational characteristic. This relationality has three interrelated foci: the relation between humans with God, the relation of humans with each other, and the relation of humans with all other creatures. These three foci correspond to three disorders emphasized in Christian theology, namely: sin, evil, and death, respectively. Furthermore, Heim tries to associate each of the three pairs of human relation and disorder with each of the three Triune persons, by using the Augustinian idea of appropriation. "The tradition," he says, "often associates each of the three persons of the trinity with redemption in one of these dimensions."[177] But, this tradition is also balanced with another principle that the external works of the Trinity are undivided. What is of importance here is that Heim sees the distinction between the immanent Trinity and the economic Trinity as having direct correlation with the problem of threefold relational disorder. In this sense, "salvation is a deliverance from certain conditions as well as a positive fulfillment."[178] We can make sense of both aspects through the lens of the Trinity. I will discuss more deeply Heim's understanding of the immanent Trinity and the economic in chapter 3.

For the present, it suffices to note that Heim also maintains explicitly that the third dimension derives from "*perichoresis* or mutual communion of the three divine persons."[179] Interestingly, the divine perichoresis also makes it possible for other dimensions, within the larger context of a relation between creatures and God, to exist with their own integrity. Heim argues for two imaginative ways of picturing the perichoretic communion in relation to different dimensions of religious ends. First, it is possible to emphasize "the pure independence of each one as parallel and non-converging absolutes."[180] Their incommensurable feature is drawn precisely from autonomous divine realities. A second vision is rather complex, in which the Trinitarian communion-in-difference becomes a pattern for a unity-in-distinction of the religious dimensions.

177. Heim, *Depth of the Riches*, 60.
178. Ibid., 67.
179. Ibid., 211.
180. Ibid., 212. This approach, I believe, comes closer to ones proposed by John B. Cobb, Jr. and Stephen Kaplan, although each of them argues from very different theoretical approach. While the former employs the Whiteheadian process thought resulting in a "deep religious pluralism" or "complementary pluralism" in which multiple ultimacies are recognized, the latter uses Bohm's holographic model where "three different ultimate realities could be simultaneously existing, equally real and mutually interpenetrating." Griffin, "Religious Pluralism"; Kaplan, *Different Paths*.

S. Mark Heim has demonstrated the possibility of a Trinitarian theology of religions that is theoretically solid and theologically perspectival. By employing orientational pluralism, Heim is able to defend his particular perspective as a Christian, based on the notion of the Trinity, without losing his openness to other religions, including the possibility of multiple and even conflicting ultimate ends. Compared to Panikkar and D'Costa, Heim shows us a "middle way." On the one hand, he is closer to D'Costa in maintaining that any theological position must have a theoretical basis. On the other hand, we find a clear similarity between Heim and Panikkar in their common use of appropriation to relate the Trinity to the issue of religious diversity, although each has a very different model of appropriation.

In this chapter, I have surveyed the work of three theologians who use the Trinity as the central category for developing a theology of religions. In the following chapter, I will analyze their proposals more deeply, giving special attention to the importance of perichoresis within each approach.

3

Comparative Analyses

In this chapter I offer my critical comparison of Panikkar's, Heim's, and D'Costa's models of a Trinitarian theology of religions. In particular, I focus on two key aspects of each model: its *theoretical* framework and its *content*. The comparative analyses that I offer here are not limited to looking at the strengths and weaknesses of the three projects; they also locate certain elements of each that I will retrieve for my own theological *bricolage*.

From Post-Pluralism to Transversal Attitude toward Others

Radical Pluralism or Post-Pluralism?

In spite of the differences in the constructions of Trinitarian theology of religions by Panikkar, D'Costa, and Heim, each of these theologians has several things in common. One of the similarities that they share is their rejection of pluralistic theologies. The question that I address in this regard is whether they reject pluralism for certain failures inherent within such a theory or that pluralistic theologies propounded by some contemporary theologians are in fact not pluralistic enough and are in need of serious revision in order to be even more pluralistic. In brief, are these three theologians suggesting a post-pluralism or radical pluralism?

To answer the question, however, the twofold principle that I have mentioned in chapter 1 needs to be presented again: "Any Christian theology of religions should maintain dialectically the commitment to Christian truth and openness to the truths of other religious traditions." In the light of this principle, we can reformulate the question as follows: Are Panikkar,

D'Costa, and Heim successful in maintaining the above-mentioned dialectic through their criticisms of pluralistic theologies?

Each of the theologians has provided an excellent critique of pluralistic theologies as well as constructed a particular model that tries to transcend the weaknesses found in pluralistic theologies. Yet, each model also demonstrates certain problems that need to be addressed. My purpose in this part is threefold: first, I demonstrate some similarities among Panikkar, D'Costa, and Heim in the light of the dialectic principle that I have set earlier; second, in light of the insights of the three thinkers under discussion I suggest avoiding the usage of the classical typology of exclusivism, inclusivism, and pluralism; third, I propose my own theoretical standpoint based on the strengths and weaknesses in the previous models.

First Similarity: Anti-Absolutism and Universal Particularism

The first similarity shared by the three theologians is their rejection of pluralistic theologies insofar as each attempts to absolutize itself and to superimpose its truth on other particularities. It does not mean any universal truth-claim cannot be made, but such a claim should be exercised through the recognition of its own particular standpoint. What they reject in pluralistic theologies is when a theory, in making its truth-claim, tries to elevate its status as being *one* theory or system among many others into a supersystem that domesticates other particularities within its own particular scheme. In short, Panikkar, D'Costa, and Heim share the same spirit that maintains the dialectic between universality and particularity without eagerly resolving it.

Panikkar, for instance, makes a strict distinction between his notion of pluralism (both as human consciousness and perichoretic interrelatedness of all reality) and other versions of pluralism that try to be an overarching supersystem and include all particularities. In so doing, Panikkar insists that an authentic pluralism does not belong to *logos*. Rather, it belongs to *mythos* and *pneuma*.

This is the basic argument that Panikkar frequently makes in answering those who criticize him through the rational-theoretical category. Gerald J. Larson, for example, argues that Panikkar's theoretical pluralism "becomes unintelligible in a two-valued (truth-falsehood) logic, inasmuch as the principle of the excluded middle is violated," and therefore, "the notion of pluralism so formulated is as self-defeating as any formulation of relativism and as tripped up by the problem of self-referentiality as any formulation of universalism or absolutism."[1] In answering Larson's critique, Panikkar returns to his distinction between *logos* and *mythos* (and *pneuma*). He acknowledges the problem by saying, "We have a situation of pluralism only when we are confronted with mutually exclusive and respectively contradictory ultimate systems. We cannot, by definition, logically overcome a pluralistic situation without breaking the very principle of noncontradiction and denying our own set of codes: intellectual, moral esthetic, and so forth."[2]

Thus, if we want to hold on to pluralism, we cannot avoid the breaking of logical principles belonging to *logos*. On the other hand, to place pluralism in the realm of *logos* is to open the necessity of having a universally absolutized theory. However, Panikkar argues, a universal theory is always a denial of pluralism, because "any alleged universal theory is one particular theory, besides many others, that claims universal validity, thus trespassing the limits of its own legitimacy."[3] Thus, the best way available for us is to hold pluralism, not as belonging to *logos* (theory), but as belonging to *mythos* and *pneuma* (human consciousness and cosmotheandric reality).

Along with the primacy of pluralism as *mythos* and *pneuma* over pluralism as *logos*, Panikkar also employs the principle of perspectivism. This principle keeps him from the danger of absolutism. He frequently insists that any position that he suggests comes out of a particular perspective. His perspective—or "window," to use Panikkar's metaphor—is certainly the combination of the Christian, Hindu, and Buddhist traditions. Nevertheless, while explicitly acknowledging his particular standpoint, Panikkar still makes universal truth-claims. What he rejects is not that one makes a universal claim of truth, but that one absolutizes one's universal theory and fails to recognize one's own particularity as well as the particularity and universality of other theories. Robert M. Parks, Jr. provides a clear summary of this aspect of Panikkar's thought, "Panikkar still makes claims to truth, which necessarily have universal intention. He still criticizes other theories, and presents his own perspective as better. Why would he make it his own if he did not think it better? But Panikkar insists that one must never absolutize one's solutions or criticisms. In other words, the pluralistic attitude forces one to recognize the other as source of understanding from whom one can

---

1. Larson, "Contra Pluralism," 72. Borrowing from Larson, Kärkkäinen advances the critique by arguing that Panikkar always resorts to his advaitic or mystical principle when he "encounters a real theological/logical problem" and in so doing he lacks of "a proportional network" supporting his doctrine. Kärkkäinen, *Religious Pluralism*, 131.

2. Panikkar, *Invisible Harmony*, 153.

3. Ibid., 161.

learn, it forces an awareness of the freedom of being, of one's own limitations and contingency."[4]

In a similar vein, D'Costa argues against pluralistic theologies. The key idea in D'Costa's critique of pluralistic theologies is that any theological position must be tradition-specific. This idea, however, results in two implications. On the one hand, he can firmly uncover the exclusivistic character of pluralistic theologies. What pluralists have done is no more than act as brokers of disputing parties and invite the disputing parties to leave their tradition and to join the pluralists' own tradition. Pluralistic theologies are not a neutral position; rather, their tradition is the Enlightenment or liberal modernity and their gods are Unitarian, deistic, or agnostic. Thus, there is no such thing as a universal theory that can claim its universal overarching position over particular religious traditions. On the other hand, D'Costa must also apply the same principle to his own position. Otherwise, he would commit the same mistake as the pluralists have done. Therefore, if the tradition-based characteristic is inevitable, exclusivism must be the only one valid position in the theology of religions.

We also discover in D'Costa's theological career an interesting shift from inclusivism to exclusivism by way of his dissatisfaction with Rahnerian inclusivism, resulting in his critical distancing from the classical typology itself, as well as his engagement with MacIntyre's and Milbank's critique of liberal-modern ideas. In both phases, however, we can still see D'Costa's consistent position with regard to the universal dimension of Christian faith. Both inclusivists and exclusivists, he argues, believe that "their tradition finally contains the truth regarding ontological, epistemological, and ethical claims. This particular narrative helps to narrate all creation."[5] Thus, both universality and particularity of truth are not firmly anchored in some alien epistemological, ontological, or ethical framework, as he finds in pluralistic theology, but in the Christian narrative itself. It is through the dialectic of Christ's particularity and Spirit's universality—as the equal and mutual expressions of the Irenaean two hands of God—that D'Costa comes to this conclusion.

Now, we turn to S. Mark Heim. He argues against pluralistic theologies by showing that Hick's, Smith's, and Knitter's versions of pluralism fail to fulfill their own premises. Religious paths are considered salvific only if they are in agreement with the conceptual frameworks the pluralists have set beforehand. Thus, pluralistic theologies become some sorts of meta-theologies

---

4. Parks, "Trinitarianism," 242–43.
5. D'Costa, *Meeting of Religions*, 22.

An Imaginative Glimpse

canopying all particular traditions. They tend to provide a God's-eye view that places them "above" any other theories of religions. Here, we find similar accusations of pluralism as a universal theory in Panikkar and Heim. Like Panikkar, who believes that an alleged universal theory is in fact a particular theory claiming to be universal, Heim also clearly demonstrates that pluralistic theologies convey "cultural structures of plausibility against which modern Western Christianity has been defined."[6] Unlike Panikkar, however, Heim does not want to resort to a non-theoretical pluralism, but to maintain his inclusivist-pluralistic model from theoretical perspective.

After uncovering the absolutist tendency of pluralistic theologies, Heim argues that the problem of pluralistic theologies is not in their universal dimension, but their tendency to superimpose their truth-claims on other theories. Drawing from Rescher's orientational pluralism, Heim suggests that one can make a universal claim from one's particular orientation and even critically reject other orientations, but it does not mean that one can claim a God's-eye perspective transcending other theories. The orientational pluralism allows Heim to argue that, from a particular perspective, only one theory of reality is appropriate. Thus, all theoretical interpretations are perspectival. In other words, any theory of religion is on the same plane as others.

The argument for the universal dimension of a theory makes it possible for Heim to construct an inclusivist framework, grounded in Christian faith, which affirms all religious traditions. He maintains, "It is appropriate then for each to argue for and from its own universal view, so long as the diversity and actuality of religious ends are recognized."[7] Within such a universal framework, Heim argues that the Christian religious end (communion) is the ultimate end attainable for Christians, while other religious ends from other religions are posited as penultimate. Nevertheless, the distinction between ultimate and penultimate is valid only from the side of that which claims its end as ultimate. Those from other traditions could and should claim their religious end—penultimate in the Christian framework—as ultimate in their own framework, while acknowledging the Christian end—ultimate in the Christian framework—as penultimate. In so doing, Heim is able to do two things simultaneously: claim the universality of Christian faith and invite other religious believers to claim their own universality. The combination of orientational pluralism and his inclusivist framework enables Heim to use the terms "pluralistic inclusivism" and "inclusivist pluralism" interchange-

6. Heim, *Salvations*, 103.
7. Ibid., 215.

ably. On one hand, Heim's model is pluralistic, in the sense that it opens the possibility of recognizing religious ends other than the Christian end and to allow other traditions to claim their own universality. On the other hand, it is inclusivist, in the sense that its universal scope may include other religious ends within its framework, while recognizing their validity on their own terms. Even more, Heim allows the possibility of other religions to include the Christian end as a penultimate fulfillment within their own traditions.

Thus, with regard to the question whether we can maintain a theory of religions, Heim comes closer to D'Costa than he does to Panikkar. Using different theoretical approaches, both D'Costa (with his postmodern critique from Milbank and MacIntyre) and Heim (through his Rescherian orientational pluralism) are in agreement in claiming the possibility of constructing a theoretical alternative to pluralism. They differ, however, in depicting what kind of post-pluralistic model to construct. Where D'Costa argues for a post-pluralism that is based on the idea that all positions are basically exclusivist, Heim believes that post-pluralism should mean a more radically pluralistic acceptance of religious difference within the scope of inclusivism.

I have thus far demonstrated one commonality among Panikkar, D'Costa, and Heim, which bring us to conclude that each of the theologians can be reasonably associated with the post-pluralist position. They all reject pluralistic theologies as universal attempts to absolutize a particular view and impose it on others. They believe in the possibility of making universal truth-claims without abandoning the particularity of their own traditions. This observation, however, deals only with the first side of our task: *commitment to the Christian faith*. We still need to analyze another common feature among them with regard to the question whether they show *openness to other religious truths*. I would argue that they do, each with a different route as to how to affirm other religious truths.

Second Similarity: Respect for the Auto-Description of Other Religions

Panikkar is exceptional in demonstrating openness to non-Christian traditions. Unlike other pluralists, he has immersed himself into the depths of Hinduism and Buddhism, combining these two religious traditions with the Christian tradition without wanting to baptize them in the sacred Christian water. He has enacted pluralism through his own spiritual journey. Far from being a theoretical rationalization, pluralism is for Panikkar a mystical human attitude that engages with pluralistic reality itself.

An Imaginative Glimpse

Moreover, Panikkar's greater openness to non-Christian traditions is demonstrated through his engagement with those traditions. It is so real to him that he is able to say, "I consider myself 100 percent Hindu and Indian, and 100 percent Catholic and Spanish. How is that possible? By living religion as an experience rather than as an ideology."[8] Since radical openness exists on the experiential level, it is the person who experiences multiple traditions who needs to engage with those traditions *within* her or his life. Thus, Panikkar takes the primacy of *intra*-religious, rather than *inter*-religious, dialogue.[9] In this regard, he argues superbly, "We must distinguish between *inter*religious dialogue and *intra*religious dialogue. The first confronts already-established religions and deals with questions of doctrine and discipline. Intrareligious dialogue is something else. It does not begin with doctrine, theology and diplomacy. It is intra, which means that if I do not discover in myself the terrain where the Hindu, the Muslim, the Jew and the atheist may have a place—in my heart, in my intelligence, in my life—I will never be able to enter into a genuine dialogue with him."[10]

In D'Costa, apparently, we have a totally different case. While Panikkar embraces pluralism, D'Costa rejects it. He supports the shift of his position, from inclusivism to exclusivism, with his engagement with Milbank and MacIntyre. It is commonly known that both thinkers have significant affinities in criticizing modern liberalism and rejecting any tradition-free rationality. D'Costa's agreement with the two thinkers results in his total rejection of pluralistic theologies and his emphasis on the tradition-specific nature of any theological reflection.[11]

A key idea dominating in D'Costa's theology is that exclusivism is a logical consequence of any tradition-specific position. Thus, since all positions are always situated in a certain tradition, they all must be exclusivists. He painstakingly demonstrates that all alleged pluralists are basically exclusivists

---

8. Panikkar, "Eruption of Truth," 834. A good discussion for the issue of multiple religious belongings, see Cornille, *Many Mansions?*. In this book, Panikkar is also one of the contributors.

9. Panikkar, *Intrareligious*.

10. Panikkar, "Eruption of Truth," 835. In this respect, Cousins comments on Panikkar's personal life that he characterizes as one among a few mutational persons, in whom "the great cultural traditions—formerly distinct through their diverse historical origin and development—now converge, making these mutants heirs, for the first time in history, to the spiritual heritage of humankind." Cousins, *Christ*, 73–74.

11. Jeffrey Stout provides a very illuminating analysis on what he calls "the new traditionalism" advocated by Milbank and MacIntyre (along with Stanley Hauerwas). See Stout, *Democracy and Tradition*, Part 2.

and that inclusivism collapses into exclusivism. The question now is whether D'Costa's exclusivist, tradition-specific, position shows openness to other religious traditions? He tries to affirm his openness—even, greater openness than Christian pluralistic theologies as well as non-Christian pluralists such as Dalai Lama—through three principles.[12] First, the Trinitarian doctrine of God that he suggests always maintains openness in history and that is only "closed" eschatologically. In this sense, he boldly urges that "being inattentive to other religions is a form of idolatry." Second, the fact that the history of religions is still in progress makes him believe that no *a priori* judgment of other religions can be permissible. Consequently, thirdly, Christian theology should take the primacy of other religions' auto-interpretation over Christianity's hetero-interpretation of other religions.

Moreover, D'Costa argues that his Trinitarian position, based on the Catholic tradition, provides a better treatment of other religions than merely viewing the other as "rival" (MacIntyre) or as the object of "out-narration" (Milbank). D'Costa's position attempts to maintain that "the other is always interesting in their difference and may be the possible face of God, or the face of violence, greed, and death.... Trinitarian theology provides the context for a critical, reverent, and open engagement with otherness, without any predictable outcome."[13]

In conclusion, unlike Panikkar (and Heim) whose main methods are to propose a positive and "descriptive" appropriation of the Trinity to other religions, D'Costa avoids such an attempt and chooses to remain silent as to how other religions should be descriptively appropriated within the Trinitarian framework. This silence, D'Costa believes, reflects the silence demonstrated by Vatican II as to whether salvation is mediated through non-Christian religions. Nevertheless, D'Costa does not seem to be successful enough in his refraining from "including" other religions into Christian Trinitarianism. For example, James Fredericks argues that "D'Costa's interest in interreligious prayer also leads him to a form of theological inclusivism."[14] Fredericks maintains that D'Costa's exclusivism results from his more restrictive understanding of inclusivism. When viewed from a less restrictive understanding of inclusivism, D'Costa's idea of the work of the Spirit in interreligious prayer can legitimately be classified as inclusivism

---

12. D'Costa, *Meeting of Religions*, 133.

13. Ibid., 9. D'Costa's favor of the postmodern notion of "difference" has appeared since his 1998's article, "Trinitarian Différance."

14. Fredericks, "Review," 298. Kärkkäinen offers a similar evaluation that D'Costa is basically still in the inclusivist position; see Kärkkäinen, *Religious Pluralism*, 78–79.

and as such it "shares in the major shortcoming of the pluralist theology of religions, *viz.*, differences are domesticated. Other religious traditions, in the final analysis, are the work of the same Holy Spirit that Christians know to be at work within their own tradition."[15] Fredericks's assessment, I believe, is correct. D'Costa, indeed, frequently "includes" other religions within his theological framework makes them *loci* in which the works of the Spirit prevailing. For instance, D'Costa agrees with Paul John II who acknowledges "the inchoate reality of the Kingdom" present within other religions, yet "remains incomplete unless it is related to the Kingdom of Christ in the Church and straining toward eschatological fullness."[16] In this sense, we can ask the same question that D'Costa asks to Heim: "Does his proposal really secure what he set out to do: to accept other religions in terms of their own self-description?"[17]

If Fredericks is right in judging that D'Costa's model is basically inclusivist, the next question is—using the distinction that he employed earlier—whether he promotes an open or closed inclusivism. The fact that he interprets the silence of Vatican II as a denial of the salvific structure of non-Christian religions has ambiguously made him go farther from being an open inclusivist that, by definition that he makes, should never claim to possess the truth. It would have been better if he follows the lead left by Vatican II to remain silent regarding this issue. D'Costa should have refrained from interpreting the silence as denial of the possible salvation of non-Christian religions, since it would also be consistent with his respect for the otherness of other religious traditions.

Heim's main concern differs from Panikkar's and D'Costa's. He sees that each model of the classical typology (exclusivism, inclusivism, and pluralism) deals with a wrong question: whether there is one path or many paths toward the one ultimate end. The question should rather be whether there is one ultimate end or many ultimate ends. When the question is posed that way, none of the classical models can escape from the judgment of being exclusivist. Even pluralism, as the most radical critique of exclusivism, shows in itself an exclusivist tendency, when the radical differences among religions are reduced into a single ultimate end. Through his theological model of multiple religious ends, Heim attempts to maintain the real religious differences—represented in their different religious ends or fulfillment—and

---

15. Fredericks, "Review," 298–99.
16. D'Costa, *Meeting of Religions*, 114–16, 64; *Redemptoris Missio* 20.
17. D'Costa, "Review," 139.

it means he must demonstrate that his model allows other religions to be recognized in his model on their own terms.

Heim's recognition of other religions, nevertheless, cannot be separated from Heim's basic assumption, that "all theories of religions are either exclusivist or inclusivist in nature."[18] Arguing that his orientational pluralism is consistent with inclusivism, Heim emphasizes that the key element in inclusivism is "the recognition of other orientations and the defensibility of other views from those orientations."[19] The inclusivist version that he suggests, however, is not one that assumes that "the other defensible views will ultimately dissolve into recognition and realization of the religious end of the inclusivist's 'home' tradition, if their adherents are to achieve 'salvation' at all," but rather that those defensible views becomes penultimate ends (from the perspective of the inclusivist) that "could endure as the religious fulfillments of those who pursue various religious ends."[20] Not only is such an endurance of other religious ends maintained both historically and eschatologically, it is also affirmed theologically through the multiple relations anchored in the Trinitarian framework.

While Rescher's orientational pluralism supports Heim's perspectivism, it has nothing to say about the content of Heim's theological inclusivism. Rescher reminds his readers about the agnostic character of his orientational pluralism with regard to the substantive or ontological question. Thus, it would be misleading to ask whether orientational pluralism provides a good support for Heim to respect other religious auto-descriptions and accept their truths on their own terms. Orientational pluralism justifies Heim's argument that every theory of religions is both perspectival and universal. But, it is the task Heim sets for himself to demonstrate whether his model is able to create enough rooms for other religions without being modified or domesticated. It is precisely at this point that some critics find Heim's inclusivism problematic.

Heim incessantly assures his readers that his version of inclusivism is also at the same time more pluralistic than the pluralistic theologies of Hick, Smith, and Knitter. It is inclusivist in its eagerness to "include" other religious ends within its Trinitarian framework. It is pluralistic in the sense that it recognizes the validity of other religious ends. But, whether his serious attempt and good intentions about taking into account the differences of other religions is successful is still unsettled. Gavin D'Costa, for example,

18. Heim, *Salvations*, 152.
19. Ibid.
20. Ibid.

expresses his doubts by writing, "... Advaita, in terms of its own self-understanding, eschatologically radically negates the category of 'relation,' a point which Heim does acknowledge, such that it is difficult to see the *telos* of Advaita being eternally preserved within a trinitarian framework. 'Identity' in Sankara cannot be assimilated to immanence or coinherence within three divine persons, or at least without a lot more argument."[21]

With the same spirit, Kärkkäinen criticizes Heim's inclusivism as "nothing other than a typical inclusivist reading of other religions, totally against their own self-understanding."[22] Heim, in reply, would reject the accusation by arguing that, on the one hand, his version of inclusivism is similar to other versions of inclusivism in that they both "include" other religious traditions within the Christian framework. That is the point of proposing an inclusivist position. Otherwise, the only other option left would be to "exclude" other religions from the divine salvific economy (or economies). This is the logical consequences of Heim's model, which allows only two alternatives: either inclusivism or exclusivism. On the other hand, Heim would also argue that his "pluralistic inclusivism" is radically different from the classical forms of inclusivism and the difference lies on the "principle of inclusion" employed by each of them. The principle of inclusion employed in the classical versions of inclusivism is monistic. The inclusion of other religions into the Christian framework thus means that their ultimate ends are insufficient and need to be fulfilled by the Christian faith. Thus, the acceptance of other religions occurs only half-way and continues with their absorption into a single, yet alien, principle provided by Christian faith. On the contrary, Heim's inclusivism recognizes the internal sufficiency of other religious ends and such fulfillments are maintained fully and continually within the Trinitarian framework functioning as the principle of inclusion, which is in itself not monistic but pluralistic. While I believe D'Costa and Kärkkäinen have offered fair criticisms of Heim's inclusivism, I can also see that Heim is not very explicit in expressing his inclusivist appreciation of other religions. My constructive proposal to develop a theoretical view that transcends the limitations will be discussed further below.

---

21. D'Costa, "Review," 139.
22. Kärkkäinen, *Religious Pluralism*, 149.

Revisiting the Typology

In the next section I summarize my evaluation of the theoretical aspects of three theological models suggested by Panikkar, D'Costa, and Heim and propose my own idea based on the strengths and weaknesses found in the three theologians. However, I need to pause a moment to clarify my position regarding the classical typology of exclusivism, inclusivism, and pluralism. We have seen in the three theologians, as well as in the larger theological context, that the classical typology has been employed with various meanings and categories. More specifically, Panikkar, D'Costa, and Heim use the typology in various ways. While D'Costa and Heim discuss the typology extensively, Panikkar rarely addresses it, even though he also proposes a revised fourfold typology in his book, *The Unknown Christ of Hinduism*.[23] Panikkar also clearly advocates pluralism, even though his view is different from that of the other pluralists co-authoring *The Myth of Christian Uniqueness*. Pluralism is, for him, not a theoretical position but rather a human attitude. In this sense, he is critical of pluralism as a theory.

S. Mark Heim calls for an "inclusivist pluralism" or "pluralistic inclusivism," while harshly criticizing some pluralists such as John Hick, Paul F. Knitter, and Wilfred C. Smith. In the final analysis, however, it is safe to conclude that Heim only allows two final options: either inclusivism or exclusivism. Heim prefers the former. At last, Gavin D'Costa, initially holding an inclusivist position, ends up making a strong claim that there is only one plausible position with regard to other religions, namely, exclusivism; it includes those who call themselves pluralists. However, by identifying exclusivism with tradition-specific positions, it is obvious that he also does not want to identify his exclusivist version with the classical versions. In conclusion, each theologian employs a particular position already known in the classical typology (pluralism in Panikkar, inclusivism in Heim, and exclusivism in D'Costa), but each also revises the meaning of the position so that each position has a new and different meaning than what is commonly used (at least, as described by Alan Race).

We have also noticed that each revised position suggested by each theologian can be criticized, interestingly, by using the popular understanding of the typology. Panikkar, in rejecting pluralism as a theoretical position and accepting it as a human attitude, has been criticized as having failed

---

23. Along with exclusivism, inclusivism, and pluralism, he adds a fourth type (or a third in his typology): parallelism. While he holds pluralism, it seems to me that he identifies parallelism with the theocentric pluralism.

An Imaginative Glimpse

to show that his position is not another theory. Also, Heim's inclusivism is criticized as having been collapsed to a typical inclusivism in its failure to respect other religions' auto-descriptions. Finally, we can still find a clearly inclusivist tendency in D'Costa's tradition-specific exclusivism.

Interestingly, whatever position each thinker holds, all theologians under discussion have a similar stance against pluralistic theologies. At least, there are two main similarities found in the three theologians with regard to their rejection of pluralistic theologies of religions. First, they reject the superimposing tendency in pluralistic theologies while still believing that a universal truth-claim can be made from a particular perspective. Second, they try to respect the auto-description of other religions. These two similarities, therefore, permit us to conclude that, despite the different positions that they hold, Panikkar, D'Costa, and Heim can be understood as post-pluralist theologians.

Besides naming their positions post-pluralist, I also prefer not to use any typology in describing the Christian attitudes toward non-Christian religions. In my opinion, it has created ambiguity rather than helping us deal with the theological complexity that we have in performing our theological task. The twofold principle that I have frequently mentioned—commitment to Christian faith and openness to other religious truths—is sufficient to guide my attempt at constructing a perichoretic theology of religions.

Transversal Attitude toward Others

The purpose of this section is to provide a theoretical support for my theological construction. It, however, is not a full-fledged theory pretending to solve all problems inherent in our discussion. Rather, I start from what has already been suggested by the theologians under discussion. I then analyze their strengths and weaknesses and suggest some revisions. I begin in the first part with the discussion of Panikkar's rejection of pluralism as a theoretical system or model. Since my project is to construct a theological model that also implies a theoretical necessity, I need to argue against Panikkar's position on this matter. Then, in the second part, I aim to show that Rescher's orientational pluralism borrowed by Heim is the most plausible model for fulfilling the objective of my project. Since I have discussed it at length in chapter 2, I just briefly summarize the theory. What is more important, however, is to demonstrate some weaknesses of the theory and make some suggestions to address the weaknesses left by orientational pluralism. I argue for transversality as a form of rationality that is able to transcend the static and self-enclosed characteristics of orientational pluralism. Let's begin now with Panikkar's problem.

Panikkar's Problem

Panikkar frequently argues against the intelligibility of pluralism as a theoretical system. Since pluralism occurs only if there are incompatible yet coexistent systems, the construction of pluralism as a theory—thus, putting it in the realm of *logos*—would inevitably create a supersystem that becomes ideological and oppressive. Panikkar's solution is radical. He rather places pluralism on the realm of *mythos* and *pneuma* and links it to a human attitude toward reality. Panikkar's proposal is certainly advantageous in avoiding the longstanding issues of the conflict between multiple theories or systems. The only possible way to approach pluralism is through mystical or spiritual attitude or, in Panikkar's words, "cosmic confidence."[24]

The problem is, of course, once pluralism is "elevated" to the level of *mythos* and is sanitized from the dimension of *logos*, we cannot have a firm basis to argue reasonably. Panikkar himself acknowledges that the linking of pluralism to cosmic confidence would result in the breaking of (although it is superior to) the principle of noncontradiction, which is essential in any theoretical and rational discourse.[25] If this is the case, does it not mean that an authentic dialogue among religious adherents can only be limited to non-rational ways?

Another problem relevant to the purpose of this project is that Panikkar's proposal makes my intention to construct a theoretical model (in a theological sense) seem impossible and illegitimate. For this reason, it is necessary for me to address Panikkar's objection. Stephen Kaplan, who also struggles with the same issue, has some important insights into this issue. Kaplan's main objective in his book, *Different Paths, Different Summits*, is to construct a model, based on Bohm's holographic idea. This model allows three or more different ultimate realities to exist concurrently and to mutually interpenetrate each other. Kaplan acknowledges, however, that this model falls under the category of Panikkar's supersystem, even though it is not a developed or complete one.

Kaplan begins his discussion with Panikkar's caution that pluralism entails "the dethronement of reason and the abandonment of the monotheistic

---

24. Panikkar, *Invisible Harmony*, 145–82.
25. Panikkar, *Cultural Disarmament*, 95; cf. Panikkar, *Invisible Harmony*, 153.

An Imaginative Glimpse

paradigm."[26] Kaplan agrees with Panikkar that pluralism entails the monotheistic paradigm, which should be interpreted not literally but as referring to any philosophical system that maintains an idea of singular truth. Kaplan, however, disagrees with Panikkar's second observation, that pluralism also entails "the enthronement of reason." Drawing from Krishnachandra Bhattacharyya and Stephen Pepper, Kaplan asks: "Why can one not develop a model for religious pluralism that allows us to employ a variety of types of reason, different types of logic, different theories of negation?"[27] According to his analysis, Panikkar's "dethronement of reason" is unnecessary for pluralism, since "it would seem that any one model for religious pluralism would have to represent *one* type of rational process," and it means, "any model that was utilized for religious pluralism would reflect the enthronement of a particular type of rationality."[28]

Kaplan argues that Panikkar is wrong in this matter. Through his holographic model, Kaplan demonstrates the possibility, even necessity, of a pluralist proposal "to entertain more than one of . . . philosophical, rational systems."[29] Thus, the problem is not the rational or theoretical model *per se*, but how a particular model can destroy pluralism. He goes further by pointing out three ways through which a model could destroy pluralism.[30]

First, when a model presents a single ultimate reality and supersedes other ultimate realities, it would be in opposition to an authentic pluralism.[31] Second, it would destroy pluralism when a model presents a single type of negation or rationality. Finally, a model is against an authentic pluralism if it is rooted in a non-pluralistic framework that makes different ultimate realities inaccessible to different people. None of the options, Kaplan believes, appears in his holographic model.

While I agree with all of indicators that Kaplan identifies, I need to add a fourth marker of how a model could destroy pluralism, that is, when a

26. Kaplan, *Different Paths*, 49; Panikkar, *Invisible Harmony*, 153.

27. Kaplan, *Different Paths*, 49.

28. Ibid., 51. Kaplan also discusses a second reason of why Panikkar rejects any model for religious pluralism, that is, that Reality cannot be totally comprehensible. For Panikkar, any theoretical model attempts to comprehend the incomprehensible, then it must fail.

29. Kaplan, *Different Paths*, 50.

30. Ibid., 53.

31. In the light of my rejection of using the classical typology of exclusivism, inclusivism, and pluralism, I use the terms "pluralism" and "pluralistic" here only as having been used by Kaplan, or in that the terms refer not to "pluralism" as a particular theory but as generic terms for religious diversity.

model rejects its particular starting point and claims its neutral position. In other words, a non-perspectival model cannot be pluralistic.

Kaplan's criticism of Panikkar is important for my project in two respects. First, he demonstrates the possibility of a constructive model that respects different ultimacies. Second, he is successful in pointing out that different rational systems inherent in different religious traditions can mutually exist. However, while these two insights help us confront Panikkar's critique of pluralism as a theoretical system, we cannot ignore Panikkar's valuable claim that interreligious encounter is always in need of a non-logical "cosmic confidence." I now turn to the discussion of orientational pluralism.

Transversality: Beyond Orientational Pluralism

Among the three theologians, S. Mark Heim has provided the most plausible and convincing theoretical framework, especially with the orientational pluralism that he borrows from Nicholas Rescher. Since I have discussed the theory at length in the previous chapter, it is sufficient to highlight some of its main points.

Orientational pluralism, working on the meta-philosophical level, is an attempt to safeguard the perspectival aspect of every interpretive theory and, at the same time, to maintain that there is only one correct theory for a particular perspective. Thus, as there are many culturally-situated orientations, there are also many realities, each corresponding to one perspective or orientation. With regard to the notion of a single and absolute truth, the orientational pluralists would absolutely agree, but they also claim that every theory cannot reach such an absolute truth. What is possible is to interpret the truth from a single perspective. Any attempt at transcending and combining different perspectives is also perspectival. Thus, orientational pluralism allows one to make a universal truth-claim, but rejects that such a claim comes from a God's-eye viewpoint.

It is important to note that for Rescher, as for Heim, there is a significant difference between the multifaceted approach to reality and the perspectival approach to reality. The multifaceted approach views reality as so complex that diverse systems can only grasp different aspects or facets of the truth—every one is right in its own way. On the contrary, the perspectival or orientational approach holds the position that "one and only one position is appropriate from a given perspective of consideration; but there is a variety of perspectives."[32] While in the former approach facets of truth could and

32. Rescher, *Strife of Systems*, 176.

should be combined into one coherent truth, for the latter approach such a conjunction is impossible. Perspectives cannot be combined, since each perspective offers "the *whole* reality, not only some *part* of reality," but once again, it is the whole reality from a given perspective, not from a God's-eye, neutral position.[33] This point is very important for me in analyzing how Panikkar, D'Costa, and Heim deal with different religious tradition. But, before turning to this subject, a second important issue needs to be addressed.

Is orientational pluralism a form of relativism? Apparently it is, as Rescher painstakingly distinguishes between different models of relativism, particularly between truth-relativism and justification-relativism. Orientational pluralists reject the former and accept the latter. Rescher argues, "the relativism of orientational pluralism is epistemic, not ontological. It is a relativism of *acceptability*, not a relativism of *truth*."[34] Consequently, we can only address truth-claims not the absolute truth.

Orientational pluralism, undoubtedly, provides a tremendous basis for dealing with the issue of religious plurality, as we have seen in its appropriation through Heim's works. However, the elements of perspectivism and relativism that I discussed above, if held together, would also create some serious problems. For example, with regard to Rescher's argument that perspectives cannot be combined, how could we justify Panikkar's theology that has obviously "combined" three different, even contradictory, perspectives (Christian, Hindu, and Buddhist)? Here, we might be able to understand better Panikkar's dissatisfaction with pluralism as a theoretical system or model. On the other hand, Panikkar's proposal would certainly seem implausible for genuine orientational pluralists. They might also argue that Panikkar's position is closer to the multifaceted approach than to perspectival approach. But, Panikkar would disagree with this accusation, since he rejects any *theoretical* possibility for pluralism, while Rescher offers his orientational pluralism as a theory. Thus, one cannot say that Panikkar has combined three theoretical perspectives. Moreover, granted that Panikkar's position has a theoretical element, even though he does not acknowledge it, we can reconcile Rescher's orientational perspectivism and Panikkar's pluralism. When we see more closely Panikkar's metaphor of "windows"—that we see the *totum* from our window—it is obvious that he has employed the same perspectival idea, though unintentionally. It is of course possible to offer a satisfactory solution both from the perspectival approach and from Panikkar's points of view. We can say that what Panikkar has combined

33. Ibid., 179.
34. Ibid., 195.

are not different epistemological perspectives but different metaphysical systems. This would neither contravene the principle held in orientational theory nor abandon Panikkar's affirmation of perspectivism.

By the same token, we can understand Heim's inclusivist position. His revised inclusivism has not violated the principle of non-conjunction in orientational pluralism, since Heim's inclusion is not one of perspectives but one of multiple religious ends. Moreover, this form of inclusivism is to be viewed as a *Christian* proposal, even Heim's *personal* proposal. Heim himself also recurrently offers an invitation for non-Christians to propose their universal inclusivist model, even though it would result in the Christian fulfillment being penultimate in relation to the ultimate fulfillment taught in the non-Christian religions.

With regard to D'Costa's model, orientational pluralists can give a serious critique. To say that every position is tradition-specific is a justification or *epistemological* claim, but to say that every position is exclusivist is a *truth* claim. D'Costa seems to fail to distinguish the two claims. In other words, a tradition-specific position is not necessarily identical with exclusivism.[35]

I have demonstrated that orientational pluralism can be employed to analyze the three theologians that we discuss. It also provides valuable insight for maintaining the balance between particularistic perspectivism and universalistic truth-claims. However, there is a major problem with this theory with regard to the *relation* between different religious perspectives or orientations. In my opinion, orientational pluralism is seriously deficient in providing a dynamic opportunity for different perspectives to engage with one another. Interestingly, this is also the critique of John B. Cobb, Jr. toward what he calls "conceptual relativism." He says,

> The problem with conceptual relativism is not that it sees a circularity between beliefs and the norms by which they are judged. This is the human condition. The weakness is that it pictures this as a static, self-enclosed system, whereas the great religious traditions can be open and dynamic. This does not justify someone claiming to stand outside all the relative positions and to be able to establish a neutral, objective norm over all. But it does mean that

---

35. Beside multifaceted and perspectival approaches, Rescher also discusses two other approaches: no-reality and unique reality approaches. While no-reality approach says everybody is wrong because there is ultimate truth accessible for anyone, the unique reality approach says maintains that only one privileged party is right and others are wrong. Clearly, D'Costa holds the unique reality approach.

normative thinking within each tradition can be expanded and extended through openness to the normative thinking of others.[36]

We need, however, to carefully discern this critique within the larger context of Cobb's proposal to solve the dichotomy of absolutism and relativism. Cobb realizes that his strong rejection of absolutism has often been interpreted as an endorsement of relativism. Even more, he acknowledges that this interpretation is not fully wrong, since the radical pluralism that he proposes can indeed lead to "conceptual relativism." This is a view in which "each tradition is best [evaluated] by its own norm and there is no normative critique of norms."[37] The problem with conceptual relativism, Cobb argues, is that it pictures each tradition as "a static, self-enclosed system, whereas the great religious traditions can be open and dynamic."[38] He also stresses that this problem makes it almost impossible for us "to bridge the chasms that lie between alternative systems of concepts."[39]

Cobb's insights, I believe, are valuable if we want to minimize the relativistic bent of orientational pluralism. His solution is twofold. First, he makes a distinction between conceptual relativism, which he rejects, and his own version of relativism, which simply means "the affirmation that every event, every assertion, every belief, is *conditioned* by a multitude of factors: physical, social, historical, psychological, biographical, and so forth."[40] A key word here is "conditioned." If every system or concept is conditioned, then there is no way we can escape from relativism. But, secondly, Cobb also argues that the conditionedness of all beliefs should lead us into a more dialogical openness toward others. He believes that the discovery of consensus and the process of creative transformation among two or more different and conflicting systems are possible. But, we cannot assume those praxis-oriented common grounds are already present. "Commonalities are to be found, not posited."[41]

Cobb's idea of the conditionedness of all religious systems is congruent to the principle of perspectivism in Rescher and Heim's orientational pluralism. Cobb's hope for creative transformation for religions, however, is more constructive in proposing a more dynamic encounter among conflicting

---

36. Cobb, "Beyond 'Pluralism,'" 86.
37. Cobb, *Transforming Christianity*, 66.
38. Ibid.
39. Ibid., 97.
40. Ibid., 96, italics mine.
41. Ibid., 105.

systems. The next question is, if the transformative commonalities among different religious systems are to be found, rather than posited, how do we pursue them in a rational way? To answer this question, the idea of transversal rationality from Calvin O. Schrag would be greatly beneficial.

Calvin O. Schrag's *The Resources of Rationality*, sketches his argument for a transversal logos as a solution to the problem of universalism versus particularism, one that is "passing between the Scylla of a hegemonic and ahistorical universalism and the Charybdis of a lawless, self-effacing particularism and enervated historicism."[42] Schrag formulates the importance of transversal play as a third alternative to modernity and postmodernity in many different ways. For example he says, "We submit . . . that an unavoidable task of philosophy for the new millennium is that of installing the dynamics of transversal rationality and transversal communication across the landscape of difference within an increasingly global and pluralistic world order. Only this can save us from the impasse created by the collision of a hegemony of universally legislated belief systems and policies with a rampant relativism of chaotic particularity and multiplicity."[43]

He also observes that the ahistorical grand story of modernity and the historically localized story of postmodernity always confuse the *ahistorical* with the *transhistorical*. While the former affirms the ahistorical logos, the latter rejects it. Yet, both share the idea that logos is ahistorical. In contrast, Schrag proposes transversal rationality under the category of the transhistorical and the advantage of using this transversal grammar is obvious, as he writes, "[I]t facilitates a thinking beyond the dichotomies of transcendentalism versus historicism, the essential versus the contingent, the absolute versus the relative, and is thus able to avoid confusing the transhistorical with the ahistorical. The dynamics of the transversal logos, in its extending over and lying across the multiplicity of social practices and conventions, makes it possible for us to visit different times and places without either requiring a panoptic standpoint outside of history or having recourse to an incommensurability of local narratives."[44]

Thus, the transversal rationality enables us to cross multiple systems, each of which claims its universality, without being trapped either in the universal ahistorical foundationalism of modernity or the radical historical

---

42. Schrag, *Resources*, 9. I am indebted to J. Wentzel van Huyssteen's works for introducing me to Schrag's transversal idea. Huyssteen, however, applies transversality to the issue of religion and science. See Van Huyssteen, *Shaping of Rationality*.

43. Schrag, *Convergence*, 80.

44. Schrag, *Resources*, 173.

particularism of postmodernity. The dynamics of transversal rationality work through various systems. It is neither vertically transcendent to those systems (as in modern universalism) nor horizontally immanent within them (as in postmodern particularism), but diagonally, that is, "between" them, "in such a manner that it is able to critique, articulate, and disclose them without achieving a coincidence with any particular form of discourse, thought, or action."[45] The expected results of employing the concept of transversality are clearly promising: "a convergence without coincidence, an interplay without synthesis, an appropriation without totalization, and a unification that allows for difference."[46]

When put within the context of our conversation, the transversal grammar for multiple religious traditions transforms the perspectival dimension of orientational pluralism, from a static and self-enclosed approach into a more dynamic and relational approach. Orientational pluralism has certainly laid a solid basis for maintaining the balance between one's situatedness in a particular context *and* the possibility of its claims for universality. Heim rightly utilizes the insights from orientational pluralism to support his idea that there can be multiple religious ends; each is valid in its given perspective. But, when it comes to his revised inclusivism, he moves beyond orientational pluralism, particularly because orientational pluralism has nothing to say beyond justification-claims. Heim's inclusivism, as a truth-claim, in other words, is not necessarily a logical implication of his subscription to orientational pluralism. The only thing orientational pluralism can contribute in Heim's inclusivism is to give a warning that, even when other religious ends are included in Heim's Trinitarian framework, it is still a particular perspective and not a universally absolute truth.

Moreover, from Schrag's perspective, Heim's inclusivism could be seen as having not fully employed the transversal grammar. Heim might be considered at a "halfway house" from the universal to the transversal. Schrag, interestingly, uses the image of "halfway house" to refer to Merleau-Ponty, who distinguishes "lateral universal" from "overarching universals."[47] Merleau-Ponty's text that Schrag quotes is worth reintroducing here, since it reflects to a great extent what Heim has suggested in him inclusivism.

> This provides a second way to the universal: no longer the overarching universal of a strictly objective method, but a sort of lateral

---

45. Ibid., 158.
46. Ibid., 158–59.
47. Ibid., 171–72.

universal which we acquire through ethnological experience and its incessant testing of the self through the other person and the other person through the self. It is a question of constructing a general system of reference in which the point of view of the native, the point of view of the civilized man, and the mistaken view each has of the other can find a place—that is, of constituting a more comprehensive experience which becomes in principle accessible to men of a different time and country.[48]

This is precisely what Heim suggests in his Trinitarian inclusivism. The multiple religious ends are recognized fully, yet also included, within the dimension of otherness inherent in the Christian Trinity. In the Schragian perspective, this is not enough. Merleau-Ponty's lateral universal is only a halfway in the journey from the universal to the transversal. The transversal unification that Schrag seeks—convergence without coincidence—cannot be achieved by seeking "the metaphysical comfort of stable beginning and universal telic principle" nor "via a vertically ordered and hegemonic decision-making arrangement that simply subordinates the lower to the higher."[49] Rather, "what is required is a transversal ordering and communication that is achieved through a diagonal movement across the group, acknowledging the otherness and integrity of each, while making the requisite accommodations and adjustment along the way."[50] In short, transversal rationality operates primarily in the context of communication among different systems, not in the constructive modeling done by an individual *bricoleur*.

My proposal is therefore as follows. First, any constructive model of theology of religions, as Heim has done and I am doing now, can never be claimed as a perfect product of the transversal rationality. It will always be a "halfway house" in our journey to fulfill the goal of transversality. To use Panikkar's idea loosely, what is done in the constructive theology of religions is more an *intra*-religious than *inter*-religious dialogue. Second, any constructive theology of religion, however, always needs to employ the transversal rationality in its imagining the model that it creates by using the principles of transversality as well as in following up its constructive attempt with a real communicative praxis with people from other traditions. Third, both constructive theology of religions and interreligious communicative praxis that follows from it need always to be in an ongoing process. "It is a dynamic of unification that is always an 'ing,' a process of unifying, rather than an 'ed,'

---

48. Merleau-Ponty, "From Mauss," 120; Schrag, *Resources*, 171.
49. Schrag, *Self after Postmodernity*, 129–32.
50. Ibid., 132.

An Imaginative Glimpse

a finalized result," says Schrag.[51] A fourth proposal, which is also my critical evaluation of Schrag's total rejection of the universal, is that there is still a possibility and necessity of talking about universality, although it should be joined with a transversal grammar.[52] Even, Schrag admires Merleau-Ponty's attempt to reinterpret the universal—from the overarching universals to lateral universals. Despite the fact that Merleau-Ponty's reinterpretation of universality is considered to be an attempt that only goes "halfway," Schrag also admits that Merleau-Ponty's idea of lateral universal that seeks for "a more comprehensive experience which becomes in principle accessible to men of a different time and country" is "the effect of a transversal rationality."[53]

In conclusion, we are still in a need of a constructive theology of religions that has "universal relevance"[54]—or "universal intent," in Polanyi's words[55]—but one that is guided by transversal rationality. Hence, universality that works transversally. Such a transversal universality recognizes the universal scope of its own and of others. There are, thus, many *uni*-versals (or pluriversal, so to speak); each argues for its *uni*-tive claim and respect of the unitive claims of other universals.

Trinity and Religious Diversity

Economic and Immanent Trinity

The distinction between the economic and immanent Trinity has played a significant role in Trinitarian theology for centuries. The term "economic Trinity" refers to the threefold way through which the triune God works and

---

51. Schrag, *Self after Postmodernity*, 129.

52. James Crosswhite provides an excellent comparative analysis of Calvin O. Schrag's rejection of the notion of universality and Chaim Perelman's retrieval of the notion of universality. He offers three reasons why he inclines more to Perelman. First, our history and our argumentation are already suffused and dependent on the notion of universality. Second, transversality fails to capture the pragmatically open intention of reasoning that attempts to succeed before a universal audience. Third, the notion of universality can still be preserved by keeping the argumentation open to criticism. See Crosswhite, *Rhetoric of Reason*, 155–59.

53. Schrag, *Resources*, 171.

54. Heim argues that we his project is always guided by two principles: "advocacy of the universal relevance of our conviction, and recognition of the integral otherness and universal scope of varying approaches." Heim, *Salvations*, 209.

55. For Polanyi's idea of universal intent, see Polanyi, *Personal Knowledge*. Lesslie Newbigin has also applied Polanyi's idea to the issue of religious diversity; see Newbigin, *Gospel*.

relates to creation. This idea is distinguished from the "immanent Trinity," which refers to the eternal and internal life of the triune God apart from creation. The distinction between these two notions is commonly used to deal with the tension between the absoluteness and the relatedness of God:[56] "On the one hand, to affirm the immanent-economic distinction risks subordinating the economic Trinity and hence protecting transcendent absoluteness at the cost genuine relatedness to the world. But, on the other hand, to collapse the two together risks producing a God so dependent upon the world for self-definition that divine freedom and independence is lost."[57]

I begin my comparative analysis with the issue of the relationship between the immanent Trinity and the economic Trinity because—as I will go on to argue—a robust Trinitarian theology of religions can be constructed only if it is based on a clearly defined relationship between the economic Trinity and the immanent Trinity. In chapter 5 I will explain my own understanding of the two, drawing upon LaCugna's book, *God for Us*. For now, however, using the basic ideas introduced above suffices for a comparative analysis of how each theologian deals with this issue.

Panikkar reinterprets the Christian doctrine of the Trinity through the lens of cosmotheandrism. We may ask whether the cosmotheandric reality reflects the divine Trinity, or the other way around. This question may be successfully answered through engagement with the Christic principle (a claim I make further below). For the present, however, it is sufficient to note that Panikkar gives cosmotheandrism primacy over the Christian Trinity. By using the term "radical Trinity" as another term for cosmotheandric reality, Panikkar wants to emphasize that neither Christianity nor the divine holds a monopoly on the Trinity. He writes, "[The Trinity] does not belong in an exclusive way to what some call God. Besides what Christian tradition has called the immanent Trinity (*ab intra*) and the economic Trinity (*ad extra*), I submit, there is the radical Trinity (*in omnibus*)."[58]

Even though the notion of radical Trinity is crucial in Panikkar's writings, by no means does he diminish the classical notions of immanent and economic Trinity. On the contrary, he wants to assign even deeper meaning to the Christian Trinity by enlarging the scope of the Trinitarian radicality (or, radical relativity) to include extra-divine reality. His basic principle is clear: "Every bit of reality has this trinitarian imprint."[59] Unlike the classi-

56. Peters, *God as Trinity*, 20.
57. Ibid., 22–23.
58. Panikkar, "Cosmic Evolution," 70.
59. Panikkar, *Blessed Simplicity*, 128.

cal ideas of immanent and economic Trinity that only refer to the divine, Panikkar's radical Trinity includes God, humanity, and the world. The three make up the radical Trinity.[60]

Contrasted with Trinitarian ideas from the Western tradition, Panikkar's radical Trinity seems unorthodox. Trinitarian theology in the West has been characterized by *Logos*-oriented thinking, in which Christ, the *Logos*, becomes the center of the Trinity. Panikkar tries to support his Trinitarian theology with insights he receives from Eastern Christianity as well as from other religious traditions, especially Hinduism and Buddhism, without abandoning the importance of Christ the Logos. Ewert H. Cousins rightly summarizes Panikkar's program by saying, "Panikkar is attempting to evoke in his *logos*-bound Western readers these primordial modes of perception [the silence of the Father in Buddhism and the non-differentiation of the Spirit in Hinduism] which have not been directly mediated by their culture."[61]

It is also obvious that the idea of perichoresis plays a significant role in Panikkar's theology. While in the economic Trinity the idea of perichoresis refers to the mutual indwelling of the Father, Son, and Spirit as the three persons relates to creation, in the radical Trinity the idea of perichoresis points to the mutual indwelling of God, humanity, and world. Thus, the shift from the economic Trinity to the radical Trinity is followed by the shift from person-perichoresis to reality-perichoresis. The emphasis is placed on all of reality, instead of only on the economy—or history—of salvation.[62]

D'Costa's infrequent use of the distinction between the immanent and economic Trinity demonstrates that he accepts the validity of this distinction as a part of how the Christian tradition talks about the Trinity. Like Heim, he emphasizes the importance of the doctrine of Trinity in the context of salvation-history.[63] Unlike Heim, however, D'Costa makes an explicit positive claim as to how the Triune God works in history. The Trinitarian

---

60. Panikkar's attempt to include the whole of reality into the trinitarian structure is shown clearly in his *The Silence of God*: "I can assert that God's radical relativity *ad extra* is a mirror of the same radicality *ad intra*: that is to say, the whole universe, as image or 'vestige' of the Trinity, is endowed with the trinitarian character of radical relativity." Panikkar, *Silence of God*, 142.

61. Cousins, "Panikkar's," 128.

62. Keith Johnson harshly criticizes Panikkar as having posited three economies—the economy of the Father, the economy of the Son, and the economy of the Spirit—that "ultimately constitute a form of economic tritheism." Johnson, "'Trinitarian' Theology," 298–301. Although Johnson's analysis of the presence of "three economies" in Panikkar is plausible, I argue that, at the end, those three economies constitute a single larger cosmotheandric economy, so to speak.

63. Kärkkäinen, *Religious Pluralism*, 143

Comparative Analyses

economy of salvation always takes place in and through the life of the church that orients herself toward the kingdom of God.[64] Obviously, the explicit relation between the Trinity and the church is undermined both in Panikkar's and in Heim's theologies.

Another important aspect in D'Costa's Trinitarian theology that brings him closer to Heim is his salvation-history perspective, which—as does Heim's—emphasizes the importance of eschatological consummation or fulfillment. Such an eschatologically-oriented perspective, which is predominant both in his earlier phase of inclusivism and in his latest phase of exclusivism, provides him with a basis for reinterpreting Rahner's Rule: "the economic Trinity is the immanent Trinity, and vice versa."[65] He agrees fully with the first part of Rahner's axiom that the economic Trinity *is* the immanent Trinity. This statement expresses the conviction that we do not have two trinities, one economic and the other immanent. Rather, we only have one Trinity that can be viewed in two ways, that is, in its relation to creation (the economic Trinity) and in itself (the immanent Trinity).

Based on this idea, D'Costa agrees with the Catholic Church that God's revelation is already "closed" insofar as "God has truly revealed Himself in Jesus Christ" and "the 'closed' operates centrifugally to relate *all* truth as being present, hidden, disclosed, and concealed in Christ *in so much* as God is present in Christ."[66] Also, the first part of Rahner's Rule implies that "we cannot discover anything new about God, *in the sense* of ontologically unrelated or contrary to Christ."[67]

However, D'Costa disagrees with Rahner's "vice versa" part, precisely because God's revelation was "closed" in Jesus Christ. He explains this by borrowing Rahner's claim that revelation is closed because it is "open to the concealed presence of divine plenitude in Christ. . . . That revelation has been closed is a positive and not a negative statement, a pure Amen, a conclusion *which includes everything and excludes nothing* of the divine plenitude, conclusion as fulfilled presence of an all-embracing plenitude."[68]

D'Costa seems reluctant to place too much emphasis on his exclusivist position. His rejection of the second part of Rahner's Rule, which is based on his eschatological revaluation of the Trinity, as well as his borrowing

64. D'Costa, *Meeting of Religions*, 113.
65. Rahner, *Trinity*, 21–22.
66. D'Costa, *Meeting of Religions*, 38.
67. Ibid.
68. Rahner, *Theological Investigations*, 49, italics his; cf. D'Costa, *Meeting of Religions*, 38–39.

from Rahner in regards to how to interpret the "closed" nature of divine revelation, gives him an opportunity to show, however faintly, his openness to other religions. He concludes his argument by saying, "[O]penness can be genuinely said to exist within my trinitarian orientation . . . since the trinitarian doctrine of God is only eschatologically 'closed,' and is always also a doctrine about the shape of the church, it means that the very doctrine of a trinitarian God within Christianity allows Christianity to maintain a real openness to God *in history*."[69]

Heim, I believe, would agree with D'Costa's reformulation of Rahner's Rule, but not with his exclusivist arguments. Heim would be more prepared to accept D'Costa's arguments from the earlier inclusivist phase, and extends D'Costa's respect for Otherness to a more positive construction of how other religions take their places in the Trinitarian structure.

We have seen that Panikkar enlarges the scope of the Trinity from person-perichoresis to reality-perichoresis. This enlarged scope makes Panikkar's Trinitarianism differ from Heim's, whose Trinitarian theology focuses more particularly on the salvific-economic dimension of the Trinity.[70] Heim's project concerns how the Trinity becomes the principle of fulfillment for all religions. While Panikkar understands that God, Humanity and World are mutually indwelling within each other, constituting a Trinitarian reality, Heim believes that Humanity and World are within yet dependent on the Triune God. Panikkar's Trinity is radical because it expresses a "symmetry," so to speak, between God, Humanity, and World.

Heim, on the other hand, accepts the "radical asymmetry" or "obvious hierarchical character of the disparity between God and humanity," even though such an asymmetry "could be assimilated or transposed to the key

---

69. D'Costa, *Meeting of Religions*, 133. D'Costa argues differently in his earlier inclusivist phase. While agreeing with the first part of Rahner's Rule and disagreeing with the "vice versa" part, he provides an argument from the viewpoint of "open inclusivism." He says, "While we know God, we do not know everything about God." D'Costa, "Trinitarian Différance," 38. Also, the rejection of the second part of Rahner's Rule, in this phase, means that the truth "is never our possession but, rather, we are possessed by it," so that "it is in this surplus that genuine Otherness can become a question mark to my own Christian self-understanding, a question mark to the location of my questioning, and the question mark that bears the trace of revelation." D'Costa, "Trinitarian Différance," 38–39.

70. This is also the conclusion drawn by Kärkkäinen, "Whereas Panikkar's trinitarianism is based on a generic idea of the trinitarian structure of reality (and thus of religions), Heim builds on the biblical salvation-history and subsequent Christian tradition." Kärkkäinen, *Religious Pluralism*, 143.

of Trinitarian communion," with each remaining "distinct."[71] However, it is important to note that transposition of the humans into the Trinitarian communion refers only to the Christian religious end. No other religions are geared toward attaining "communion," even though the various religious ends can still be assimilated to the divine through different aspects of the Trinity. The assimilation of non-Christian ends to the Trinitarian life both reflects the fact that "they are part of the network by which all can be drawn into closer communion with God and to salvation" and affirms that "God always will relate with creation under the terms of freedom granted it."[72]

Heim seems to reject the separation between the economic and immanent Trinity. First, he affirms that the economic Trinity is grounded in the immanent (or ontological) Trinity, implying that "relational images of God express something of God's true nature."[73] Second, having settled the connection between the economic and immanent Trinity, Heim proceeds by saying that those relations are manifested in different religious ends. He frequently emphasizes that multiple religious ends grasp different but genuine dimensions of the triune life and aspects of God's economic activity.[74]

Nevertheless, it is arguable whether Heim suggests a single economy or many. John G. Flett observes that Heim has proposed "alternate economies" apart from the divine economy centered on Christ.[75] To be sure, Heim would agree with Flett's charge, since precisely the main proposal of Heim's theology is that there are not only multiple means or ways, but also multiple ends. If in using the term divine economy we refer only to Christ as the means of salvation, then it is true that Heim proposes many economies. However, if such economy is focused more broadly on the triune God, who works indivisibly, then it would be more proper to say that there is a *single yet multidimensional economy*. It is a single economy insofar as it refers to the same triune God. Yet, it is also multidimensional insofar as all religious ends are encompassed within different dimensions of the Trinity. Heim neatly expresses his idea:

> God is related to us in complex and distinct ways. The channels between God and humanity are open on several frequencies. Salvation consists in a particular enrichment, intensification, and harmonization of all of these, in interrelations that allow each its

71. Heim, *Depth of the Riches*, 176.
72. Ibid., 268.
73. Ibid., 126.
74. Ibid., 268, 72.
75. Flett, "In the Name," 9.

own scope. There is a "hierarchy" between full communion with the triune God and lesser, restricted participations. But all the types of relation with God are grounded in God, in the coexisting relations in God's own nature.[76]

Heim assures his readers that, in the end, the Trinity accommodates multiple religious ends. Thus, in this sense, he comes close to Panikkar's notion of cosmotheandrism. Unlike Panikkar, however, Heim argues that such an overarching Trinitarianism occurs only in an eschatological sense. It is through the idea of Trinitarian and eschatological plenitude that Heim explains the Christian hope for universal salvation, without trying to solve the problem of universalism and division.[77]

To conclude discussion of this issue: we have seen two very different approaches in representing the dialectic of the immanent and economic Trinity. The first approach is that of the *reality-based* idea proposed by Panikkar, in which the scope of the immanent and economic Trinity is enlarged to include all reality in a radical way. It is through the idea of the "radical Trinity" that Panikkar tries to transcend the limitations of Trinitarian theology in the West by utilizing the silence of Buddhism and the unity of Hinduism.

The second model, the *salvation-history-based* approach, can be found in D'Costa's and Heim's theologies, in which emphasis is placed on the economy of salvation from creation to consummation. The advantage of this approach, compared to Panikkar's, is in its greater respect for and engagement with history.[78] However, while D'Costa chooses to remain silent about other religions, Heim maximizes this historical engagement by respecting other religions on their own terms and, at the same time, including them within his Trinitarian plenitude. This difference results in Heim producing what may be termed a more eschatological version of Panikkar's cosmotheandrism. In short, Heim shows the middle way between Panikkar's reality-based approach and D'Costa's salvation-history-based approach.

---

76. Heim, *Depth of the Riches*, 179.

77. It is clear that Heim does not go further to accept Origen's notion of *apokatastasis* or universal restoration that makes hell empty. He allows the possibility of hell and annihilation as true options.

78. Camilia G. MacPherson argues that, in his early writings, Panikkar attempts to combine the idea of linear history of the West with the idea of mythic history of the East, resulting in a "total history." Later, however, he argues that "the Christian way of viewing history as linear must collapse in order to open the door to a recognition of the true universality of the Blessed Trinity." MacPherson, *Critical Reading*, 116. See also Rowan Williams' critique, from the Western theological perspective, of Panikkar's limitations in dealing with history; see Williams, "Trinity and Pluralism."

The Father, Son, and Spirit

This section discusses how our theologians understand the relation among the three "persons" of the Trinity and how they place other religions in relation to the three. I put the term "persons" in quotes since the notion of person has been disputed in the history of the Christian tradition, especially in today's theological discourse. While the usage of the terms throughout the history generates complex problems, it is important to underscore how it has created a special issue in the modern time.

With the rise of the modern era, a person is identified in terms of a unique and self-determining subject. Ted Peters succinctly summarizes the problem, "From the modern point of view . . . we understand a person to be a unique individual who is a self-initiating and self-determining subject. Each person is a distinct seat of subjectivity and, hence, independent of other persons and things. One's personhood signals one's autonomy. If, then, we were to apply without qualification the modern understanding of person to the trinitarian formula of 'one substance in three persons,' we could not avoid positing three distinct subjectivities only tenuously tied together. It would constitute a thinly veiled tritheism."[79]

For this reason, Karl Barth and Karl Rahner suggest the replacement of the term "person" in the Trinity with "mode of being" (*Seinsweise*) and "distinct manner of subsisting" (*Subsistenzweisen*), respectively.[80] Even though these proposals are admirable as attempts to avoid the tendency of tritheism in modern Trinitarian theology, they have also been severely criticized. LaCugna, among others, argues that Barth's and Rahner's rejection of using the term "person" in the light of a modern psychological definition end up using the same definition to refer to the divine essence. "The one self-conscious Subject [that is, the divine essence] thus subsists or exists under three modalities."[81] Moreover, LaCugna also sees a problem with the two Karls in that they do not take into account other concepts of person available in the nineteenth and twentieth centuries that provide better alternatives to the Cartesian notion. Those alternatives, she says, interpret a person as always existing in relation.

Drawing from many thinkers, LaCugna suggests a reconstruction of Trinitarian theology that highlights the notion of person-in-relation. Along with LaCugna, there are many contemporary theologians taking the same

---

79. Peters, *God as Trinity*, 35.
80. Barth, *Church Dogmatics, Vol. I.*1, 411–13; Rahner, *Trinity*, 109–13.
81. LaCugna, *God for Us*, 254.

An Imaginative Glimpse

path. This new tendency reflects both the emergence of postmodern notion of interpersonal personhood and the reemergence of the Orthodox idea of communion.[82] Against this brief backdrop, I will now compare Panikkar, D'Costa, and Heim in their attempts to articulate the three persons of the Trinity.

Panikkar is very cautious in his use of the term "person." He sharply makes a distinction between "person" and "individual", identifying the latter as a product of modern thinking. He believes that many problems will be solved if we can unravel the modern Western "myth of individualism."[83] He sees the idea of individual as problematic because it refers to a human being who can be quantified and, at the same time, is taken out of its communality. On the contrary, the concept of person is ultimately relational and communal. In one of his clearest statements of the idea of person, Panikkar says,

> the person disappears if we freeze those centres of relationships and handle them as if they were independent knots, which can be manipulated separately.... [T]he term "person" does not, properly speaking, allow for plural, not only because each person is unique and non-quantifiable, but also because a peculiar plural is internal to the very concept of person: a person being is always society, always relation between several centres or focusses [sic], so that the very concept of an individual and individualized person would be a contradiction in terms.[84]

Not only does person have a relational characteristic, Panikkar argues, person *is* relation. Panikkar goes even further by saying that, since person is relation and all reality is mutually interrelated, "every person represents and symbolizes all of reality," and that "each person reflects the harmony of the universe, when this person is in his or her proper place, and is not alienated."[85] Thus, for Panikkar, the idea of person indicates uniqueness and equivocal meaning, and acts as a symbol for all reality.

This understanding also influences his discussion of the "persons" of the Trinity. He urges that the notion of person can only be assigned properly to the Son. "Only the Son is Person, if we use the word in its eminent sense and analogically to human persons: neither the Father nor the Spirit is a Person."[86] He provides two reasons for this position. First, the term "person"

---

82. Peters, *God as Trinity*, 35–36.
83. Panikkar, "Self-Critical Dialogue," 265.
84. Panikkar, "Christ's Name," 254.
85. Panikkar, *Dwelling Place*, 141; Panikkar, *Cultural Disarmament*, 59.
86. Panikkar, *Religious Experience*, 52.

Comparative Analyses

is not a univocal term. If it were univocal, then there must be a *quaternitas*, "a God-divine nature, outside, inside, above or beside the Father, Son and the Holy Spirit."[87] This would be theologically improper. To say that there are three persons of the Trinity is to imply that the term "person" has been used as an analogy, which means that there must be a primary reference or an analogous factor (*quid analogatum*) appropriate for the three. Second, the divine personhood is properly ascribed to the Son because it is only through the Son that we can have a personal relationship with the divine. It is the Son who acts and creates. Here, Panikkar employs the classical Christian idea that the Son is the mediator, in and through whom everything comes into existence.

Panikkar maintains that the idea of the God-Person, applied only to the Son, is the unique contribution of Christianity. With regard to the Father and the Spirit, he borrows descriptions from Buddhism and Hinduism. The Father is the true transcendence and the Spirit is the true immanence. The idea that we can have a personal relationship with the Father or the Spirit would imply the necessity for both the Father and the Spirit to be persons, and this would destroy the true transcendence of the Father and the true immanence of the Spirit.[88]

Panikkar's idea of person as only appropriate for the Son provides him a solid basis for acknowledging the authentic differences among religions. While the Son corresponds to the personalistic religions such as Christianity, Judaism, and Islam, the Father corresponds to Buddhism and the Spirit to Hinduism. Nonetheless, this position also has a weakness in its inconsistency with the Christian traditional language of the three persons of the Trinity. If the Son is the only "person" in the Trinity, how do we make sense of the terms "Father" and "Son" and the relation between both? Does not this traditional language mean that we use an analogous factor (*quid analogatum*) familiar to human relationship for both the Father and the Son? Of course, Panikkar's idea of limiting the person to the Son is consistent with his entire framework, which attempts to appropriate the Father to Buddhism and the Spirit to Hinduism. Thus, based on Panikkar's understanding that person implies relationality and communality, he finds it problematic to say that the Father and the Spirit are "persons," since Buddhism and Hinduism

87. Panikkar, *Religious Experience*, 52.

88. Interestingly, he often uses the term "persons" for the threefoldness of God by placing it between quotes. It indicates that, while he is critical of the idea of "three Persons," he cannot avoid the fact that it has been historically used in the Christian traditions. What he offers, however, is a proper understanding of the person, informed by his engagement with Buddhism and Hinduism.

do not recognize any relation/communion with the ultimate in a "personal" sense as Panikkar understands it.

Panikkar, I believe, leaves this problem unsolved. Heim, on the other hand, provides an answer to this issue. Heim maintains two important aspects in Panikkar while at the same time revising them significantly: the idea of person as relational-communal and the advantage of using an appropriation method.[89]

D'Costa does not provide a deep reflection of the meaning of "person" and how to apply this term to the Triune persons. I suspect that, by explicitly affirming the Catholic tradition as his starting-point, he simply follows what is traditionally held by the Catholic Church. More specifically, D'Costa employs the Irenaean idea of Son and Spirit as the "two hands of God," although he does not explicitly refer to Irenaeus. D'Costa's intention is clearly to avoid separating the economy of Christ and the economy of the Spirit, or particularity and universality. However, unlike Irenaeus who coins this metaphor to explain the divine act of creation, D'Costa uses it for a soteriological purpose. While D'Costa never talks about a direct relation to the Father, the first person of Trinity, it is clear that he argues that humanity and the rest of creation can relate to the other two persons, Christ and the Spirit.

In his earlier phase of inclusivism, the mutual combination of both "hands" is more strongly emphasized, which makes it possible for him to reject both the possibility of using the economy of the Son apart from the economy of the Spirit (a characteristic of exclusivism) *and* the primacy of the Spirit over the Son (a possible path taken by pluralists). "The Holy Spirit allows the particularity of Christ to be related to the universal activity of God in human history."[90] In rejecting the dangers of exclusivism and pluralism, D'Costa also expresses the proper relation between the Father and the Son in such a way that an *exclusive identification* of God and Jesus (as in exclusivism) and a *non-identification* of God and Jesus (as in pluralism) are avoided.[91]

The mutual engagement between the Son and the Spirit shifts to the background as D'Costa moves to an exclusivist position. In this phase, the relation between the two persons is still maintained, although no longer in a symmetrical manner. The particularity of Christ is now related more closely to the universality of the Logos and, therefore, the universality of the Spirit

---

89. For an analysis of Panikkar's appropriation method, see Cenkner, "Interreligious Exploration."

90. D'Costa, "Trinitarian Theology," 19; cf. D'Costa, "Christ," 150.

91. D'Costa, "Christ," 18.

is now subordinated to the universality of the Logos.[92] This does not mean, however, that the role of the third person of the Trinity is less important. On the contrary, the main purpose of D'Costa's latest position is to demonstrate that the Spirit actively and significantly works in other religions. Yet, the freedom of the universal activity of the Spirit is framed within the particular-universal normativity of the Son, even within the particularity of the church. It is only within such a Christological and ecclesiological framework that we can see the Spirit working in the salvific economy. Thus, in the other words, the universality of the Spirit, who works actively in other religions, is anchored to Christ and the Catholic Church.

Similar to Panikkar, Heim emphasizes the relational nature of the term "person." Unlike Panikkar, who argues that person is only applicable to the Son, Heim is in line with the Christian traditional language that the Father, the Son, and the Holy Spirit are three persons of the Trinity. Comparing Panikkar's approach with that of Konstantine and Smart, Heim observes that Panikkar offers a more pluralistic outlook, although the latter model provides a "more fruitful direction."[93] Heim finds that he is in agreement with Konstantine and Smart, insofar as "they outline dimensions of the life of God that stem from the triune nature but which are not identified exclusively with individual persons. God has these dimensions by virtue of being triune, by virtue of the communion among the persons."[94] What is problematic about Konstantine and Smart, however, is that they "see that various religions may tune themselves to different aspects of the Trinity, but they hold that religions all lead to a single end."[95] Heim seeks to solve the limitation in the Konstantine and Smart model by radicalizing their insight to the point where different dimensions of the Trinity correspond to different—yet real—religious ends.

Heim agrees in particular with their idea of the social character of the Trinity as well as with the doctrine of "social Trinity" generally taught in the Eastern Orthodox tradition. To support his own social notion of the Trinity, Heim borrows from John D. Zizioulas's exploration of personhood

---

92. D'Costa also accepts the idea suggested by John Paul II that relates the universality of the Spirit to the particularity of the church. The church, however, should be seen as the "body of Christ." Thus, the church is the proper locus for the meeting of the universality of the Spirit and the particularity of Christ.
93. Heim, *Depth of the Riches*, 164.
94. Ibid.
95. Ibid., 165.

An Imaginative Glimpse

in the Orthodox tradition.[96] It is worth quoting at length Heim's statement summarizing the whole idea:

> [I]n the Christian understanding person becomes the most basic category of the triune God, whose divinity is constituted by the relation of the persons.... "Person" is the most basic category of divinity, and not one person or three in isolation, but person as constituted by relation with others. The nature of God's being is the communion of persons. God's nature is to be a person constituted by the communion of persons. This is a social view of the Trinity, which does not so much stress threeness as it does the one communion among the three.[97]

In short, being is defined as person-in-communion. This idea takes the primacy of person and communion over being and nature, without diminishing the latter. In this sense, difference among persons is affirmed through their communion. Thus, God's being is not only person-in-communion but also communion-in-difference.

Of importance here are the implications for divine-human relations. Heim believes that the Orthodox idea of person-in-communion, as explained by Zizioulas, can become a solid basis for acknowledging the possibility of creation's full participation in the divine communion, even though the world has a separate existence, different from God's.[98] The enlargement of the scope of communion to include creation is not a zero-sum game. "In sharing such a nature with creatures, God does not have less of it."[99] Heim, furthermore, intensifies this idea of the "social analogy" of the Trinity by demonstrating three different dimensions of the divine-human relationship: impersonal, iconic, and communal. These three dimensions correspond to different religious ends or fulfillments.

Two important notes regarding Heim's treatment of Christ and the Spirit are necessary. First, Heim's treatment of Christ or the Son seems to be ambiguous, yet he approaches the same kind of universalistic mode provided by Panikkar. In Panikkar's scheme, Christ is the symbol of cosmotheandrism, "a living symbol for the totality of reality: human, divine,

---

96. Zizioulas, *Being as Communion*.

97. Heim, *Depth of the Riches*, 171.

98. Flett criticizes Heim as having developed and reimagined notion of *analogia entis*; see Flett, "In the Name," 8–9. I doubt, however, that this accusation is accurate. The analogical language that Heim employs, in my opinion, is much closer to Barth's *analogia relationis* than to *analogia entis*; see Barth, *Church Dogmatics*, Vol. III.2, 323–24.

99. Heim, *Depth of the Riches*, 176.

cosmic."¹⁰⁰ Thus, the universal value of Christ comes to the fore, although at the expense of severing the relation between the cosmic Christ and the historical Jesus. In Heim, a similar way of thinking is apparent. Heim argues that the three dimensions of the triune life, corresponding to multiple religious ends, "are each embodied [and] reflected in Christ. . . . Christ not only reconciles us with God, but reconciles our varied ways of relating to God."¹⁰¹ Unlike Panikkar, however, Heim painstakingly seeks to bridge the gap between the second person of the Trinity and the historical Jesus. He finds in the resurrection story the universal meaning of Jesus for all creation and all human relations. He says, "The resurrection of Christ then creates a situation unique in human experience: it universalizes a normal human relation. . . . In the resurrection, the mundane type of human relation in which Jesus participated is universalized."¹⁰²

Nevertheless, in my view, Heim goes too far in his attempt at universalizing the meaning of the resurrected Jesus. Not only is Jesus Christ the unique path toward the Christian end, he is also the reconciler of multiple religious paths and, consequently, multiple religious ends. This overstatement, I believe, results from his understanding of the role of Christ in overcoming *sin*. He argues strongly, "People can attain these fulfillments without faith in Christ. *But sin stands between humans and these ends*, as it does between humans and salvation. The work of Christ plays its role in clearing the path to these ends as well as to salvation."¹⁰³ Heim is aware of the traditional inclusivist idea of Christ working anonymously in other religious people or even other religions. Clearly, he rejects this view as having diminished the particularity of different religions. Nonetheless, Heim cannot escape from the universal meaning of Christ, either. His solution, therefore, is to offer a more restricted claim: "The work of Christ is always involved in the overcoming of sin necessary for the achievement of any of the discrete religious ends. The work of Christ is necessary for such ends, but explicit relation with Christ is not constitutive of them."¹⁰⁴

The problem is, of course, whether Heim does justice to other religions by implanting the particularly Christian view of sin in other religious beliefs, which might not include the idea of sin. Heim recognizes this problem.¹⁰⁵

100. Panikkar, *Unknown Christ*, 27.
101. Heim, *Depth of the Riches*, 200.
102. Ibid., 57.
103. Ibid., italics mine.
104. Ibid., 286.
105. Ibid., 289.

An Imaginative Glimpse

But, he argues, if sin *truly* hinders the realization of multiple relations with God, then the redemptive work of Christ is *necessary*. He writes, "The limitation and loss of other religious ends arise because dimensions of sin that are unacknowledged cannot be redeemed, and thus prevent the realization of relation with God through those same dimensions which fill up the integral pattern of salvation.... Sin and redemption are known together. Where one sees no possibility of estrangement or corruption, there can be no reconciled and restored relation."[106]

In conclusion, by employing the sin-redemption narrative uniquely taught in the Christian tradition and applying it to multiple religious relations with the Triune God, Heim's idea of the universal Christ is still shadowed by the same logic as in the classical inclusivism. The redemptive act by Christ works anonymously as *the* answer to "anonymous" sin. If my conclusion is correct, his statement that the "explicit relation with Christ is not constitutive" for other religious ends seems to be trivial, if not untrue.

Panikkar, with his Reality-based model, is free from the burden that Heim must bear, although both of them come to a similar conclusion regarding the universality of Christ. For Panikkar, Christ is the universal symbol of the cosmotheandric reality, not because the other two "persons" are less universal. On the contrary, the universalizing attempt of Christ is necessary because the transcendence of the Father (coming from the Buddhist idea of "silence") and the immanence of the Spirit (coming from the Advaitic "unity") already touch the whole of reality, so to speak. It is the person of the Son that possibly has less universal bearing. Of course, the cost that he has to pay is to diminish the exclusive identification between the Son and the historical Jesus.[107] In Heim, on the contrary, the identification between the Son and the historical Jesus is unavoidable precisely because of the sin-redemption framework that he employs. In my opinion, Heim can escape from repeating the failure of the classical inclusivism by freeing his notion of sin as taught in the Christian faith and adopting a vaguer definition of the human condition.[108]

A second note concerns Heim's treatment of the Spirit. Interestingly, while the Spirit is of course constitutive of the triune communion for Heim,

---

106. Ibid., 288–89.

107. Panikkar writes, "When I call this link between the finite and the infinite by the name of Christ, I am not presupposing its identification with Jesus of Nazareth." Panikkar, *Religious Experience*, 53.

108. See for instance the second of three books of The Comparative Religious Ideas Project, edited by Neville, *Human Condition*.

his Trinitarian theology of religions does not give enough attention to the third person of the Trinity. Thus, he puts much more weight on the Son than that on the Spirit. Heim seems to acknowledge this fact by saying that, even though Jesus Christ cannot be an exhaustive and exclusive source for knowledge of God and God's action, the Trinity is always Christocentric. This is so for two reasons. First, viewed from below, the doctrine of God's triune nature is historically developed on the basis of Jesus Christ. Second, viewed from above, we must say that God's hidden mystery manifests in its particularity through Jesus Christ.

Heim is absolutely correct in demonstrating the two-way relation between the mystery of God and the particularity of the divine presence in Jesus Christ. However, this relation would be limited and static without the universalizing dimension of the divine presence in the Spirit.[109] Thus, to Christocentric notions of the Trinity we must add Pneumatocentric conceptions.[110] The role of the Spirit, which Heim does not develop in detail, is predominant in D'Costa's model.

Which Perichoresis?

Perichoresis in Panikkar's works is ubiquitous and is the most important characteristic of his whole theology of religions. If cosmotheandrism is Panikkar's overarching concept, perichoresis is its very heart. He borrows the term from the Christian tradition, which usually applies to the inner life of the triune God. In his extremely broad interpretation, perichoresis includes, even focuses on, the interpenetration of all cosmotheandric reality. Since all reality is characteristically cosmotheandric, perichoresis can be found everywhere.

It is true that Panikkar uses the term primarily to refer to cosmotheandric reality. "I am transient, or rather, I share in the *perichorêsis*, in the dance of the entire universe, in the constant rhythm of all, in the trinitarian

---

109. As a matter of fact, Heim is fully aware of the role of the Spirit when he maintains, "The fullness of God's mystery is never grasped by us. It is hidden in the divine source (Father), overflows in Christ beyond the measure of our means to receive it, and is *continually active in all of creation through the Spirit*." Heim, *Depth of the Riches*, 134, italics mine. Nonetheless, he does not elaborate on this statement.

110. A pneumatocentric theology of religions has been advanced by Amos Yong. He, for instance, argues that this approach suggests the Spirit as "the key to overcoming the dualism between Christological particularity and the cosmic Christ." Yong, *Beyond the Impasse*, 47. For a brief introduction to Yong's model, see Kärkkäinen's *An Introduction to the Theology of Religions*, 277–81.

An Imaginative Glimpse

or cosmotheandric display of reality."[111] But, he acknowledges that the fundamental meaning of perichoresis is transposed from intra-Trinitarian (the Triune God) to extra-Trinitarian realm (reality other than God), and finally to all reality (cosmotheandric: God, world, humans). He maintains that perichoresis, "is not reduced to the intra-Trinitarian realm, but *extended to all creation*. Is there anything 'outside' the Trinity?"[112] Such an extension of perichoresis makes it possible for Panikkar to see the imprint of the Trinity everywhere. For instance, he allows for the application of perichoresis to interreligious relationships, saying that "every religion can be a dimension of the other in a kind of trinitarian *perichoresis* or *circumincessio*."[113]

There are two important issues in Panikkar's idea of perichoresis that must be addressed here. First, despite the genius of Panikkar in using the perichoretic idea to demonstrate the "radical relativity" not only of the triune inner life but also of all reality, we can ask whether there is a radical distinction between the perichoretic relation among the three divine persons (called *person-perichoresis*) and the perichoretic relation in the cosmotheandric reality (called *reality-perichoresis*). Panikkar seems to see no significant distinction.

A problem then arises. On the one hand, Panikkar acknowledges that reality-perichoresis is an extension of person-perichoresis. Thus, God becomes the source of cosmotheandric reality or—in Panikkar's use of a mandala metaphor— the "seed" or the "center" of both the world ("circle") and humanity ("circumference").[114] More precisely, Panikkar argues that the creation (world and humanity) come to be through and in the Son. In this sense, the Son is the origin of all reality other than the triune God. Creation cannot participate in the divine perichoretic relation other than through the Son. Otherwise, we would have to treat the creation as a fourth "member" of the Trinity.

On the other hand, Panikkar argues that God is a constitutive part of reality-perichoresis, as he frequently maintains, "There is no God without Man and the World. There is no Man without God and the World. There is no World without God and Man."[115] My problem with this idea is that God

---

111. Panikkar, "Mysticism," 167.

112. Ibid., 151, italics mine.

113. Panikkar, *Dwelling Place*, 151. Panikkar also argues that synonyms of perichoresis can be found in other religions, such as *pratītyasamutpāda* in Buddhism, or *sarvam sarvātmakam* in Shaiva spirituality. See Panikkar, *Dwelling Place*, 97.

114. Panikkar, *Cosmotheandric Experience*, 76.

115. quoted in Raj, *New Hermeneutic*, 86; cf. Panikkar, *Dwelling Place*, 72.

seems to be dependent on the other two, in order for Reality-perichoresis to be truly authentic. To be sure, Panikkar's position here must be seen in the context of his loose borrowing of the Buddhist notion of *pratītyasamutpāda* or co-dependent origination. In Panikkar, the causal dimension of this concept is replaced by the emphasis on "radical relativity of all things and their interdependence."[116]

In short, while in person-perichoresis the entire creation is dependent on the Son in its participation in the triune perichoresis, in reality-perichoresis God, cosmos, and humanity are interdependent. If my analysis is correct, we find here an inconsistency in Panikkar's notion of perichoresis. How could God be part of reality-perichoresis, while all reality other than God participates in the intra-Trinitarian life or person-perichoresis? This confusion, however, could be cleared up if the two perichoretic relations have an overlapping "member," and if one of the two is greater than the other. My proposal is that person-perichoresis is greater than reality-perichoresis, with the latter being part of the former. It requires that the divine in cosmotheandric reality-perichoresis is also a constitutive member of the person-perichoresis. In the Christian tradition, as it is in Panikkar's theology, this overlapping "member" is the Son.

Thus, *theos* in cosmotheandrism must be the Son, in and through whom all creation comes to be. God in cosmotheandrism cannot be *totum Dei* (the whole of God), since it implies that the whole reality is greater than God. But, God in cosmotheandrism is the Son as *totus Deus* (wholly God). Consequently, since all reality is created in and through the Son, creation can participate in person-perichoresis. This clarification is hopefully consistent with Panikkar's original intention.

With Panikkar, therefore, we can say that Christ is the "link between the finite and the infinite."[117] He also maintains the same basic idea in a different way; that is, that Christ is the symbol of the whole of reality. "When we say that 'Christ is the symbol of the whole of reality,' we intend to say that not only are 'all the treasure of divinity' included in Christ, but that 'all the

---

116. Panikkar, *Intrareligious*, 124. Komulainen also sees this issue. He writes that in Panikkar's idea of *pratītyasamutpāda*, "Different aspects of reality are interwoven and thereby in mutual interplay. It is not a question of causal relations, but one of the simultaneity of all components and phenomena.... Panikkar gives us to understand that the relational character of his ontology is more fundamental than that of Buddhism: for him, relations are not only constitutive of the whole, but the relational nature of reality 'flashes forth, ever new and vital, in every spark of the real.'" Komulainen, *Emerging*, 185; cf. Panikkar, *Cosmotheandric Experience*, 60.

117. Panikkar, *Religious Experience*, 53.

mysteries of man' as well as the thickness of the universe are also hidden in him. He is not only the 'first-born' but the 'only begotten,' the symbol of reality itself, the cosmotheandric symbol par excellence."[118]

Secondly, a suggestion can be made with regard to the term cosmotheandrism itself. If reality-perichoresis is the result of person-perichoresis being extended, then the term cosmotheandrism does not correspond perfectly with the Trinity. Peter C. Hodgson rightly draws attention to this issue. He makes an excellent suggestion by saying, "The correlation would be more successful if, instead of a theanthropocosmic vision, we thought in terms of a "theo-cosmic-pneumatic" vision, with *anthropos* (humanity) understood to belong to *cosmos*, and the whole of *cosmos* being understood as that moment of difference in which *theos* (God) mirrors and knows Godself; the third trinitarian moment would be that of spiritual mediation in which the freedom, mystery, and wholeness of God are consummated."[119]

This revision is beneficial in that the term theo-cosmic-pneumatic expresses the structure of the Trinity more clearly. It is consistent with Panikkar's understanding that perichoresis is extended from three person of the Trinity to all reality or creation, with the second person acting as the principle of extension from the divine to creation as well as the principle of participation of the whole creation in person-perichoresis.

D'Costa approaches the notion of perichoresis differently; that is, from the perspective of "ecclesiological trinity."[120] Commenting on the text about the *Paraclete* in the Gospel of John, he maintains that "the Spirit's perichoretic indwelling of the disciples is predicated upon the indwelling of the Son and the Father . . . such that the Spirit's indwelling the disciples will be enacted in their keeping the commandment of love—learning to love as Jesus had loved."[121]

Thus, the role of the Spirit is significant in enabling human participation (in this context, the disciples' participation) in intra-Trinitarian love. In making this case, D'Costa he builds a basis for the necessity of the Catholic Church for the theology of religions.

Nevertheless, he makes a substantial move by expanding the scope of this perichoretic relation, not only for the church but also for other religions. "[P]erichoretic relations do not stop at the boundaries of the church."[122]

118. Panikkar, *Christophany*, 147.
119. Hodgson, *Winds of the Spirit*, 110.
120. D'Costa, *Meeting of Religions*, 121.
121. Ibid.
122. Ibid., 143.

Thus, D'Costa is ready to move from his ecclesial-perichoresis to reality-perichoresis, even though he does not elaborate on the latter. D'Costa sees the act of interreligious prayer as an obvious example of how non-Christian religions can participate in the perichoretic relation. It is in interreligious prayer that all religions "come together in love."[123] Yet, his argument that such participation is imperfect and fragmented is consistent with his overall position about the possible presence of "the inchoate reality of the Kingdom" in other religions.[124] The fact that we may only glimpse the "inchoate" presence of the Spirit in the interreligious prayer tells us that we are all still waiting for eschatological fullness.

The idea of perichoresis is also important in Heim's model, although it does not receive as much attention as it does in Panikkar's. Heim differs from Panikkar in that he is more restrictive in employing the notion of perichoresis. He does not use the term to describe relations of anything other than one of the triune persons. For Heim, perichoresis or mutual communion of the three divine persons becomes the basis for Christian salvation. However, it also opens the possibility for Christians to engage with other dimensions of the Trinity and "to include them *as* other."[125] In such a way, difference is celebrated and each of the dimensions is viewed as co-equal with the others.

The problem with Heim's perichoresis, however, lies in the way he defines and uses the term. In the Christian tradition, perichoresis can be rightly translated as "mutual communion" or "mutual indwelling" or "coinherence" of persons. On the one hand, Heim limits perichoresis only to the third dimension of the Trinity corresponding uniquely to communion as the Christian end. On the other hand, interestingly enough, Heim also sees the importance of the concept of perichoresis for other dimensions of the Trinity. For instance, Heim discusses in a more detailed fashion a second variant of the first impersonal dimension of the Trinity; that is, immanence. He argues that the divine unitive immanence reflects "the impersonal mutual indwelling of the three triune persons" or "the coinherence or complete immanence of each of the divine persons in the others."[126] This proposal is brilliant, since traditionally perichoresis refers to the real coinherence among the three divine persons. Here, he suggests that there is also an impersonal

---

123. Ibid., 154.

124. In addition, he reminds his readers that the possible presence of the Spirit in interreligious prayer should also mean that "Christ, the kingdom, and the Father are also present, even if 'inchoately.'" D'Costa, *Meeting of Religions*, 164.

125. Heim, *Depth of the Riches*, 213.

126. Ibid., 210.

dimension of such a perichoretic relation. Heim supports his proposal by expanding the idea of divine self-contraction (making space for creation) to the inner life of the Trinity. He writes, "Each of the divine persons 'makes space' for the others (as God makes space for creation). But each person also lives by coinherence with the others."[127]

The point that I want to make here is that perichoresis, in Heim's model, is not one among other dimensions (communion as salvation). It can also be found in other dimensions, as reflected in Hinduism's immanence. It is true, nevertheless, that Heim does not try to elaborate the possibility of seeing perichoresis in *all* dimensions. My project seeks to expand what Heim has left unclear and undeveloped, that is, by employing perichoresis as the central category. In short, unlike Heim who argues for different dimensions of the Trinity (impersonal, iconic, and communion), in which perichoresis belongs to the third dimension (with an underlying presence in the first dimension), my proposal is based on different dimensions, with perichoresis as the central category.

The Need for a Modest Approach

We have seen three different models of theology of religions, each of which construes a different way of understanding the Triune "persons" and the notion of perichoresis. We have seen Panikkar's appropriation method that gives full recognition to religions other than Christianity, especially Buddhism and Hinduism, by identifying them as the religion of the Father and the religion of the Spirit, respectively. In order for this model to be truly respectful of the non-personal characteristics of Buddhism and Hinduism, unfortunately, it has to avoid using the term "person" for the Father and the Son. In so doing, Panikkar has to face a problem of reconciling his Trinitarian model with the Christian traditional understanding of the three persons of the Trinity. The genius of Heim's model is in its attempt to employ the same appropriation method as Panikkar's, but by using a different category. While Panikkar uses the "persons" of the Trinity, Heim uses the "dimensions of relation" of the Trinity. Nevertheless, while this alternative solves Panikkar's problem, it poses its own problem. As Flett correctly argues, "The Father, Son and Spirit *as* Father, Son and Spirit have no bearing in Heim's proposal—they make no systematic difference."[128] In short, the question is

127. Heim, *Depth of the Riches*, 191.

128. Flett, "In the Name," 10. Flett's critique is worth quoting at length: "The phrases 'persons-in-communion' and 'communion-in-difference' result in a neutered

not only "Why should there be three," but also, "Why should there be Father, Son, and Spirit?" I find Flett's critique compelling, especially when we see that Heim's treatments of Jesus Christ and the Spirit are quite imbalanced.

D'Costa differs from both Panikkar and Heim. Instead of systematizing or conceptualizing other religions within the Trinitarian framework through the appropriation method, he seeks to construct rules of engagement with the religious others. D'Costa's refusal to conceptualize non-Christian religions within the Trinitarian framework is consistent with his idea that, however positive the affirmation that one makes in including other traditions within one's framework, "[it] is not that tradition as it understands itself, but what the alien theologian chooses to prioritize and select."[129]

D'Costa's approach, on the one hand, is commendable. Heim has been criticized, by D'Costa and others, as having done injustice to other religious traditions by including them as part of his (Christian) Trinitarian framework. According to this critique, in so doing he is not truly respectful of the otherness of non-Christian religions. In Panikkar's case, a similar case can possibly be made, but only in that he includes all religions within his cosmotheandric scheme. On the other hand, D'Costa's model, due to his reluctance to systematize a model that explicitly includes other religions, cannot contribute optimally to construct a reality-based theology of religions like the one proposed by Panikkar (and to a lesser extent that proposed by Heim). Despite his emphasis on the universal dimensions of the Son, the Spirit, and even the Catholic Church, D'Costa's model provides no ontological clue that different religious traditions may be positive parts of reality as a whole.

To bridge the above differences, I offer a modest proposal, which seeks to transcend the limitations shown in Panikkar's, Heim's, and D'Costa's models while embracing their valuable insights. This attempt, thus, is both a work of *bricolage* and of systematic construction. On the one hand, I side with the conviction that the Trinity functions as a grammar of Christian faith, which enables us to engage with the problem of the relationship between the triune God and the whole of creation. This principle is also consistent with my entire argument that a perspectival yet universal framework can be constructed without falling into either relativism or absolutism. Such

---

abstraction, meaning little more than an adjectival 'relational collectivity'. The particular acts and relationships of the three trinitarian persons determine neither the nature of communion, nor God's 'dimensions'. . . . His position . . . is both formally and materially non-trinitarian no matter the linguistic inference." Flett, "In the Name," 10.

129. D'Costa, *Meeting of Religions*, 23.

An Imaginative Glimpse

a universal and orientational view, centered on the Christian doctrine of the Trinity, can still be open to the differences and otherness of non-Christian religions, at least on the theoretical level.

My modest approach focuses on certain possibilities, such as participation and freedom, contingency and interdependency, recognition and embrace, and unity and diversity.[130] If those dialectic features characterize the relation between the divine and creation, they must also be reflected in the theology of religions that I wish to construct in this project. In this sense, Panikkar's and Heim's models (especially the former) are admirable.

On the other hand, D'Costa's reluctance to provide a cartographic model, in which all religions have their own places in the Trinitarian framework, must be considered as a valuable contribution to my model. It warns us about the dangers of an overly Christian conceptualization of other religions into our own framework.

I believe my proposal is modest in the sense that it is less restrictive in its attempt to include other religious traditions within a Christian Trinitarian framework. Such an attempt should be guided by what I call "an imaginative glimpse." This attitude allows construing other religions in the Trinitarian framework without a total confidence in its certainty. There are at least two reasons supporting this position. First, along with D'Costa I argue that we cannot include the totality of other religions into our grand conceptual structure.[131] Any Christian theology of religions should pay respect to the otherness of non-Christian religions. Nevertheless, unlike D'Costa, I argue that we still can make a universal claim that embraces other religions insofar as we admit that their places in our imaginative reality are far from certainty and absoluteness. Such an act of embracing also requires mutuality, in the sense that we need to be open to respecting universal claims made by other parties. The maximum that we can affirm is that we are glimpsing within our Trinitarian reality the presence of other religions as the others. They are touchable, yet uncontainable. The others always transcend our ability to

---

130. In chapter 5, I will develop the idea of "embrace" as an alternative to exclusion and inclusion acts.

131. James Fredericks makes a very good argument for comparative theology as a more plausible alternative to theology of religions. He maintains, "Unlike theologies of religions, comparative theology does not start with a grand theory of religion in general that claims to account for all religions. . . . Instead of theories about religion in general, comparative theologians are interested in studying other religions on their own terms and then exploring their own Christian faith using what they have learned about the other religions." Fredericks, *Faith among Faiths*, 167–68. Panikkar's case, however, is unique, since he claims himself as a Christian and Hindu at the same time. Thus, his theology of religions is at the same time parallel with his comparative theology.

conclude our final words about them. The end has not come yet. An imaginative glimpse, therefore, is a theological and interreligious approach with an eschatological outlook.

A second point, related to the first above, is that my approach employs the notion of perichoresis as its central category. My argument is that this notion offers a possibility to synthesize certain important aspects of Panikkar's, Heim's, and D'Costa's models, which otherwise would be difficult to reconcile. We have already seen that each of the three theologians discusses perichoresis, although in different ways. Interestingly, all agree that perichoresis does not only refer to intra-Trinitarian communion but also opens the possibility of creation's participation. In the following chapters, my attention will be devoted to constructing my own model based on this possibility.

4

Perichoretic Indwelling of and in the Triune God

Three Forms of Perichoresis in the Church Fathers

JÜRGEN MOLTMANN CALLS PERICHORESIS AN ANCIENT CONCEPT THAT focuses on "community without uniformity, and personality without individualism."[1] Moltmann's statement correctly points out the central value of perichoresis in maintaining the principle of person-in-communion, in which the unity and difference in the Trinity are maintained. Although the concept may have been used to explain ideas in the Scriptures and in the first three centuries of the early patristic works, it is through the writings of Gregory Nazianzus that it is used theologically for the first time. Thus, my analysis begins with him and continues with three other significant fathers: Maximus the Confessor, Pseudo-Cyril of Alexandria, and John of Damascus. It is interesting to note that the doctrine of perichoresis in the Greek church fathers developed from nature-perichoresis (two natures of Christ) to person-perichoresis (three persons of the Trinity) and finally to reality perichoresis (cosmic participation in the Triune life). This development, obviously, follows the general observation that the doctrine of Trinity is an unavoidable consequence of the doctrine of Christology and its soteriological implications, in which the participation of creation in the Triune life is mediated through the Son. The structure of this section follows such a development.

---

1. Moltmann, "Perichoresis," 113.

Nature-Perichoresis

Gregory Nazianzus (c. 330–390) is the first church father who employs the idea of perichoresis in its verb form (*perichōréō*). The term originated in Stoic philosophy, where it can mean both interpenetration and rotation.[2] In his famous *Epistle* 101, Gregory applies the idea to the natures of Christ. He writes, "As the natures, so also the appellations are mixed (κριναμένων) and they penetrate (περιχωρουσων) into one another (εἰς ἀλλήλας) by reason of their coalescence."[3] Here, perichoresis refers specifically to the mutual transfer or interpenetration of Christ's divine and human attributes (*communicatio idiomatum*, the technical term from the latter period) that follows from the union of Christ's two natures. Regarding the two natures of Christ, Wolfson argues that Gregory Nazianzus discusses the mutual penetration of natures in other places but without employing perichoretic language or providing a clear explanation as to how it happens.[4]

Maximus the Confessor (580–662) follows closely Gregory's idea and develops it further. He is the first theologian who introduced the noun *perichoresis* into Christological discourse. In one of his statements concerning perichoresis, he writes, "The [human] nature, by being inconfusedly united with the [divine nature], has penetrated through the whole (δι ὅλον περιχώρηκε) [of the divine nature]."[5] Michael G. Lawler offers an interestingly different translation: "The human nature totally makes room for (*perikechoreke* [sic]) the divine nature, to which it is united without any confusion."[6] Both translations clearly emphasize the fact that interpenetration does not confuse the two natures; however, they differ in translating *perichoreke*. While both translations emphasize the dynamism and action of Christ's human nature, Lawler employs a more spatial picture of the perichoretic act. Nevertheless, what we have here is an obvious development in comparison with previous theologians, in that Christ's human nature plays a significant role in perichoresis. The human nature of Christ is not in a passive position. Thus Maximus is able to say "the whole power of his humanity, with all its openness to suffering, [is] quite unimpaired by the union."[7] The

---

2. Wolfson, *Church Fathers*.
3. *Epistle* 101.5., quoted in Wolfson, *Church Fathers*, 421.
4. Wolfson, *Church Fathers*, 422.
5. *Ambiguorum Liber* 112b, quoted in Wolfson, *Church Fathers*, 424.
6. Lawler, "Perichoresis," 50.
7. *Ambiguorum Liber* 5, quoted in Vishnevskaya, "Divinization," 133.

dynamic role of human nature, however, does not diminish the primary role of the divine nature.

Pseudo-Cyril of Alexandria, following Gregory Nazianzus, employs the idea of perichoresis as the proper way to explain the interchange of Christ's properties or attributes, but as opposed to the other theologians he bases it on "the identity of hypostasis."[8] In section 24 of *De Sacrosancta Trinitate*, Pseudo-Cyril uses the concept not only to explain the interchange of Christ's properties but also of Christ's divine and human natures. In the interchange, the two natures do not change into one composite nature, but rather they are united hypostatically and "receive an inconfused and unchangeable penetration into one another."[9] Unlike Gregory, who does not describe how the hypostatic union happens, Pseudo-Cyril explains it very clearly, "This penetration [*perichoresis*] springs not from the flesh but from the divinity, since it is impossible for the flesh to penetrate through (διά) the divinity; still the divine nature, having once penetrated through (διά) the flesh, bestows on the flesh an ineffable penetration with (πρός) itself, which in particular we call union."[10]

Thus, the double-penetration of the divine and human natures of Christ occurs not mutually but in a causal relation. The process begins with the divine that penetrates *through* the flesh; then follows the penetration of the already penetrated flesh *with* the divine. Wolfson interprets the first step of process ("the penetration of the divine nature into the human nature") as the deification of the human, while the second step of the process ("the penetration of the already deified human nature into the divine nature") as the humanation or incarnation.[11] Pseudo-Cyril adds nothing new to the Christological use of perichoresis. His significant contribution lies more in developing the concept in Trinitarian discourse, which is discussed further below.

The Christological use of perichoresis in John of Damascus (c. 676–749) introduces another new development with regard to the relation between nature-perichoresis and person-perichoresis.[12] Theologians before

8. See Wolfson's translation of Pseudo-Cyril's *De Sacrosancta Trinitate* 27 in *Church Fathers*, 422.

9. Quoted in Wolfson, *Church Fathers*, 423.

10. *De Sacrosancta Trinitate* 24, quoted in Wolfson, *Church Fathers*, 423.

11. Wolfson, *Church Fathers*, 424.

12. Angus Steward argues that John of Damascus is an important figure for several reasons: First, as the last of the Greek fathers, John is a great summarizer of the Greek theologies; second, his *Exposition* is one of the earliest systematic theologies; third, his works influences both the Eastern and Western churches; fourth, John's writings becomes

him had always applied the concept of perichoresis to Christ first and only later to the Trinity. According to Verna Harrison, in John the order is reversed. Consequently, "because of the eternity of God he emphasizes the static aspect of perichoresis as a state of coinherence rather than a movement of interpenetration. The use of the preposition ἐν both for the Trinity and for Christ highlights this point."[13] In short, the reversal that John does has undermined the dynamic nature of nature-perichoresis.

Apart from this issue, elsewhere John of Damascus also talks about the two natures interpenetrating into (εἰς) each other. His concern is to maintain the balance between the *mutual* and *asymmetrical* process of perichoresis between Christ's two natures, as reflected in this statement, "Although we say that the natures of the Lord coinhere in each other (περιχωρεῖν ἐν ἀλλήλαις), we know that this coinherence (περιχώρησις) arises out of the divine nature. For this last pervades all things and penetrates (περιχωρεῖ) as it wishes, but nothing pervades or penetrates through it."[14]

To conclude, we have seen an interesting development of the idea of perichoresis applied to Christology. It shifts from the interchange between Christ's divine and human properties (*communicatio idiomatum*) to the interpenetration of the two natures. In the developments of Pseudo-Cyril and John of Damascus, the tension between asymmetrical process and mutual penetration appears. It has become canonical to say that the interpenetration of the two natures (*mutuality*) is only acceptable insofar we talk about human nature as already deified or penetrated by divine nature (*asymmetry*). The church fathers also stress that the hypostatic union between the two natures is the fundamental basis for nature-perichoresis, in which the two are unconfused with one another. The last words from Wolfson regarding perichoresis might be useful to summarize the general meaning of perichoresis, "The result of our discussion is that the term *perichoresis*, with either εἰς or ἐν or διά or πρός, is used by the Fathers in the sense of a 'thorough penetration,' as a physical analogy for the purpose of explaining the *communicatio idiomatum*, just as other physical analogies were used by them for the purpose of explaining the trinity of persons in the Godhead and the unity of person in Jesus."[15]

---

the earliest response to Islam. See Stewart, "John of Damascus."

13. Harrison, "Perichoresis," 61–62.
14. *De Fide Orthodoxa* III.7, quoted in Harrison, "Perichoresis," 62.
15. Wolfson, *Church Fathers*, 428.

An Imaginative Glimpse

Person-Perichoresis

Pseudo-Cyril is the first theologian who applies the idea of perichoresis to the Trinity. Once used as a vital tool in explaining the interpenetration of Christ's two natures, perichoresis in Pseudo-Cyril now refers to the mutual indwelling of the Triune persons. His main purpose is to counter the charge of tritheism directed to the Christian idea of the Trinity.[16] Through such a notion he can emphasize the equality of the three hypostases in essence as well as their differences in relation to their origin. The three hypostases, he argues, "possess coinherence in each other (τήν ἐν ἀλλήλαις περιχώρησιν ἔχουσαι), though without confusion or division."[17] This affirmation of the perichoretic unity-in-difference is followed by his quoting and revising of Gregory's text from *Oration* 31.14 that strongly emphasizes both the oneness and threeness of God.[18]

After Pseudo-Cyril, Prestige argues, "nothing of importance remained to be added to the Greek patristic definition of the Trinity."[19] Later, the text from Gregory embedded in Pseudo-Cyril's text is "doubly embedded" in John of Damascus's *De Fide Orthodoxa* 1.8.[20] John fully follows Pseudo-Cyril in emphasizing the unity of substance and the distinct personhood of the three. Moreover, he makes the Trinitarian perichoresis the starting point for his discussion of the Christological perichoresis. "As in the Holy Trinity the three hypostases, through natural identity and coinherence in each other (ἐν ἀλλήλαις περιχώρησιν), are and are called one God, so in our Lord Jesus Christ the two natures, through hypostatic identity and coinherence in each other (ἐν ἀλλήλαις περιχώρησιν), are one Son."[21]

John's Trinitarian starting point is also evident in the following statement: "Three persons are united in a holy trinity undividedly and without

---

16. Harrison, "Perichoresis," 59.

17. *De Sacrosancta Trinitate* 10, quoted in Harrison, "Perichoresis," 59.

18. Egan, "Trinitarian Perichoresis," writes an excellent paper arguing that Pseudo-Cyril's revision of Gregory's *Oration* 31.14, demonstrates both his satisfaction with some and dissatisfaction with other aspects of Gregory's statements. Also, he concludes that Pseudo-Cyril's use of Trinitarian perichoresis in his writings shows his attempt to reinforce the unity of God, which he finds not too strongly expressed in Gregory's *Oration* 31.14. The basic problems in Gregory's *Oration* 31.14, which are also revised by Pseudo-Cyril, are the monarchy of God the Father and its implication to the divine causality. For an extensive survey of the scholarly discussions of the issue, see Beeley, "Divine Causality."

19. Prestige, *Patristic Thought*, 299.

20. Harrison, "Perichoresis," 59–60.

21. *De Fide Contra Nestorianos* 36, quoted in Harrison, "Perichoresis," 61.

any confusion. They are undivided because of their unity of nature and they mutually make room for one another without any confusion (ἐν ἀλλήλαις ἀσύγχυτον περιχώρησιν). Similarly, through incarnation of the Word of God, two natures are united without confusion. They are without division both because of the unity of the person and because they make room for one another without confusion (ἐν λλήλαις τῶν φύσεων ἀσύγχυτον περιχώρησιν)."[22]

From these two statements, we can see that, in John's Christological treatment, the indivisibility of the two natures of Christ is anchored *both* in the unity of three hypostases of the Trinity and in perichoresis. Without the concept of perichoresis, it is difficult to maintain the Christian faith in God as simultaneously the one and the three and it is even more difficult to preserve the Christian faith in Christ's hypostatic union. John, moreover, summarizes his perichoretic idea in *De Fide Orthodoxa* 1.14:

> The subsistences dwell and are established firmly in one another. For they are inseparable and cannot part from one another, but keep to their separate courses within one another, without coalescing or mingling, but cleaving to each other. For the Son is in the Father and the Spirit: and the Spirit in the Father and the Son: and the Father in the Son and the Spirit, but there is no coalescence or commingling or confusion. And there is one and the same motion: for there is one impulse and one motion of the three subsistences, which is not to be observed in any created nature.[23]

As he makes clear, the three persons indwell in one another, in that each contains the two others and is contained by the two others as well. At the same time, the differences between the three persons are still firmly maintained. John also argues in the above statement that the perfect perichoretic relation and unity in God's inner life "is not to be observed in any created nature." The radically qualitative difference between God the creator and creation is therefore explicitly sustained.

Before concluding this section and moving to the analysis of reality-perichoresis some important issues need to be addressed. First, although the technical term perichoresis is absent, the idea of mutual inclusivity in the Trinity appears in the writings of other church fathers, from both the Latin and Greek traditions, such as Athanasius, Gregory of Nyssa, Hilary of Poitiers, Augustine, Basil of Caesarea, Didymus the Blind, and others.[24]

22. *De Natura Composita* 4, quoted in Lawler, "Perichoresis," 52
23. John of Damascus, "Exposition," 160.
24. See Torrance, *Christian Doctrine*, 168–73.

An Imaginative Glimpse

Gregory of Nyssa, for example, employs other terms such as *peripheresis* (from the Greek verb περιφέρω meaning "to whirl 'about' each other and inside each other") and *anacyclesis* (ἀνακύκλησις meaning "interchange" or "circular intermingling").[25] These two terms are used to express an idea similar to perichoresis.

Second, as regards the employment of perichoresis in the Latin fathers, the term perichoresis was adapted to be compatible with Latin theological understanding of personhood. There are two Latin translations of perichoresis: *circumincessio* and *circuminsessio*. The former, *circumincessio*, reflects the active dimension of perichoresis (from *circum-incedere*, to move around); the latter, *circuminsessio*, captures the passive dimension (from *circum-insedere*, to sit around).[26] Moltmann gives an interesting comment on the relation between the two translations, "With the Latin translations *circumincessio* and *circuminsessio* the double meaning of the trinitarian unity is expressed: movement and rest.... In the eternal life of the Trinity there are simultaneously absolute silence and total whirlwind, just like the 'eye' of a hurricane. More importantly, there is on the level of the trinitarian perichoresis no priority of the Father, but total equality of the divine persons."[27]

In conclusion, it is clear that the application of perichoresis to the Triune life is derived from its earlier usage with regard to Christ's two natures. The difference between nature-perichoresis and person-perichoresis is obvious. The former maintains the mutuality between two natures based on an asymmetrical relation, in which the divine nature penetrates the human nature first, whereas the latter preserves the radical mutuality and equality among the three persons as a nonnegotiable principle. Such a distinction is also evident in that the church fathers change the preposition, from perichoresis "to" or "into" (εἰς) one another to perichoresis "in" (ἐν) one another. Regarding this issue, Prestige provides a clear explanation: "Perichoresis 'to' one another might imply that the Persons were equivalent or alternative; perichoresis 'in' one another implies that they are coterminous and co-extensive."[28]

---

25. Stramara, "Gregory of Nyssa's," 261–62.

26. While the first translation, *circumincessio*, is employed by Bonaventure in *Commentaria in Quatuor Libros Sententiarum* I.1.4, the second translation, *circuminsessio*, is not used explicitly but reflected in Thomas Aquinas's *Summa Theologica* I.42.5, and the council of Florence in 1440.

27. Moltmann, "Perichoresis," 114.

28. Prestige, *Patristic Thought*, 298.

Of course, the issue of divine monarchy, in which the unity of God belongs to the Father, also occurs. However, the idea of perichoresis itself can be seen as a significant attempt to overcome the subordinationist element that may be attached to the idea of the monarchy of the first person. Even more, as LaCugna observes, perichoresis emerges as a substitute for the idea of monarchy in the Greek fathers.[29] On the other hand, LaCugna also points out that the perichoretic idea, by emphasizing "a true communion of persons," also avoids the pitfall of locating the divine unity in the divine substance, as the Latin fathers did.[30] Thus, perichoresis can truly provide a middle way or bridge between Latin and Greek Trinitarian theologies.

Reality-Perichoresis

I borrow the terms nature-perichoresis and person-perichoresis from Oliver Crisp.[31] He, however, does not discuss another type of perichoresis that I call reality-perichoresis, which refers to the perichoretic relation between the Triune Creator and creation. The notion of reality-perichoresis deals with the mutual indwelling of the divine and creation, mirroring what we find both in nature-perichoresis and person-perichoresis. Thus, in this sense, the idea of the perichoretic relation between the Creator and creation results from the ideas of the perichoretic relation of the Triune persons and the perichoretic relation between Christ's two natures.

The concept of reality-perichoresis plays a central role in my constructive model. Here, I will limit myself to discussing how this idea is introduced in the church fathers by Maximus of Confessor.[32] We have observed that Maximus' employment of perichoresis primarily focuses on its Christological dimension. He does not deal directly with the perichoretic relation of the Trinity. By focusing the idea of perichoresis on Christ's two natures, Maximus has an opportunity to deal with its soteriological implications. In this regard, one of his fascinating statements from *Quaestiones ad Thalassium* 59 is worth quoting in full.

> The soul's salvation is the consummation of faith. This consummation is the revelation of what has been believed. Revelation is the

---

29. LaCugna, *God for Us*, 270.
30. Ibid., 271.
31. Crisp, *Divinity and Humanity*.
32. My discussion of this subject is greatly indebted to Elena Vishnevskaya's article, "Divinization."

> inexpressible interpenetration (περιχώρησις) of the believer with (or toward, πρός) the object of belief and takes place according to each believer's degree of faith. Through that interpenetration the believer finally returns to his origin. The return is the fulfillment of desire. Fulfillment of desire is ever-active repose in the object of desire. Enjoyment of this kind entails participation in supranatural divine reality. This participation consists in the participant becoming like that in which he participates. Such likeness involves, so far as this is possible, an identity with respect to energy between the participant and that in which he participates by virtue of the likeness. This identity with respect to energy constitutes the deification of the saints.[33]

Maximus argues that divine revelation makes it possible for a believer to penetrate the divine so that the believer "finally returns to his origin." In the rest of the statement, Maximus explores the process and meaning of the human penetration into the divine. It happens through the "participation in supranatural divine reality" where the participant becomes like God (*theosis* or deification), not in *ousia* but in *energia*. Thus, in the context of reality-perichoresis, as Butler maintains, "perichoresis *is* participation."[34]

Therefore, human-divine perichoresis is possible, even though it must always begin with divine revelation. Maximus appears to understand that the revelation through which God penetrates the believer occurs through incarnation. Here, we find a common idea of the twofold incarnation-deification in Greek theology. I would argue, however, that similar to Maximus' understanding of nature-perichoresis, his reality-perichoresis also demonstrates an asymmetry in which the divine initiative (revelation or incarnation) is primary.

The asymmetrical characteristic of perichoresis, nevertheless, does not diminish its reciprocity. Maximus employs the idea of unity-in-difference, in which differences between God and creation are united without confusion.[35] Drawing from the unity-in-difference occurring in human life, Maximus argues for the possibility of "the interpenetration of the extreme into each

---

33. Quoted in Harrison, "Perichoresis," 57–58.
34. Butler, "Hypostatic Union," 166.
35. *Scholia in Librum* 4, quoted in Balthasar, *Cosmic Liturgy*, 235. Törönen argues that in Maximus perichoresis is almost identical with "union without confusion." He writes, "With the interpenetration, natures are utterly united but not altered *qua* natures. . . . Maximus is careful in pointing this out by making it clear that there is a *peri-chôrêsis* but not a *meta-chôrêsis*, that is, there is an interpenetration but not a change of one nature into the other." Törönen, *Union and Distinction*, 122.

Perichoretic Indwelling of and in the Triune God

other" so that wholly different elements can be brought into "a friendly cohabitation," as he explains in the following statement: "Again, what is [the meaning of] the intertwining of the opposites of our bodies according to the mixture by means of synthesis? [The intertwining] brings things opposite by nature into a friendly cohabitation and tames the harshness in extremes by moderation, and prepares them to advance through each other without injury, and taking care of the things synthesized in this way, [by causing] the interpenetration of the extremes into each other according to the mixture."[36]

Maximus, interestingly, seems to talk about humanity as the representative of the whole creation. In this context the role played by Christ, the God-human, is essential. He writes that "with us and through us [Christ] encompasses the whole creation."[37] Moreover, "God will penetrate (χωρήσαντος του θεού) everything in general and each in particular, filling up everything with a measure of His grace."[38]

In addition to the cosmic participation in God's life, Maximus also recognizes the differentiation within the created universe, which results from the theophanic manifestation in and through creation. Such differentiation exists through the *logoi* of beings, that is, God's will for each part of God's creation. Thus, as Törönen concludes, "Differentiation in the cosmos springs from God's very own purpose for the universe. It is his pre-eternal will that there is multiplicity and variety in the universe."[39]

The *logoi* themselves are united by and pre-existent in the Logos. Therefore, the interpenetration between God and creation is mediated through Christ, the Logos. If human penetration to and participation in the divine life is based on revelation, and revelation points to incarnation, then the role of Christ must be central. In this sense, I would argue that, for Maximus, Christ becomes the principle of both difference and unity.

I have demonstrated the presence of reality-perichoresis in Maximus of Confessor's writings. He insists that the perichoretic relation between God and creation occurs both asymmetrically and reciprocally. It is asymmetrical in the sense that the divine revelation through incarnation is prior to human participation; it is reciprocal in the sense that both God and creation interpenetrate to each other. Creation is also able to penetrate the divine reality through participation.

---

36. *Ambiguorum Liber* 17, quoted in Butler, "Hypostatic Union," 168
37. *Ambiguorum Liber* 41, quoted in Vishnevskaya, "Divinization," 140
38. *Opuscula Theologica et Polemica* 1, quoted in Vishnevskaya, "Divinization," 140.
39. Törönen, *Union and Distinction*, 129.

Interestingly, since the idea of person-perichoresis is not developed in Maximus, he does not discuss any direct relation between reality-perichoresis and person-perichoresis.[40] A close relation, however, between reality-perichoresis and nature-perichoresis is crystal clear. Both asymmetry and reciprocity are present in both types of perichoresis, precisely because reality-perichoresis flows from person-perichoresis. Balthasar's statement might be helpful in clarifying this point: "In Maximus' view . . . the liturgy is ultimately always 'cosmic liturgy': a way of drawing the entire world into the hypostatic union, because both world and liturgy share a Christological foundation. This is something new and original and must be regarded as Maximus' own achievement."[41]

We have discussed briefly the development of the idea of perichoresis in the church fathers' writings, especially those from the Greek tradition. Starting from its Christological usage, in which the two natures of Christ interpenetrate in each other (*nature-perichoresis*), the idea of perichoresis is later applied to the Trinity (*person-perichoresis*). The three persons of the Trinity mutually indwell in each other. While nature-perichoresis demonstrates a mutual yet asymmetrical reciprocity between divine nature and human nature, with the former being the primary cause, person-perichoresis emphasizes a perfectly mutual and symmetrical reciprocity among the Triune persons. In Maximus' writing we find a third type of perichoresis, namely that of *reality-perichoresis*, where humanity and the whole universe participate in God's life by virtue of Christ's mediation.

After the doctrine of perichoresis was fully developed, it became a valuable treasure for the Christian churches, both Greek and Latin, in expressing their faith in the Triune God and in Christ's salvific work. Interestingly, as Randall Otto maintains, while the Trinitarian use of perichoresis has increased, the use of perichoresis in the Christological discussion decreased.[42] Meanwhile, the application of the doctrine in discourse on the

---

40. Similarly, Charles C. Twombly's study of John of Damascus' usage of perichoresis in the doctrines of God, Christ, and salvation shows that the relation between person-perichoresis and reality-perichoresis is obscure in John Damascus. He concludes, "The case for using mutual indwelling in relation to John's understanding of salvation is less clear because perichoresis invariably refers to a constancy in the union of the realities so united which does not encompass the fluctuation of faith and obedience represented by human response to God. Here, the language of participation and communion, a language which allows for the possibility of flux, is more fitting and is indeed that which John uses in connection with salvation." Twombly, "Perichoresis," 183.

41. Balthasar, *Cosmic Liturgy*, 322.

42. Otto, "Use and Abuse," 384.

relationship between the Creator and the created is the least developed of all. My project focuses on the universe's perichoretic participation in the Triune life, and how this notion opens up the possibility of construing an "imaginative glimpse" of different religions having their unique places in such a perichoretic space. In the following section, however, it is imperative to first look at the use of perichoresis in modern theology with special attention to Jürgen Moltmann's open Trinity.

Jürgen Moltmann's Open Trinity

Karl Barth and Karl Rahner have always been credited as the theologians who "rediscovered" the doctrine of the Trinity in the twentieth century. Post-Barth and Rahner, the Trinity has come to the fore in many theological sub-disciplines. Along with this development, the notion of perichoresis, which was central in the Greek tradition, has also gained attention throughout a broad spectrum of theological discussion. This section will focus on Jürgen Moltmann, who employs the doctrine within the broader context of his "open Trinity."

In the 1980s Moltmann felt that his way of doing theology, in which he concentrated only on "a single point," namely theology of hope and theology of the cross, was no longer sufficient. Since then, he has embraced "a new Trinitarian thinking," by which he meant "thinking in relationship, in community, and in transition."[43] Such a new thinking has a twofold purpose. First, the two Trinitarian approaches based on the notion of supreme substance and absolute subject are no longer adequate; second, a third alternative based on the relationship or sociality of God is much more promising for contemporary theological tasks.[44]

Thinking of God as communion makes it possible for Moltmann to distinguish Trinitarianism from monotheism. Unlike Barth and Rahner, Moltmann does not believe that tritheism is the real danger for Christianity. Rather, it is monotheism that becomes the nemesis of Christian faith,

---

43. Moltmann, *Broad Place*, 287. It must be clear, however, that Moltmann had already begun to develop his ideas about the Trinity in his book, *Crucified God*.

44. There are two types of analogy commonly used in Trinitarian theology: psychological analogy and social analogy. While the former is based on "a view of personhood as constituted by differentiated but inseparable activities of the self," the latter "takes the human experience of life-in-relationship as the best clue to an understanding of the triune life of God." Migliore, *Faith*, 78. The first analogy has traditionally dominated within the Western tradition, whereas the second analogy has been more common within the Orthodox tradition; recently, the latter has become more popular in the West.

since monotheism can easily shadow the Christian idea of God in the form of Sabellian modalism. This is precisely the trap that threatened Barth and Rahner, who both attempt to save the Christian Trinity from tritheism but end up with overemphasizing God as a single divine subject.[45] Moltmann's rejection of monotheism is based on his examination that monotheism is monarchism and therefore it "provides the justification for earthly domination" and "legitimates dependency, helplessness and servitude."[46] In short, monotheism is contrary to the idea of freedom implied in the concept of the Trinity.

The Trinity, Suffering, and Free Love

The primacy of Trinitarianism over monotheism is also evident in the discussion of suffering. Moltmann goes so far as to affirm that only the Trinitarian God can suffer, "The suffering of love does not only affect the redeeming acts of God outwards; it also affects the trinitarian fellowship in God himself. In this way the extra-trinitarian suffering and the inner-trinitarian suffering correspond. . . . For we *can* only talk about God's suffering in trinitarian terms. In monotheism it is impossible."[47]

Moltmann finds in the Trinity a firm basis upon which the engagement with the problems of suffering and theodicy can take place. Since I do not focus on this issue,[48] it is sufficient for now just to highlight three important insights. First, Moltmann always relates the problem of the world's suffering to the cross of Jesus Christ in such a way that we cannot talk about "the death *of* God" but "the death *in* God" or "tragedy in God."[49] Through his concept of *theopathy*, he is enabled to proclaim, "The Son suffers death in this forsakenness. The Father suffers the death of the Son. . . . [H]ere the innermost life of the Trinity is at stake. . . . What happens on Golgotha reaches into the innermost depths of the Godhead, putting its impress on the trinitarian life in eternity."[50] In other words, the suffering of the world affects God's inner self.

Second, the suffering of the world and the suffering of the Son on the cross become the reason for Moltmann to accept Rahner's Rule: the

---

45. Moltmann, *Trinity*, 139–48.
46. Ibid., 192.
47. Ibid., 25.
48. For a deeper analysis of Moltmann's discussion of the issue of suffering in relation to the Trinity see Moltmann, *Crucified God*; Moltmann, *Trinity*, ch. 2.
49. Moltmann, *Crucified God*, 207; Moltmann, *Trinity*, 42–52.
50. Moltmann, *Trinity*, 81.

economic Trinity is the immanent Trinity, and vice versa. Arguing that the rule concerns the interaction between the "inwardness" and "outwardness" of the Triune God, Moltmann affirms that the cross of the Son in the economy of salvation has "a retroactive effect" on the inner life of the Trinity.[51] It is important to note, however, that Moltmann does not simply conflate the immanent Trinity and the economic Trinity. While the identification between the two results from the history of the Son, or the cross, the distinction between the two results from the doxological aspect of his Trinitarian theology, in which "the history of the Spirit moulds the inner life of the triune God through the joy of liberated creation when it is united with God. That is why Christian doxology always ends with the eschatological prospect, looking for 'the perfecting of thy kingdom in glory, when we shall praise and adore thee, Father, Son, and Holy Spirit, for ever and ever.'"[52] "[When] God is all in all . . . the economic Trinity is raised into and transcended in the immanent Trinity."[53]

Third, Moltmann relates the issues of suffering and divine passion to the question of God's freedom and love. He never separates divine freedom from divine love. But, unlike Barth who sees freedom and love as complementary, Moltmann argues that God's freedom *is* "his vulnerable love, his openness, the encountering kindness through which he suffers with the human beings he loves and becomes their advocate, thereby throwing open their future to them."[54] Thus, divine freedom is demonstrated only through love. It is in the loving friendship between God and creation that freedom finds its perfect place. In mutually loving friendship, God's freedom corresponds with human freedom. I will discuss the issue of human freedom, which is important for my larger project.

With regard to the notion of love, Moltmann develops certain theses that eventually become the foundation of his open Trinity.[55] He begins with redefining love as *the self-communication of the good*. The good has power to "go out of itself, to enter into other beings, to participate in other being,

---

51. Ibid., 160–61.

52. Ibid., 161.

53. Ibid., 161. The eschatological idea that "God is all in all"—God in the world and the world in God—is very predominant in Moltmann's theology and expresses fully his panentheistic position; see Moltmann, *Trinity*, 29, 82, 38, 61, 91–92, 105. The place of the world *in* God, nevertheless, is not only eschatologically proper. It is also reflected in the creation of the world through God's self-withdrawal, as we see later.

54. Moltmann, *Trinity*, 56.

55. Ibid., 57–60.

and to give itself for other beings."⁵⁶ Thus, love is always ecstatic—directed toward others. Furthermore, Moltmann applies this particular definition of love to Godself. *Every self-communication presupposes the capacity for self-differentiation.* Here, Moltmann employs the Augustinian metaphor of lover-beloved-love for the Trinity: "If God is love, he is at once the lover, the beloved and the love itself."⁵⁷ Consequently, God's self-communication and self-differentiation expresses God's revelation, in which "he *discloses his inner being through his* decision[;] . . . his being, his goodness and his own being flow into this decision, and through that into the world."⁵⁸

These three theses are followed by Moltmann's explanation of what they mean for the inner-Trinitarian and extra-Trinitarian Others. According to Moltmann, divine love is both necessary and free. In *Trinitarian* terms, on the one hand, love means "love of like for like." But, beautifully, Moltmann expands the scope of divine love to creation, by saying: "[God's love] is no longer addressed to the Other in the like, but to the like in the Other. Like is not enough for like. If his free and creative love is responded to by those it calls to life, then it finds its echo, its answer, its image and so its bliss in freedom and in the Other. God is love."⁵⁹

Having explained his own view of the meaning of love both to divine inner life and to the world, Moltmann argues that creation is the sign of God's external love, since a free love is also a *creative* love. It can only take place through God's self-humiliation, self-limitation, and even self-withdrawal. However, free love is not only a creative love but it is also a suffering love. By creating the world through self-humiliation, God takes up the suffering of the world into Godself. He says, "The suffering love of God with the world, the suffering love of God from the world, and the suffering love of God for the world are the highest forms of his creative love, which desires free fellowship with the world and free response in the world."⁶⁰

---

56. Ibid., 57.

57. Moltmann, *Trinity*, 57. McDougall provides an excellent analysis of Moltmann's treatment of Augustine's psychological model of the Trinity; see McDougall, *Pilgrimage of Love*, 104–7.

58. Moltmann, *Trinity*, 58.

59. Ibid., 59.

60. Ibid.

God is All in All

The above description of the divine passion in relation to God's freedom and love expresses "the entire trajectory of the trinitarian history of God from creation to eschatological consummation."[61] The Trinitarian history of God—Moltmann's favorite term—culminates in the total and reciprocal union between God and the world, when God is in the world and the world in God.

The eschatological idea that "God will be all in all"—another favorite term for Moltmann, drawn from 1 Corinthians 15:28—is also predominant in his theology, clearly expressing his panentheistic position.[62] For Moltmann, the conviction that the world is *in* God is not only appropriate eschatologically, but is also reflected in the creation of the world through God's self-limitation (*zimzum*) as well as through the incarnation of the Son.[63] In this sense, Trinitarian panentheism, Moltmann contends, is the best alternative to the pantheistic and the theistic approaches to the doctrine of creation.[64] While pantheism is inaccurate in making everything a matter of indifference, theism is also wrong in seeing creation as merely an external and arbitrary act of God.

Nevertheless, panentheism is also limited in its incapacity to link God's immanence in the world with God's transcendence. Here, Trinitarianism comes to be very helpful. Moltmann maintains that the Creator Spirit indwells the whole creation and makes it a "dynamic web of interconnected processes." Also, "The Spirit differentiates and binds together. The Spirit preserves and leads living things and their communities beyond themselves. This indwelling Creator Spirit is fundamental for the community of creation. . . . If the cosmic Spirit is the Spirit of God, the universe cannot be viewed as a closed system. It has to be understood as a system that is open—open for God and for his future."[65]

He, furthermore, explains that the self-limitation of the Triune God as an attempt to appropriate the doctrine of *zimzum* suggested by the Kabbalist Isaac Luria for the Christian context. Taking up the Jewish doctrine of

---

61. McDougall, *Pilgrimage of Love*, 75.

62. Moltmann, *Trinity*, 29, 38, 61, 82, 91–92, 105.

63. Whether Moltmann's treatment of God's self-limitation (*zimzum*) is coherently related to his Trinitarian theology of creation has been an interesting issue in the contemporary theological discourse. Wolfhart Pannenberg, for example, gives a harsh criticism of Moltmann on this issue. See Pannenberg, *Systematic Theology, Vol. 2*, 89.

64. Moltmann, *God in Creation*, 98, 103; Moltmann, *Trinity*, 107.

65. Moltmann, *God in Creation*, 103.

Shekinah, which originally refers to the presence of the infinite God in the temple, Luria applies the same notion to the divine presence in creation. In this doctrine, God limits Godself by withdrawing God's omnipresence and making room for creation. Moltmann, in turn, addresses Luria's *zimzum* for two purposes: to appropriate it into his Trinitarian doctrine of creation and to reconcile it with the classical doctrine of *creatio ex nihilo*.[66]

The Spirit fills the whole creation with her own life, bridging the gap between the Father's love for the Son and their love for the world. Also, it is the Spirit who works in creation as the divine internal self-limitation through two mutual processes: through "a contraction of the Spirit," in which the Father alters his love for the Son, *and* through "an inversion of the Spirit," in which the Son alters his response to the Father's love. All these "inward" processes result in the divine act of creating that opens up "outwardly" the space, the time and the freedom for creation. God, according to Moltmann, "throws open a space for those he has created, a space which corresponds to his inner indwellings: he allows a world different from himself to exist before him, with him and *in him*. . . . So the space of creation is at once outside God and within him. Through his self-restriction, the triune God made his presence the dwelling for his creation."[67]

Moltmann moreover tries to systematize his idea of God's self-withdrawal in conversation with the classical doctrine of *creatio ex nihilo*. This classical doctrine depicts creation as occurring *extra Deum*. By using the zimzum theory, Moltmann is able to demonstrate that creation is principally an inward act of God. In *God in Creation* he explicates his idea in a more sophisticated way. He writes, "God makes room for his creation by *withdrawing his presence*."[68] The result of this self-withdrawing is a *nihil*. Here, creation in the proper sense is not yet present and the *nihil* refers to the partial negation of the divine Being. While *creatio ex nihilo* has not happened,

---

66. It must be clear, however, that Moltmann does not address the ontological question of the one and the many. He is more interested in the historical engagement of the Triune God with creation. To fill this gap one must consult a different perspective provided by other philosophers or theologians such as Robert C. Neville. See Neville, *God the Creator*, 81–88, especially his comparison between creation *ex nihilo* and divine contraction. To be sure, the contraction theory that Neville addresses here is one that is originated from the neo-Platonic tradition, while Moltmann's theory of divine self-contraction is borrowed from the Kabbalist tradition. Also, the fact that Moltmann does not attempt to replace the doctrine of creation *ex nihilo* with the doctrine of contraction, but rather combines both theories, needs a special treatment, which is beyond the scope of this project.

67. Moltmann, *Coming of God*, 298–99.

68. Moltmann, *God in Creation*, 87, italics mine.

what we have now is *vacatio ex Deo*, in which the primordial space is not created but vacated out of Godself.[69]

Since Moltmann's idea of referring the vacated space within God as *nihil* is highly problematic, it deserves a special discussion here. He understands the *nihil* as "a literally God-forsaken space" or "hell, absolute death" that is contrary to life that God gives in creation.[70] A feminist theologian, Catherine Keller, criticizes Moltmann precisely at this point.[71] On the one hand, she praises Moltmann's "less conventionally unilateral, masculinizing creativity" with a "feminizing signal." On the other hand, Moltmann's identification of the *nihil* with God-forsakenness and even hell and absolute death obviously "reinscribes stereotypes of masculine creation vs. the feminine passivity" and "disappointing." She laments, "What is his 'literally God-forsaken space' but that of the hinted-at divine maternity?"

While Keller is correct in showing Moltmann's problem from the feminist perspective, we can also criticize Moltmann's *nihil* from the perspective of evil's origin.[72] The consequence of equating *nihil* with evil is that God becomes the author of evil, precisely through God's act of vacating space within Godself to make "room" for creation. Moltmann identifies this vacated space as God-forsaken, hellish and deadly. I will attempt later to redeem Moltmann's doctrine of creation by suggesting the identification of the vacated space as *khora* and demonstrating the perichoretic value of such a proposal for my own model of theology of religions.

It must also be clear that Moltmann's version of panentheism does not merely depict creation as the reality *inside* Godself but also at the same time as the reality *outside* Godself. "If creation *ad extra* takes place in the space freed by God himself, then in this case the reality outside God still remains *in* the God who has yielded up that 'outwards' in himself."[73] Finally, Moltmann relates God's self-withdrawal to the idea of kenosis (self-emptying) and thus relates creation to incarnation. "The divine kenosis which begins

---

69. Gunton, *Doctrine of Creation*, 90.
70. Moltmann, *God in Creation*, 87–88.
71. Keller, *Face*, 17–18.
72. I am indebted to Dr. Kirk Wegter-McNelly for showing, in our personal conversation, the difference between the problems of evil's origin and of evil's destiny. While he praises Moltmann's proposal for resolving the latter through the idea of the cross as death *in* God, he criticizes Moltmann's apparent solution to the former. Wegter-McNelly also suggests the term *creatio ex inferno* to express Moltmann's attempt to relate *vacatio ex Deo* to *creatio ex nihilo*.
73. Moltmann, *God in Creation*, 88–89.

An Imaginative Glimpse

with the creation of the world reaches its perfected and completed form in the incarnation of the Son."[74]

Whether Moltmann's treatment of God's self-limitation (*zimzum*) is coherently related to his Trinitarian theology of creation has been an interesting issue in the contemporary theological discourse. I need to treat this issue more detailed here. It is true that Moltmann's discussions of *zimzum* and of Trinitarian creation seem to be not explicit and even incoherent. When talking about the former, one can easily have an impression of a single God who limits and empties Godself, not a Triune God. It is only in the latter—the creation of the world—that Moltmann talks more explicitly in a Trinitarian mode. It is also obvious that the link between the former and the latter is the idea of self-limitation. If *zimzum* demonstrates God's humility to limit Godself, then this "characteristic" must also be reflected in the other moments of the Trinitarian history of God, especially in the *kenosis* of the Son. I suspect Moltmann's reluctance to depict God's self-contraction as a more Trinitarian act relates to his idea that *nihil*, as the result of self-contraction, bears a negative sense as God-forsaken space, hell, and absolute death.

Wolfhart Pannenberg, for example, criticizes Moltmann on this issue. Arguing that the notion of *zimzum* was originally used in Jewish mysticism to emphasize "the independence of the creaturely existence alongside God," Pannenberg rejects Moltmann's *nihil* within Godself as "a materially unfounded mystification of the subject."[75] He complains that Moltmann's idea of God's self-contraction lacks any Trinitarian basis and proposes to replace it with an explicitly "Trinitarian explication of the doctrine of creation."[76]

Colin E. Gunton also gives strong criticisms on Moltmann's idea of God's self-contraction as an inward act.[77] He argues that "if the world is truly to be the world, it needs to be 'outside' of God, not in such a relationship according to which it is in some way enclosed within God."[78] However, I do not find Gunton's arguments convincing. Moltmann's solution to the issue of "inward versus outward" is promising, in which he suggests that "the space of creation is at once outside God and within him."[79] The underlying issue

---

74. Moltmann, *Trinity*, 118. Later on Moltmann even stretches the idea of the divine kenosis to the consummation of the world. See his contribution article in Moltmann, "God's Kenosis," 137–51.

75. Pannenberg, *Systematic Theology, Vol. 2*, 15.

76. Ibid.

77. Gunton, *Doctrine of Creation*, 140–42.

78. Ibid., 142.

79. Moltmann, *Coming of God*, 299.

behind the outward-inward or outside-inside problem is whether the freedom of creation can be maintained without diminishing its close relationship with the Creator. I will argue later to resolve this issue by proposing two things. First, I propose the metaphor of "a permeable or porous membrane" between God and creation so that creature beings can still lives as other-than-God in the Triune life, while at the same time the Spirit can penetrate the whole creation through divine immanence. Second, Moltmann's negative *nihil* needs to be remedied by understanding the vacated space within Godself as *khora*, which becomes an affirmative space for the dynamic life of creation as well as one of the perichoretic dimension pointed to certain religious ultimacies.

However, Moltmann's solution does not make any excuse of his lack Trinitarian dimension of God's self-contraction. Here, Gunton is correct in pointing out the problem. He writes, "There is a great deal of difference between saying that all things were created in God, *simpliciter*, and that it happened and happens in Christ."[80] Gunton also quotes Pannenberg's main idea of the Son as the principle of the intra-Trinitarian self-distinction as well as the principle of distinction between God and the world, which I agree fully. But, interestingly, by suggesting the latter, Gunton has answered his own complaint against Moltmann's idea of the world being inside God. To say that creation happens "in Christ" is to say that it happens "in the Triune God." Thus, the Trinitarian idea can resolve all of this complexity by centering the whole issue on the Son, both as the second person of the Trinity, *in* whom the world is created *and* the principle of differentiation between God and the world, which implies a mediatory or in-between role. Metaphorically, we can say that the in-between one is at the same time *outside* the two parties that one mediates and *inside* them so that the mediation is effectual. I will discuss the problem of "creation in and through the Son" in Moltmann further below.

When discussing the Son and the Spirit, or incarnation and glorification, Moltmann demonstrates a way of thinking similar to that used for the Father or creation. As creation is an act of the Triune God, incarnation and glorification are also characteristically Trinitarian. With regard to the incarnation of the Son, Moltmann maintains that the Son is both the Logos through whom the world is created *and* God's true and primordial image (*ikon*) who is also "the first-born among many brethren." While the incarnation is an outward act of God, it presupposes and affects the inwardness of God. "The *outward incarnation* presupposes *inward self-humiliation* . . . the

---

80. Gunton, *Doctrine of Creation*, 142–43.

An Imaginative Glimpse

incarnation intervenes the inner relation of the Trinity."[81] The kenotic incarnation of the Son, furthermore, culminates at the cross. It is on the cross that God's self-humiliation reaches its completion and perfection.

Just as freedom and love take place in the creation of the world, we can see their recurrence in the incarnation of the Son. The incarnation is the perfection of God's self-limitation characterized by freedom and love *because* God communicates Godself in incarnation not only to the like but also to God's other, that is, the world. Thus God's love directed toward the Others (the world) becomes creative love through which God "desires to find bliss through this other's responsive love. But this responsive love is a free response."[82] The incarnation of the Son, once again, reflects the openness of the Trinity toward the world. The mediating act of the Son makes the whole world exist "in God" and "God in them."[83]

The problem is, if the mediating role of the Son makes the world exist within God, "where" in God is the precise "location" of the world? Is it in the *nihil*, vacated by God through God's self-contraction? Moltmann does not give any clear clue about this, especially since he refers the nihil as God-forsaken, hellish and deadly space. The Christian tradition often says that it is "in the Son" that the whole universe is created. For Moltmann, the spatial image of "in the Son" cannot be identical with "in the vacated space" or *nihil*, since it would equate the Son with the hellish *nihil*. This, I believe, is the reason why Moltmann never talks about the creation of the world "in the Son," but only "through the Son."[84] By reinterpreting the vacated space as *khora*, and therefore redeeming its negative sense, I suggest that *khora* is the vacated space "within the Triune life" or, to be more precise, "in the Son."

When talking about the Spirit, once more, Moltmann relates closely the outwardness and the inwardness of the Trinity. The sending of the Spirit is simultaneously an outward and an inward work, as he writes, "It is a movement into which the whole creation is gathered. . . . All people and things then partake of the 'inner-trinitarian life' of God[;] . . . the triune God is at home *in* his world and his world exists *out of* his inexhaustible glory."[85] Here, the theology of Shekinah that Moltmann borrows from the rabbinic tradition finds its fullest expression. In his book *The Spirit of Life*, Moltmann explicitly elaborates the notion of Shekinah for his pneumatology

---

81. Moltmann, *Trinity*, 119.
82. Ibid., 117.
83. Ibid., 122.
84. Ibid., 113; cf. Col 1:15–16.
85. Ibid., 127–28.

and comes to certain points where the theology of Shekinah can contribute to an understanding of the divine Spirit.[86] The notion of Shekinah elucidates the personal character of the Spirit, reveals the sensibility of the Spirit, and demonstrates the kenosis of the Spirit.

In order for his Trinitarianism to reflect a true communion, Moltmanns needs to emphasize that the Spirit is not an energy proceeding from the Father or the Son. Neither is the Spirit merely a divine attribute. The Spirit is the glorifying and unifying God, in the sense that the Spirit is *"the subject* who glorifies the Father and the Son, and unites the Father and the Son."[87] Moltmann also points out that the work of the Spirit is always in a twofold order. In the *outpouring* of the Spirit upon humanity, the Spirit comes *from the Father through the Son*, while in the glorification through the Spirit the order is in reverse, *from the Spirit through the Son to the Father*. It is in glorification, as Joy Ann McDougall rightly maintains, that "one ceases altogether to speak meaningfully of God *ad extra* and *ad intra*, since the world returns to its true dwelling place within the trinitarian relations of love."[88]

Moltmann certainly understands the glorification through the Spirit as a possibility in the future, especially when he must answer the problem of evil. The divine love, in facing the reality of suffering, appears in the forms of divine patience, endurance, and waiting. God, thus, is "the supreme possibility, . . . the source of possibilities, and . . . the transcendental making-possible of the possible."[89] It is in the possible future that the freedom of creation and the creative love of God meet.

From Person-Perichoresis to Reality-Perichoresis

I have discussed the central points of Moltmann's Trinitarian theology at rather great length, especially his idea of "the Trinitarian history of God"—creation, incarnation, and glorification. In Moltmann's view, Trinity is always communal, open, and dynamic. The *communal* dimension is demonstrated in its rejection of anchoring the unity of the Trinity in a divine substance or divine subject. Rather, the Triune God is a community of three persons. Such a communal dimension of the Trinity also brings about a second dimension, namely that the Trinity is always *open* to its Other—humanity and the world—and the Other's full participation in the Triune life. The Trinity,

---

86. Moltmann, *Spirit of Life*, 51.
87. Moltmann, *Trinity*, 126.
88. McDougall, *Pilgrimage of Love*, 86.
89. Moltmann, "God's Kenosis," 150.

An Imaginative Glimpse

according to Moltmann, is also *dynamic* in that it is active in the history of creation, directing all reality to the eschatological possibility of the future, when the openness of the Trinity will reach its perfection.

To amplify these dimensions of the Trinity, Moltmann employs the doctrine of perichoresis. In *The Trinity and the Kingdom,* the term perichoresis does not appear until Moltmann moves to the issue of the unity of the Triune God.[90] Thus, I would argue that even without using the doctrine of perichoresis, Moltmann is still able to explicate his idea of the social Trinity. But, through the doctrine of perichoresis, not only is he able to reinforce his social Trinity, he also has a solid ground for dealing with the issues of the difference and unity within the Trinity.

First, Moltmann's use of perichoresis centers on the unitedness or the at-oneness of the three persons with one another. The unitedness of God furthermore presupposes the self-differentiation of God. Moltmann gives his short definition of what perichoresis is along with its significant characteristic: "The Father exists in the Son, the Son in the Father, and both of them in the Spirit, just as the Spirit exists in both. . . . In the perichoresis, the very thing that divides them becomes that which binds them together."[91]

In saying this, Moltmann can avoid both the dangers of Sabellian modalism and tritheism. On the one hand, the self-differentiation of the three persons is not "a modal difference," as we can find in Sabellianism, "for only persons can be at one with one another."[92] On the other hand, perichoresis is effective in rejecting tritheism. The perichoretic nature of God does not allow the unifying relationship to appear "after" we have three different

---

90. Moltmann, *Trinity,* 150.

91. Ibid., 174–75. Kirk Wegter-McNelly, through his "theology of entanglement," attempts to demonstrate a similar idea and even enlarges its scope to include the issue of God-world relation. Drawing from Pannenberg's theology of creation and the quantum theory in physics, he proposes the notion of nondirective God-creation entanglement based on the Trinitarian act of creation. He maintains, "Because the cooperative work of the second and the third persons of the Trinity constitutes both the formal and material principles of creation, a trinitarian notion of the relation between God and creation must be expressed both in terms of distinction and union." Wegter-McNelly, "Natural Evil," 242. He continues with his idea of the entangled relation between God and creation by saying, "The idea of a physical world nondirectively entangled with God blends these notions, making the physical world's distinction from God a product of its union with God through the entangling reality of incarnation. God's gift of being to the physical world comes precisely in the form of a relation that grants this world its relative causal independence." Wegter-McNelly, "Natural Evil," 242.

92. Moltmann, *Trinity,* 150.

persons. In short, perichoresis as the nature of God simultaneously maintains the oneness and the threeness of the divine.

Moltmann finds in perichoresis great possibilities for speaking of the socio-political reality that should reflect the perichoretic relation of the divine. His rejection of monotheistic monarchy finds its theological foundation in the doctrine of perichoresis. Whether Moltmann has misstated the problem—that is, the correlation between theology and politics—is another issue that we need to address further below. Nonetheless, what is of importance here is that his rejection of monarchism creates a certain problem in terms of divine monarchy. Clearly, he cannot abandon the divine monarchy altogether. He is aware of the danger of thinking of a "quaternity," a divine fourth—beside the Father, the Son, and the Spirit—who becomes the source of the three persons. Therefore, he still allows for accepting the Father as the eternal origin of the Son and the Spirit, only in terms of their *constitution*. The monarchy of the Father, however, "has no validity within the eternal circulation of the divine life, and none in the perichoretic unity of the Trinity."[93]

Moltmann's idea of person-perichoresis can be summarized by using his own words, "The doctrine of the perichoresis links together in a brilliant way the threeness and the unity, without reducing the threeness to the unity, or dissolving the unity in the threeness. The unity of the triunity lies in the eternal perichoresis of the trinitarian persons. Interpreted perichoretically, the trinitarian persons form their own unity by themselves in the circulation of the divine life."[94]

Here, Moltmann adopts without any reserve the idea of eternal and circulatory indwelling of the three divine persons (person-perichoresis) from the Greek fathers, especially as it appears in John of Damascus. But John does not provide him with ground for the second dimension of perichoresis, namely that in which the intra-Trinitarian perichoresis is also open *ad extra* to the participation of the whole creation in the divine life (reality-perichoresis). Thus, Moltmann creatively expands the perichoretic relation to include humanity and the world. He believes that reality-perichoresis is a logical consequence of person-perichoresis.[95] If the Trinity is a fellowship, then it cannot be a self-enclosed and exclusive unity.

---

93. Ibid., 176.

94. Ibid., 175.

95. Moltmann prefers to use the term "cosmic perichoresis"; see Moltmann, *Coming of God*, 295. In my opinion, the term reality-perichoresis is more favorable, since it refers to the whole reality (God and creation) that constitutes the perichoresis.

An Imaginative Glimpse

For this purposes, he uses biblical texts for his arguments of person-perichoresis (John 14:9; 10:30; 14:11) as well as reality-perichoresis (John 14:23; 17:21). As we have seen, this reality-perichoresis is amplified by other doctrines such as zimzum and Shekinah and is framed within the Trinitarian history of God. All these ideas, however, by no means imply that the *mutual* relation between God and creation is symmetrical. Reality-perichoresis is characteristically *mutual*, even *reciprocal*, only in an eschatological sense, when God is in all and all is in God. Moltmann goes even further by allowing the world affecting the inner life of God. Not only does God influences the world, "his world [also] puts its impress on God too."[96]

Nevertheless, the perichoretic relation between God and the world must always be *asymmetrical* when we talk about the initiator of such a perichoretic relation and when we distinguish the natures of God and creation. It is the eternally Triune God who initiates, through God's love, the mutual relation by embracing the whole universe into God's inner life, through creation, incarnation, and consummation. The world cannot take the initiative for the perichoretic relation. The mutual indwellings, Moltmann asserts, "do not take place on the same level. . . . God's indwelling in the world is *divine in kind*; the world's indwelling in God is *worldly in kind*."[97] Thus, not only is the perichoretic relation between God and creation *asymmetrical*, it also preserves the *uniqueness* of God and creation, with each indwelling the other.

Related to the reality-perichoresis that Moltmann proposes is the impact of such a panentheistic conception of perichoresis to the idea of space and time. He realizes that one of the problems with his proposal of reality-perichoresis is that of the concept of time and space vis-à-vis eternity. If reality-perichoresis occurs between the infinite God and finite creation, how do we make sense of the interpenetration between creation that is always limited by time and space and the Trinity that is not limited by time and space? Moltmann proposes his answer by arguing that reality-perichoresis between God and creation is followed logically by "a mutual perichoresis between eternity and time" in which "we can talk about 'eternal time' and

---

96. Moltmann, *Trinity*, 99.

97. Moltmann, *God in Creation*, 150, italics mine; cf. Moltmann, *In the End*, 158. Moltmann also argues that "the relationship between God and man is not a reciprocal relationship between equals." Moltmann, *Trinity*, 3. If we read this statement in light of other statements that refer to the reciprocal relation between God and humanity, the above statement could mean that the relationship between God and humanity *is not* reciprocal because it involves two unequal parties: God and humanity. But, it *is* still a reciprocal relationship in the sense that it is not a one-way communication.

... 'eternity filled with time.'"[98] Regarding space, he also suggests "a perichoretic concept of space" and finds insight in the Latin term of perichoresis itself, *circuminsessio* (mutual indwelling), and another similar term, "mutual *inhabitation*." The perichoretic concept applied to space, he maintains, refers to a "reciprocal in-existence [corresponding] on the creaturely level to the concept of the eternal inner-trinitarian indwelling of the divine Persons."[99] Moltmann, again, goes back to the idea of *zimzum* as the solid foundation of the perichoretic concept of space.

Moltmann's statement in *The Coming of God* summarizes all of his thoughts on this matter, "A mutual indwelling of the world in God and God in the world will come into being. For this, it is neither necessary for the world to dissolve into God, as pantheism says, nor for God to be dissolved in the world, as atheism maintains. God remains God, and the world remains creation. Through their mutual indwellings, they remain unmingled and undivided, for God lives in creation in a God-like way, and the world lives in God in a world-like way."[100]

In conclusion, Moltmann painstakingly attempts to apply the perichoretic idea to the relationship between God and creation without subscribing to the pantheistic framework. The mutual and reciprocal relationship between God and the world is affirmed without undermining its asymmetrical characteristic. Also, the mutual indwelling is established without any possible dissolving of either God or the world into one another.

Extra-Trinitarian Perichoresis

Moltmann seems fascinated with perichoresis. The doctrine perfectly fits into his overall panentheistic position. Perichoresis becomes the overarching principle through which Moltmann approaches almost every issue he addresses. Not satisfied with the application of the doctrine only to person-perichoresis and reality-perichoresis, Moltmann attempts to enlarge its scope to what I call the extra-Trinitarian perichoresis, by which I mean the application of the doctrine to other loci that do not involve the triune persons directly.

There are at least three loci to which Moltmann applies the perichoretic principle. The first is the perichoretic relationship between body and soul. He

---

98. Moltmann, *Coming of God*, 295.
99. Ibid., 301.
100. Ibid., 307.

An Imaginative Glimpse

argues that, based on the human likeness to God, the relationship between soul and body must be patterned by a perichoretic relationship signified by mutual interpenetration and differentiated unity.[101] Moltmann believes that, in terms of the soul-body relationship, the perichoretic idea is very close to, and can be amplified by, Gestalt psychology.

Second, Moltmann finds a pattern analogous to the perichoretic relation of soul and body in the relationship between human beings and nature. "Just as soul and body interpenetrate one another, so human beings and nature find one another in mutual perichoresis."[102] I believe the term cosmic-perichoresis, which Moltmann uses for the relation between God and creation, is more appropriate to use here. Interestingly, although such a cosmic-perichoresis is external to God's inner life, it can nonetheless be "brought into an equilibrium without that future of God which is conceived of as 'resurrection.'"[103] Thus, at the end, the perichoretic relation between human beings and nature is taken up into the larger perichoresis of God and creation. But, the point that I want to make here is that Moltmann allows perichoresis to be a pattern for other relations outside of the Trinitarian life, without fully disconnecting it from the Triune perichoresis.

The third and most important locus to which he employs perichoresis in an extra-Trinitarian sense is that of human society (I call it society-perichoresis). We have seen that Moltmann's arguments against monotheism and for Trinitarianism are based on his rejection of social monarchism. Thus, although our understanding of who God is has a direct influence on the social order, it is precisely at this point that some critics express their disagreement with Moltmann and other supporters of the doctrine of social Trinity. Moltmann, for instance, argues that "the Trinity corresponds to a community in which people are defined through their relations with one another and in their significance for one another, not in opposition to and another, in terms of power and possession."[104] Similarly, in the context of ecclesial government, Moltmann believes that the presbyterial and synodal forms of church correspond to the doctrine of the social Trinity.[105]

We find a similar way of thinking in other contemporary theologians. The Brazilian Franciscan theologian Leonardo Boff, for instance, explains the interpenetration and coinherence of the three persons by saying that

101. Moltmann, *God in Creation*, 259.
102. Moltmann, *Way of Jesus Christ*, 272.
103. Ibid.
104. Moltmann, *Trinity*, 198.
105. Ibid., 202.

Perichoretic Indwelling of and in the Triune God

each person is "to be *for* the others, *through* the others, *with* the others and *in* the others[;] . . . the 'in themselves' *is* 'for the others'."[106] In conversation with Moltmann, Boff goes so far as to claim that the inclusiveness of the Triune communion arguing is able to embrace human beings and all creation. "The united society that exists in the Trinity is the foundation of human unity; the latter is inserted in the former. . . . The union obtaining between persons and in the human community prefigures the union that exists in the Trinity."[107] It remains unclear, however, exactly what Boff means when he says that the human unity is "inserted" in the Trinity.[108]

His closeness to Moltmann is also evident in his acceptance of Rahner's Rule—the economic Trinity is the immanent trinity, and *vice versa*—yet he comments on the "vice versa" part by saying that the economic Trinity is not the whole of the immanent Trinity. There is always much more in the immanent Trinity, that is "hidden in unfathomable mystery, mystery that will be partially revealed to us in the bliss of eternal life, but will always escape us in full."[109]

Boff's idea of perichoresis then functions in his criticism of social and ecclesial structures such as individualism, isolationism, capitalism, and socialism. He maintains that the doctrine of perichoresis can serve as "the structuring principle" of his Trinitarian faith, operates as "a source of inspiration, as a utopian goal that generates models of successively diminishing differences," and become "the prototype of the human community dreamed of by those who wish to improve society and build it in such a way as to make it into the image and likeness of the Trinity."[110] Also, "the concept [of perichoresis] is central to the relevance of the Trinity to our desire for a society that lives together in more open communion, equality and respectful acceptance of differences."[111] The possibility of applying the Trinitarian model in general, and perichoresis in particular, is based on the mutual reference between the Trinity and society. "So human society is a pointer on the road to the mystery of the Trinity, while the mystery of the Trinity, as we know it from revelation, is a pointer toward the social life and its archetype. Human society holds a *vestigium Trinitatis* since the Trinity is 'the divine society'."[112]

---

106. Boff, *Trinity and Society*, 127–28.
107. Ibid., 134.
108. cf. LaCugna, *God for Us*, 312.
109. Boff, *Trinity and Society*, 215.
110. Ibid., 5–7.
111. Ibid., 136.
112. Ibid., 119.

In short, in a term borrowed from an Orthodox thinker, Boff proclaims: "The holy Trinity is our social program."[113]

Moltmann and Boff are two among many theorists of social Trinity who suggest shifting the focus from the Trinitarian perichoresis, person-perichoresis or reality-perichoresis, to the extra-Trinitarian perichoresis (cosmic-perichoresis or society-perichoresis). Other theologians who go in the same direction include Patricia Wilson-Kastner, and Paul Fiddes.[114]

Some Objections with Reality-Perichoresis and Society-Perichoresis

In this section, I discuss the most problematic aspects of the perichoretic idea, especially when it is expanded into areas outside of God's inner life. I begin with presenting the criticisms of the social Trinity proposed by Moltmann and Boff. The central issue is twofold: whether it is possible for creation to participate in the eternal perichoretic relation of the Trinity and whether the Triune perichoresis can be applied to the human community. What is at stake in both issues is the ontological difference between God and creation. The question concerns how such a difference affects our understanding of perichoresis on multiple levels.

It seems that reality-perichoresis is less problematic than society-perichoresis. There are two significant reasons for this fact. First, reality-perichoresis has long been rooted in the Eastern tradition of deification and participation. Our discussion of Maximus the Confessor demonstrates that is it possible for creation to participate in the Triune perichoresis by virtue of the embracing energy of Christ, in whom we find a perichoretic and hypostatic union of the divine and the human nature. Reality-perichoresis, in Maximus, can only make any sense insofar as its link to the nature-perichoresis is firmly established. In Moltmann, on the contrary, the link between both perichoretic relations is minimal, if not absent altogether. As Randall Otto correctly argues, "Moltmann's use of perichoresis here is very different [from that of Maximus], inasmuch as it fails to have its basis in that

---

113. Moltmann also uses the slogan to emphasize his idea of the social implication of the perichoresis; see Moltmann, *Experiences*, 322–33; Moltmann, "Perichoresis," 123–25. Moltmann recognizes Nicholas Fedorov, a friend of Dostoevsky, as the originator of the slogan cf. Volf, "Trinity."

114. Wilson-Kastner, *Faith*; Fiddes, *Participating*. Graham Buxton, in *Trinity*, discusses a number of theologians who employ the concept of perichoresis in different theological fields.

necessary hypostatic union."[115] But, Otto misses the fact that the absence of a link between reality-perichoresis and nature-perichoresis in Moltmann's theory is remedied by a clear link between reality-perichoresis and person-perichoresis. In light of his Trinitarian history of God—creation, incarnation, consummation—Moltmann is able to anchor the relation between God and creation as perichoretic.

Second, the reason why reality-perichoresis is less problematic than that of the extra-Trinitarian perichoresis (or, society-perichoresis) is found in the biblical texts. Both the Eastern church fathers and Moltmann base their reality-perichoresis on biblical texts, especially John 17:21, where Jesus says, "that they may all be one. As you, Father, are in me and I am in you, may they also be *in us*." The perichoretic unity of the believers in the Triune God is made possible by the perichoretic union between the Father and the Son, in the power of the Spirit. In such a perichoretic or mutual indwelling, the ontological distinction between Creator and creation is still maintained.

It is important to note, however, that the distinction between person-perichoresis and reality-perichoresis is strictly conceptual, not ontological, just like the distinction between the immanent Trinity and the economic Trinity is merely conceptual. We cannot say that there is person-reality without any economic relation to creation. In this sense, Moltmann is right in emphasizing the Trinitarian history of God from creation to consummation. Any talk of person-perichoresis apart from the economy of salvation culminated in reality-perichoresis would merely be speculative and worthless. Nonetheless, of course, while a separation between the two is impossible, a distinction is still necessary. In sum, person-perichoresis and reality-perichoresis are inseparable, yet distinguishable. A strict identity between the two would undermine the freedom of both God and creation. On the one hand, there must be more in God than God's relation with creation, even though we cannot think or approach God apart from God's relationship with creation. This relates to the belief that in the Triune life there is always a *surplus* or *excess* characterized by God's ecstatic free-love toward creation.[116] On the other hand, by distinguishing the two forms of perichoresis the freedom of creation is also respected, since the otherness of creation is not totally absorbed into the Triune life. I would argue metaphorically, that there must always be a permeable or porous membrane between God and creation so that creation can still live in the Triune life, while at the same time the Spirit can penetrate the whole creation through divine immanence. I be-

115. Otto, "Use and Abuse," 380.
116. Cf. Volf, "Trinity," 108.

lieve, my argument enriches LaCugna's similar ideas concerning *theologia* and *oikonomia*, discussed further below.

A more serious problem, however, occurs with regard to the second aspect of the issue; that is, whether the Triune perichoresis can be applied to the human community. I discuss two main criticisms of the social Trinity proposed by Moltmann and Boff. While both criticisms are related to some extent, the first critique is directed toward the grammatical nature of the doctrine of the Trinity, and the second deals with the problem of the ontological difference between God and creation.

Can a Second-Order Symbol or Proposition Be a Model for Human Society?

The first critique comes from Ted Peters, who argues that the doctrine of the Trinity is a second order symbol "constructed for the purpose of clarifying the more primary symbols of Father, Son, and Holy Spirit."[117] Accordingly, to step into an attempt at modeling human society based on the social doctrine of the Trinity is "to ask the tail to wag the dog."[118] Peters, moreover, proposes that the kingdom of God, as a fundamental biblical symbol, already directed toward human society, is a better option. Unlike the social Trinitarians who operate conjunctively rather than disjunctively, the symbol of the kingdom of God has a disjunctive function in criticizing all human kingship and injustice because of its centrality on God as the only king. Peters goes even further by concluding that "We as creature cannot copy God in all respects."[119]

In a similar vein, Karen Kilby argues from the postliberal perspective saying that the doctrine of the Trinity needs to be taken as "grammatical, as a second order proposition, a rule, perhaps a set of rules" for how to talk about the Christian life.[120] If this perspective is plausible, Kilby argues, theologians cannot claim authority over the doctrinal claims they make. Neither can they use the Trinitarian doctrine as "a pretext for claiming such an insight into the inner nature of God that they can use it to promote social, political or ecclesial regimes."[121]

---

117. Peters, *God as Trinity*, 185.
118. Ibid.
119. Ibid., 186.
120. Kilby, "Perichoresis," 443.
121. Ibid., 444.

Perichoretic Indwelling of and in the Triune God

I agree with Peters and Kilby regarding the status of the doctrine of Trinity (and, of course, of perichoresis) as a second-order symbol (Peters) or a second order proposition (Kilby). I argued in the previous chapter that the doctrine of the Trinity is best seen as the grammar of the Christian faith. While both argue that the Trinity is second-order because it comes after the "first-order," Peters and Kilby argue differently.

By saying that the Trinity is a "second order proposition[,] . . . a set of rules," Kilby has in her mind the distinction made by the postliberal theologian George Lindbeck, as she openly acknowledges.[122] Lindbeck suggests that we take doctrines to be "second-order guidelines for Christian discourse rather than first-order affirmations."[123] If Lindbeck's and Kilby's ideas are accepted, consequently, we cannot say that the doctrine of the Trinity claims in a descriptive manner about God *in se*. It only states what Christians believe about God.

The distinction between the first-order affirmations and the second-order rules certainly merits a special scrutiny in its own right, which involves complexities beyond the scope of my project. It is enough for now to deal with Kilby's suggestion that, while theologians may freely speculate about any social analogy of the Trinity, they "should not use the doctrine as a pretext for claiming such an insight into the inner nature of God that they can use it to promote social, political or ecclesial regimes."[124]

Instead of using Lindbeck's distinction, I suggest conceiving of the doctrine of the Trinity as second-order in terms of the distinction between pre-reflective and reflective experience.[125] As a reflective experience, however, the doctrine of the Trinity (and, of course, perichoresis) is still subject to the perspective of the theologian. It is always perspectival and contextual, rather than universal. It can surely promote its universal intent but it can never be claimed as objectively universal. I believe Kilby, with her postliberal perspective, would agree with me here. Moreover, as a reflective experience, the formulation of the doctrine of perichoresis and Trinity can still claim

122. Ibid., 445.

123. Lindbeck, *Nature of Doctrine*, 94.

124. Kilby, "Perichoresis," 444. Of course, the problem of the dualism between language and reality is already latent in postliberal theology. For a good treatment of this issue, see Adonis Vidu's critique of the postliberal theology on this issue; see Vidu, "Lindbeck's."

125. Douglas R. McGaughey makes this distinction based on Mortimer Adler's ideas. McGaughey maintains that "The activity of critical reflection . . . is a reflection about the first-order experience. Second-order reflection has its grounding in first-order experience and not vice versa." McGaughey, *Strangers and Pilgrims*, 183.

An Imaginative Glimpse

to have some insight into the inner nature of God insofar as it is grounded in the first-order experience of the Triune God in the life of believers. If my argument is acceptable, Kilby's argument that the doctrine of the Trinity cannot be used "to promote social, political or ecclesial regimes" is certainly inadequate. This does not mean, however, that I agree that we can claim the fullness of God's inner life. There is always much more in God than that upon which we can reflect.

Ted Peters differs from Kilby when he says that the Trinity is a second-order symbol. He has with him a reservoir of symbols in the Christian tradition. Some of them are first-order or, in Peters' words, "primary" or "biblical" symbols. Others have status as second-order symbols. The secondary status of the symbol of the Trinity seems to mean that it is not in the Bible, the primary source of Christian symbols. While agreeing that both the kingdom of God and the Trinity are symbols, with the former being a first-order symbol and the latter being a second-order, I do not see that the distinction supports Peters' claim that the symbol of the Trinity renders us unable to engage with realities of both God and social problems, and that therefore the symbol is empty of any praxial value. The real problem, therefore, is not that of the distinction between the first-order (or primary or biblical) and the second-order symbol. Rather, what is of importance in his critique of the social theory of the Trinity is whether we can "copy God" or link the social Trinity to the human society.

It is true that we might not be able to "copy God" *fully*, but I believe that in some respect we can still engage with who the Triune God is, and can relate the understanding resulting from this engagement to our human society; otherwise, the symbol would be completely empty.[126] This is also the case with the symbol of the kingdom of God. The term "the kingdom of God" as a symbol is not exactly the same as the reality of the kingdom of God referred to by the symbol. The *symbol* of the kingdom of God thus can mirror the *reality* of the kingdom of God in some respects. As symbols, therefore, both the kingdom of God and the Trinity are also subject to the situatedness of theologians who use the symbols. In other words, it is possible for the symbol of the kingdom of God to operate conjunctively, just as the symbol of the Trinity may operate disjunctively.

I have demonstrated the deficiency of Peters' critique of the social doctrine of the Trinity. Nevertheless, there is another serious and important issue that he addresses: can we copy God, or not? As regards perichoresis,

---

126. The idea of theology as symbolic engagement in the works of Robert C. Neville is important here; see Neville, *Scope and Truth*.

the question is whether we can use person-perichoresis as the model for constructing society-perichoresis. Peters' answer is certainly negative: "We as creature cannot copy God in all respects."[127] This issue, therefore, is closer to the second critique that I discuss in the following section.

Can Perichoresis Be a Social Program?

Joy McDougall offers a second critique of the social doctrine of the Trinity. She accuses Moltmann of a tendency "to slip into univocal predication of the same terms to the divine and human spheres, most notably the term *perichoresis*."[128] Lacking of any developed theory of divine predication, Moltmann often obscures the differences between the divine and humanity, passing over, for example, "the temporal and material condition under which human beings seek to realize their messianic destiny of fellowship with one another."[129] Consequently, McDougall continues, Moltmann's attempt to apply his social Trinitarianism "becomes far too idealized to translate into actual praxis."[130] McDougall's critique is of course applicable to Boff and other social Trinitarians.

The point that McDougall tries to emphasize is that there is a radically qualitative difference between God and creation (and human beings in particular) that makes it impossible for creation to participate in the kind of perichoretic relation with God as is found in the inner-Trinitarian life to the extra-Trinitarian community. Peters' statement summarizes the issue more bluntly: We cannot copy God in all respects! Surely, there is a obvious truth on which we must agree, which makes Peters' criticism *seem* to be correct. The term "person" cannot be applied univocally for God and creation, although we can still find an analogical dimension of the term "person" in God and creation, namely in that a person is always relational and communal. Here lies the classical discussion of whether relationality is a derivative of personhood, or if personhood is derivative of relationality, or if both are present concurrently. Despite the relational characteristic of the Trinitarian *and* human persons, the perichoretic relationships of the Triune persons are so perfect that we can say that each person is interior in the two others. For human beings, on the other hand, such interiority is impossible. In Volf's words, "Another human self cannot be internal to my own self as a subject

---

127. Peters, *God as Trinity*, 186.
128. McDougall, *Pilgrimage of Love*, 162.
129. Ibid., 162–63.
130. Ibid., 163.

of action. Human persons are always external to one another *as subjects*."[131] But, if Peters is correct in saying that we cannot copy God "in all respects," what is the praxial significance of the doctrine of the Trinity? What is the relevance of the analogous relationality between God and creation?

Here, it is worthwhile to consider Miroslav Volf's excellent article. He puts on the table two radically different views regarding the ability of the human community to copy the divine community. The first view is represented by Nicholas Fedorov whose phrase—"The Trinity is our social program"— has become a favorite motto for many theorists of the social Trinity. The second view, of course, is espoused by Ted Peters with his total rejection of any possibility of modeling of the human community based on the Trinitarian community. Volf rejects both.

On the one hand, he sees that Fedorov has strayed too far from his Orthodox tradition in saying that, because of our participation in the divine life, "God has placed in our hands all the means for regulating cosmic disorders."[132] For Volf, this certainly is a "specious" proposal and a "chimerical" vision. On the other hand, Volf's critique of Peters' position is equally harsh. In light of the Christian belief that human beings are made in the image of God, it would be anomalous to say that there are no analogues to God in creation. Also, he uses Moltmann's *The Trinity and the Kingdom of God* as an example of how the idea of the kingdom of God would only be meaningful in the narrative context of the Triune God's engagement with the whole creation. Volf asks, then, whether there is a third option between "two equally unacceptable options, the one consisting of seeking to imitate the Triune God in a blatant disregard of the fact that we are not God and the other consisting of respecting our creaturely difference from God but failing to pursue our most proper human calling to be of humanity . . . between Fedorov's divinization of humanity and Peters' total alterity of God, God's being 'shrouded in eternal mystery apart from the time in which we live.'"[133]

He suggests that we do not need to choose between Fedorov and Peters. Rather, between the two "lies the widely open space of human responsibility which consists in 'copying God in *some* respects.'"[134] Volf's proposal is interesting, and I agree with it. The question, of course, is to what extent the human community can be modeled on the Triune community. Volf, furthermore, sets certain criteria that we need to discern if we want to find those

---

131. Volf, *After Our Likeness*, 210–11.
132. Volf, "Trinity," 105.
133. Ibid., 106.
134. Ibid., 106.

"copiable" aspects of the Triune community. First, Trinitarian concepts such as persons, perichoresis and relations can be applied to human community only in an analogous rather than in the univocal sense; second, because of human sins, those analogous aspects can only be appropriated in human community historically. I would suggest a third important limitation, namely that the human community can correspond to the divine community insofar as we put the human community (and the whole universe) within the larger eschatological act of God's embracing of creation. Volf, moreover, proposes two issues through which we can apply person-perichoresis to society-perichoresis: the issue of identity and the issue of self-donation.[135] To be sure, they are only two among many other issues that we can explore.

Before moving on, it is important to restate my position as regards the two critiques directed toward the social doctrine of the Trinity, particularly in relation to the perichoretic idea. First, with regard to the first objection, coming from Peters and Kilby, about the status of the doctrine of the Trinity and perichoresis as a second-order symbol and a second-order grammar of faith, I find such objections unsound. The second objection made by McDougall and Peters, but especially the latter, is more serious. However, positing itself at the other extreme of Fedorov's stance, Peters' claim seems to be unrealistic and theologically problematic. Volf has helped me to demonstrate the possibility of finding corresponding aspects between the Triune and human communities.

In the next two sections I need to give more attention to two other fundamental issues that need clarification. First, I discuss the metaphor of dance, with special attention to Catherine LaCugna's understanding of *theologia* and *oikonomia*. Second, I need to highlight the third criterion as referred to above, that any correspondence between the Trinitarian and human communities is to be framed within an eschatological portrait of God's embrace of creation and the participation of human beings and all creation in God's life. Here, special attention is paid to Richard Kearney's idea of the possible God.

The Perichoretic Dance and the Unity of *Theologia* and *Oikonomia*

One of the most attractive metaphors for perichoresis is that of dancing, in which Triune persons move together in an eternally harmonious and

135. Ibid., 109–17.

An Imaginative Glimpse

loving dance. Etymologically, the translation of the term *perichoresis* into dancing-around is incorrect. The word *perichoresis* is derived from the verb *perichōreō* ("to encompass," with a long o in the middle), not from the verb *perichoreuō* ("to dance around" or "to dance in a ring," with a short o in the middle). From the latter, the English word choreography derives. However, despite the etymological issue, to imagine perichoresis as dancing around is still engaging. LaCugna's picturesque description of the perichoretic dancing is worth quoting in full:[136]

> Even if the philological warrant for this [translation] is scant, the metaphor of dance is effective. Choreography suggests the partnership of movement, symmetrical but not redundant, as each dancer expresses and at the same time fulfills him/herself towards the other. In interaction and inter-course, the dancers (and the observers) experience one fluid motion of encircling, *encompassing*, permeating, enveloping, outstretching. There are neither leaders nor followers in the divine dance, only an eternal movement of reciprocal giving and receiving, giving again and receiving again. To shift metaphor for a moment, God is eternally begetting and being begotten, spirating and being spirated. The divine dance is fully personal and interpersonal, *expressing the essence and unity of God*. The image of the dance forbids us to think of God as solitary. The idea of *perichōrēsis* provides a marvelous point of entry into contemplating what it means to say that God is alive from all eternity as love.[137]

LaCugna seems to incorporate the original meaning of perichoresis into the metaphor of dancing in order to demonstrate the effectiveness of the metaphor of dance. It is in the divine dance that "the essence and unity of God" (person-perichoresis), characterized by "love" and "giving-receiving," is celebrated. Interestingly, I also find a fairly similar picture of the divine dance in Elizabeth A. Johnson, yet with more emphasis on the diversity of the dancers.

> Dancers whirl and intertwine in unusual patterns; the floor is circled in seemingly chaotic ways; rhythms are diverse; at times all hell breaks loose; resolution is achieved unexpectedly. Music, light and shadow, color, and wonderfully supple motion coalesce in dancing that is not smoothly predictable and repetitive, as is

---

136. The metaphor of dance is also used by many other theologians. See Duck and Wilson-Kastner, *Praising God*, 35–36; Boersma, "Feet of God," 67–96; Moltmann, *God in Creation*, 304–7; Panikkar, "Mysticism," 167.

137. LaCugna, *God for Us*, 272, italics mine.

Perichoretic Indwelling of and in the Triune God

a round dance, and yet is just as highly disciplined. Its order is more complex. Casting the metaphor in yet another direction, we can say that the eternal flow of life is stepped to the contagious rhythms of spicy salsas, merengues, calypsos, or reggaes where dancers in free motion are yet bonded in the music.[138]

Although Johnson's picturing of the perichoretic dance seems more dynamic and diversity-respecting than LaCugna's, the latter offers a much deeper explanation of perichoresis itself. LaCugna, moreover, does not stop short at the dance of person-perichoresis. Consistent with her main thesis about "the essential unity between *oikonomia* and *theologia*"—or in a revised version of Rahner's Rule: "Theology is inseparable from soteriology, and *vice versa*"—she enlarges the scope of the divine dance so much that the whole creation is included in it.[139] She writes, "The starting point in the economy of redemption, in contrast to intradivine starting point, locates *perichōrēsis* not in God's inner life but in the mystery of the one communion of all persons, divine as well as human. From this standpoint of 'the divine dance' is indeed an apt image of persons in communion: not for an intradivine communion but for divine life as all creatures partake and literally in it."[140]

The contrast between the economy of redemption and the Latin emphasis on intradivine relatedness is the core of LaCugna's project. Her quest is to recover the unity of *oikonomia* and *theologia* in the pre-Nicene Trinitarian theology. The struggle against Arianism made the church overemphasize the impassibility of God and ended up with the separation between *theologia* and *oikonomia*, with the focus on the former. Against such a mistake, LaCugna argues that *oikonomia* is not the Trinity *ad extra*, but "the comprehensive plan of God reaching out from creation to consummation, in which God and all creatures are destined to exist together in the mystery of love

---

138. Johnson, *She Who Is*, 220–21.

139. LaCugna, *God for Us*, 211. Johnson also emphasizes this aspect. Using the metaphor of a "triple helix" as an alternative to the Greek metaphor of a "straight line" and the Greek metaphor Western metaphor of a "triangle or circle," she writes that "the triple helix twirls around in a never ending series of moves, which includes human partners and their decisions for good or ill, toward the fullness of shalom for all creatures, human being and earth, especially the most discarded." Johnson, *She Who Is*, 221. The insertion of all creatures in Johnson's metaphor is more favorable than what we find in LaCugna. Mark Samuel Medley has correctly shown that "LaCugna reduces 'all the reality' to person and God . . . and focuses exclusively on human redemption to the diminishment of a cosmocentric focus." Medley, *Imago Trinitatis*, 73.

140. LaCugna, *God for Us*, 274.

An Imaginative Glimpse

and communion" and *theologia* is not the Trinity *in se*, but "the mystery of God."[141]

LaCugna believes that the spirit of the Christian belief in the Triune God can be reflected in the chiastic model of emanation and return, in which there is "the one dynamic movement of God, *a Patre ad Patrem*."[142] By still using the metaphor of dance, she explains this point clearly, "Everything comes from God, and everything returns to God, through Christ in the Spirit. This *exitus* and *reditus* is the choreography of the divine dance which takes place from all eternity and is manifest at every moment in creation. There are not two sets of communion—one among the divine persons, the other among human person, with the latter supposed to replicate the former. The one *perichōrēsis*, the one mystery of communion includes God and humanity as beloved partners in the dance."[143]

The inseparability of *oikonomia* and *theologia* is thus affirmed, but the question is whether they are distinguished. If there is no distinction, and the two collapse into strict identity, "it would mean that one could begin at the either end, from God or economy."[144] It seems, at first, that for LaCugna the distinction lies on the mystery of God. But, interestingly, LaCugna adds that "the mystery of God is the mystery of God *with us*."[145] The God she refers to is not an isolated God. The question now is what LaCugna means by "mystery." She maintains that God is a mystery because God is ineffable, and God's ineffable mystery is found both in *theologia* and *oikonomia*. "*The economy of salvation is as ineffable as is the eternal mystery of God (theologia)*."[146] Also, "trinitarian theology can never exactly specify the character of that mystery except to say: It is the mystery of God and therefore it exceeds comprehension and formulation."[147] LaCugna furthermore bases the incomprehensibility or ineffability of the mystery of God on the notion of "person," which is by definition "an ineffable mode of existence, an elusive presence, a unique expression of a nature."[148]

In short, the mystery of God is not what distinguishes *theologia* from *oikonomia*, because both *theologia* and *oikonomia* reflect the mystery of

141. Ibid., 223.
142. Ibid., 223.
143. Ibid., 274.
144. Kärkkäinen, *Introduction*, 188.
145. LaCugna, *God for Us*, 223–24, italics mine.
146. Ibid., italics hers.
147. Ibid., 321.
148. Ibid., 323–24.

God.¹⁴⁹ In my interpretation, LaCugna's central idea is reflected through her book's title, *God for Us*. The mystery of God becomes the horizon of our relationship with God, which is embracing us yet always beyond us. The horizon of God's mystery remains transcendent and does not drain itself although it always comes to and for us. God is still the other for us and yet is always near us.¹⁵⁰ In LaCugna's own words: "God's presence to us does not exhaust without remainder the absolute mystery of God."¹⁵¹ The "remainder" of God's mystery is what I see as the surplus or excess in God's loving directedness toward creation, which saturates us without draining out itself.¹⁵²

Fully agreeing with LaCugna's main theological ideas, I nevertheless suggest that the relation between *theologia* and *oikonomia* needs to be re-interpreted or, more precisely, re-amplified by using a more eschatological perspective. Ted Peters finds a similar problem in LaCugna when he says that what is missing in LaCugna's theology is the temporality of God. "If the internal relationship of the divine life is tied to the course of world history as LaCugna seems to believe it is, then one would expect some investigation into the possible temporal dimension of God's life."¹⁵³ In the following section, I discuss the eschatological dimension of reality-perichoresis. Along with this temporal dimension, I also need to discuss the spatial dimension of perichoresis. I argue that, if both temporality and spatiality are correctly affirmed in the notion of reality-perichoresis, the "otherness" of creation from God will warrant our attempt to emphasize the ideas of difference and freedom in creation.

Time, Space, and Freedom: Eschatology of the Possible God

Many theologians have critically accepted Rahner's Rule. While they agree with the first part of the rule, that the economic Trinity is the immanent

---

149. That is why Kärkkäinen argues that there is on this matter an ambiguity in LaCugna's argument as a whole; see Kärkkäinen, *Introduction*, 187–93. Kärkkäinen, however, concludes that LaCugna's program has collapsed the immanent Trinity into the economic Trinity because of LaCugna's methodological starting point (human experience).

150. LaCugna equates "nearness" with immanence and "otherness" (not "remoteness") with transcendence; see LaCugna, *God for Us*, 322.

151. LaCugna, *God for Us*, 228.

152. cf. Volf, "Trinity," 108.

153. Peters, *God as Trinity*, 128; cf. Groppe, "Contribution," 752.

An Imaginative Glimpse

Trinity, many theologians are critical of the *vice versa* clause. D'Costa and Moltmann, whom I have discussed, are examples of such theologians. They advise accepting that the economic Trinity is the immanent Trinity, but without simultaneously accepting that the immanent Trinity is the economic Trinity. For both theologians, the eschatological characteristic of the economy of salvation cannot allow them to conflate the immanent and the economic Trinity.

For Moltmann, it is the glorification through the Spirit in the future that we find God as "the making-possible of the possible." At that time, God will be all in all—God in all and all in God. The question for Moltmann is whether God will stop being the making-possible of the possible when the possible is already actualized in the future. Moltmann does not give any clue as to the answer of this question except when he suggests the ideas of the "eternity filled with time" and "world without end" as the picture of the perichoretic relation between eternity and time.[154] Thus, temporality will always be assumed within God's inner life. If this is correct, I would argue, the temporal existence of possibility would be preserved *within* reality-perichoresis. Therefore, we might use Moltmann's terms to say that the temporal possibility puts its impress on God's life.

This more radical way of seeing God in light of possibility is similar to and extended by Richard Kearney's groundbreaking proposal of "the God who may be" or "the possible God."[155] Kearney argues that God as the possible is the best alternative to God as being and nonbeing. He begins his book by stating his thesis clearly, "God neither is nor is not but may be."[156] By taking the primacy of the *eschatological* way of interpreting God over the *onto-theological* one, Kearney suggests that the God who may be enables us to be open to the promise of God so that not only are we transfigured by transcendence but also so that we have the capacity to transfigure God,

---

154. Moltmann, *Coming of God*, 295; Moltmann, "God's Kenosis," 151.

155. Kearney, *God Who May Be*. Kearney maintains that a similar emphasis on the "futural potentiality of God" can be found in theological works of Jürgen Moltmann, liberation theology, Whitehead, and process theology; see Kearney, *God Who May Be*, 123. A special attention needs to be paid to a process theologian, Lewis S. Ford, especially in his two books, *Lure of God* and *Transforming*. In the former book, for example, he explains his idea that God's presence is derived from his nontemporality. Yet, out of the past, which God receives from the world, God creates a new future so that God transform his pure possibilities into real or realizable possibilities. Thus, for Ford, God is "a nontemporal actuality who influences us by the future he now creates; by means of the real possibilities he persuades the world to actualize." Ford, *Lure of God*, 40.

156. Kearney, *God Who May Be*, 1.

Perichoretic Indwelling of and in the Triune God

that is, "by making divine possibility ever more incarnate and alive."[157] Kearney radicalizes the mutuality between God and creation so that not only do humans depend on God, but God also depends on humans. When asking whether a new heaven and a new earth is possible, he says, "It is not impossible for God if we help God to become God."[158] Also, "God may henceforth be recognized as someone who *becomes with us*, someone as dependent on us as we are on Him."[159] Despite the insights that he offers, I disagree with his conception of a symmetrical interdependency between God and creation. Criticisms by O'Leary[160] and Westphal[161] have cogently addressed this problem.

The mutually transfiguring relation is called *persona*, which is for Kearney another word for "the otherness of the other," but here he infuses it with an aura of eschatological possibility. He furthermore proposes the idea of *possest* (as a compound term of *posse* and *esse*), which he borrows from Cusanus, to be the most proper name for the possible God. *Possest* can be best translated as "possibility-to-be" or "actualized-possibility."[162] The idea of *possest*—here, Kearney makes his wager—is much closer to the God of the Bible than that of the metaphysics and scholasticism, because the possible God "is passionately involved in human affairs and history[;] . . . promises to bring life and to bring it more abundantly."[163] This is the God whose name is neither "I am who am" nor "I am who am not" but "I am who may be."[164]

In this sense, I see a close relationship between Kearney's God who may be and LaCugna's ineffable mystery of God. God is the ineffable mystery because who God is, is still to come. Kearney's idea of the possible God also reminds us of Moltmann's idea that it is only in the future that God will be all in all. The similarity between Kearney and Moltmann is also clear in their use of spatial language as a complement to the temporal language of the future.

Moreover, the eschatological perspective makes it possible for Kearney to elaborate the idea of persona more deeply. In the eschatological persona,

---

157. Ibid., 2.
158. Ibid., 111.
159. Ibid., 29–30.
160. O'Leary, "Questions."
161. Westphal, "Hermeneutics."
162. Kearney, *God Who May Be*, 103.
163. Ibid., 2.
164. This is Kearney's attempt to translate the inaugural name of the God of Exodus 3:14 (*'ehyeh 'asher 'ehyeh*); see Kearney, *God Who May Be*, 20–38.

An Imaginative Glimpse

futurity and alterity are so conjoined that the other is irreducible just as the future is ungraspable. Yet, the idea of persona enables us to imagine what Kearney calls "the eschatological universality of the Other" that is conceived in terms of "a possible co-existence of unique *personas*."[165] Interestingly, Kearney tries to explain this idea by drawing from the perichoretic image of "differing *personas*, meeting without fusing, communing without totalizing, discoursing without dissolving[,] . . . a no-place which may one day be and where each *persona* cedes its place to its other (*cedere*) even as they sit down together (*sedere*)."[166] Perichoresis is an eschatological game, in which we find ourselves as players, "a game which we cannot master since its possibles are always beyond our possibles . . . a game that knows no end-game, no stalemate, whose ultimate move is always still to come."[167] Moreover, Kearney's perichoresis echoes Moltmann's idea that creation can put its impress on God's inner life.

> We don't *have* to dance. And the eschatological dance cannot be danced without two partners. To respond to the song of the Creator is to hear the Word which promises a possible world to come, a second creation or recreation of justice and peace, a world which the divine *posse* is always ready to offer but which can come about only when humanity says yes by joining the dance, entering the play of ongoing genesis, transfiguring the earth. God cannot become fully God, nor the Word fully flesh, until creation becomes a "new heaven and a new earth."[168]

The image of perichoresis brings a richer spatial connotation when Kearney relates it to the classical term of *khora*, the root word of perichoresis. For Kearney, perichoresis is a fascinating image of the kingdom where lack and fullness in both God and humanity meet. In this sense, any closed economy is refused. "It never closes. The economy is still bubbling, is still flowering, is still bursting into life. . . . The *perichoresis* is the dance-around the *khôra*. Peri-chôra."[169] Kearney moreover interprets perichoresis as an image through which "there is a double movement of immanence and transcendence; of distantiation and approximation. Of moving *toward* each other and the moving *away* from each other—as in a dance."[170]

165. Kearney, *God Who May Be*, 15.
166. Ibid.
167. Ibid., 109–10.
168. Ibid., 110.
169. Kearney, "Philosophizing," 57.
170. Ibid.

Perichoretic Indwelling of and in the Triune God

Obviously, the spatial image of perichoresis plays a significant role in expressing Kearney's idea of the possible God and its relation to human participation. There must be "a free space gaping at the very core of divinity: the space of the possible."[171] What is the free space that Kearney talks about? Is it the same as *khora*, around which the divine and creation dance together? I suggest it is. How does he understand the word *khora*?

Kearney discusses the notion of *khora* in conversation with Derrida, Caputo, Kristeva, Žižek, and others. The first two thinkers receive his particular attention. Kearney criticizes the deconstructionist approach of *khora* utilized by Derrida and Caputo, in that they make a strict division between God and *khora*. This radical distinction "prevents us from seeing *khora* as an open site of originary possibilities."[172] Against the backdrop of Caputo's and Derrida's either/or solution, Kearney suggests a third alternative between *khora* and *hyperousia*; that is, the possible God. He insists that "there are many degrees of latitude between the North Pole of God (qua pure hyperessence) and the South Pole of *khora* (qua anonymous abyss)."[173] Within the third alternative of the possible God, *khora* is not rejected at all. Instead, it is considered as "neither identical with God nor incompatible with God but marks an open site where the divine may dwell and heal."[174]

Kearney's idea of the possible God is important for my project. However, I want to make it clear that I am reinterpreting Kearney's idea of the possible God away from the idea that God is *less* than traditionally supposed and toward the idea that God is *more* than traditionally supposed—in particular, that there must be more in God than we know. To understand God through the perspective of possibility is important, since we cannot have an absolute certainty of who God is. The acceptance of what is more in God (the divine surplus or excess) enables us to reconstruct our attitude toward religious others. We can never have the final word on salvation, because the gracious God is always a step ahead of us and surprises us. Yet, I argue that the human experience of the surprising God can occur only in the perichoretic relation.

Thus, my reinterpretation of Kearney's idea is characteristically epistemological and theological. With regard to the former, I reinterpret the idea of the possible as the recognition of human inability to grasp the divine fully. With regard to the latter, I shift the *locus* of possibility from "the core of

---

171. Kearney, *God Who May Be*, 4.
172. Rundell, "Imaginings," 105.
173. Kearney, *Strangers*, 208.
174. Ibid., 194.

An Imaginative Glimpse

divinity" (Kearney) to the perichoretic relation between the divine and the creaturely. I am not ready to adopt the whole of Kearney's idea of "God who may be," or the possible God, since it would jeopardize the coherence of my whole project. I find it impossible to hold the image of the possible God within my larger program. In short, the possible is one of several dimensions of perichoresis; it is not the "name" of God. If this reinterpretation is acceptable, the possible needs not to be seen as an alternative to being and *khora*, as suggested by Kearney. On the contrary, it is one among many dimensions of perichoresis alongside being and *khora*.

Moreover, Kearney is correct in relating *khora* to the notion of perichoresis. Within the Trinitarian framework that I accept, the role of *khora* is significantly important in emphasizing the dimension of the abyss of the Triune God, the space which is not abandoned by the Triune God but rather is embraced through the divine dance. Here, Kearney's spatial image of perichoresis provides an imaginative stage on which the divine-human dance can occur. We can maximize the spatial image to strengthen the idea of human participation *in* the Triune life, which at the same time distinguishes the nature of person-perichoresis and reality-perichoresis. In person-perichoresis, we can say that the divine persons indwell in each other so perfectly that there is mutual interiority in each other. In the latter, in contrast, we must argue that the finite beings—humans and the world—limitedly indwell in the divine life as well as in each other. Volf correctly points out this issue by saying that "the Spirit indwells human persons, whereas human beings by contrast indwell the *life-giving ambience of the Spirit*, not the person of the Spirit."[175]

There are two important issues at play. First, Volf employs a more pneumatocentric language to maintain the perichoretic participation of human beings (and creation) in the divine life. This approach is quite different from the traditional Christocentric approach, in which human beings and creation participate through and in the Son. My argument is that we do not need to choose one of the two approaches. Rather, we can employ the Irenaean metaphor of the two hands of God and argue that it is both in the Spirit and in the Son, by way of their perichoretic interiority, that we participate in the Triune life. Thus, in this sense, we must argue that the Son *is* what Volf calls "the life-giving ambience." If this is acceptable, we can still use Hodgson's proposal to revise Panikkar's cosmotheandric reality and rename reality-perichoresis as theo-cosmic-pneumatic (see chapter 3).

---

175. Volf, *After Our Likeness*, 211.

Second, to support his idea of the "life-giving ambience" of the Spirit, Volf quotes Jesus' prayer in John 17:21, "as you, Father, are in me and I am in you, may they also be *in us*." Volf correctly observes that the prayer does not end with "may they also be *in one another*." It seems that Volf is mistaken in using the prayer to limit human participation in the divine life, since the phrase "may they also be in us" emphasizes the possibility of human participation in reality-perichoresis, while the phrase "may they also be in one another," which is not in the prayer, refers to the mutual indwelling of human beings (society-perichoresis).

To conclude, it is clear that we find an intertwining of temporal and spatial imageries inherent in Kearney's idea of the possible God. Similar appreciation of the spatial and temporal dimension of the Triune God within the historical economy is also demonstrated by Moltmann. Traditionally, temporality and spatiality are viewed as inherent features of the finitude of creation. Religious tradition also emphasizes that God cannot be determined by time and space: God is always beyond time and space. However, the idea of the Triune God to which I subscribe is one that determines Godself and assumes what is not God, or spatial and temporal creation, into Godself. This notion, therefore, tries to maintain a balance between the contingency and freedom of creation. Creation is always contingent on its Creator, yet precisely by being dependent on the Triune God does creation always experience freedom as the result of the divine love.

Recapitulation

In this chapter, I have attempted to discuss the idea of perichoresis by learning from different sources and traditions. It is obvious that the notion of perichoresis provides a tremendous opportunity to relate the Christian belief in the Triune God to the whole of creation. We have seen that the Greek church fathers set up the discursive framework through three interrelated forms of perichoresis: nature-perichoresis (the interpenetration of two natures of Christ), person-perichoresis (the mutual indwelling of the three persons of the Trinity), and reality-perichoresis (the perichoretically mutual relation between God and creation). However, when the non-divine nature is involved, as is found in nature-perichoresis and reality-perichoresis, the fathers emphasize the asymmetrical characteristic of perichoresis, in which the divine always becomes the one who takes the initiative. The result is what the fathers call *theosis* or deification, through which creation is enabled to participate fully in the divine life. Perichoretic participation, however, never

An Imaginative Glimpse

diminishes the limitations of creation, which is characterized by temporality and spatiality. Rather, the temporality and spatiality of creation are assumed by the divine in order for creation to receive its fulfillment.

My discussion of the notion of perichoresis in the modern period demonstrates its function as what Harold H. Oliver calls the "*omnium gatherum* of quite unrelated theological loci."[176] In Moltmann, we find this function operates well in gathering issues including Christology, pneumatology, cosmology, eschatology, etc. My project is intended precisely to insert theology of religion as another locus in the category of perichoresis. Borrowing from the Greek fathers, Jürgen Moltmann further develops the perichoretic idea through his notion of the open Trinity. The Trinity, which for Moltmann is a community of three persons, is a third alternative to monotheism and tritheism. Trinitarianism is signified by the centrality of love and freedom reflected in the entire trinitarian history of God, from creation to consummation. In each moment of God's economy—creation, incarnation, and consummation—the Triune persons work together throughout the historical trajectory of the past, present, and future. There are two distinctive characteristics in which the relation between the Trinity and creatures is maintained. First, using the Lurianic Kabbalist traditions of zimzum and Shekinah, the world is seen as residing in God and God in the world. This panentheistic perspective enables Moltmann to explore to a great extent the possibility of creation's participation in God's inner life. Second, as the result of this panentheistic view, Moltmann allows creation to puts its impress on God's life. The underlying principle that Moltmann tries to emphasize is that the Trinity is an open and non-exclusive communion embracing the whole creation into God's Triune life. Thus, the emphasis on reality-perichoresis seems to be a logical consequence of person-reality. Yet, Moltmann can still maintain the asymmetrical nature of mutual reality-perichoresis. This asymmetry tells us that God always takes the initiative in the perichoretic relation between the divine and creation.

The problem appears when Moltmann, followed by other social Trinitarians, attempts to apply the notion of perichoresis to the extra-Trinitarian or human reality (society-perichoresis). While we cannot reject this attempt by arguing from the symbolic and second-order nature of the Trinity, as Kilby and Peters have tried to do, we really must consider seriously another objection by Peters and McDougall, based on the ontological difference between the divine and creation. To answer the last objection, Volf offers an interesting middle way between Boff's confidence in the possibility of

---

176. Oliver, *Metaphysics*, 61.

copying God and Peters' skeptical position countering the former. I agree with Volf's argument that we can copy God *in some respects* for constructing a social and human community. However, the main focus of my project is as much on society-perichoresis as on reality-perichoresis. While the latter is my central concern, I still need to deal with the former concern when I arrive at the ethical implications of my model.

Using the metaphor of dance, LaCugna and others seek to emphasize the communal, dynamic, and open characteristic of perichoresis. More specifically, LaCugna's treatment of perichoresis in the context of her identification of *theologia* and *oikonomia* is important. Although there is no need to follow LaCugna's *exitus-reditus* pattern, her attempt to recover the separation between *theologia* and *oikonomia*, or the immanent Trinity and the economic Trinity, is consistent with Moltmann's Trinitarian history of God, as well as with my vision of the perichoretic participation of all creation. Of importance here is LaCugna's emphasis on the mystery of God, not only in *theologia* but also in *oikonomia*. It enables us to underline the ecstatic nature of God's embrace of creation without losing God's mystery. The ineffable mystery of the Triune God always reminds us that there is more in God; there is always a surplus or excess in God's love toward creation.

I have also attempted to relate the ineffable mystery of the Triune God to the idea that we experience the fullness or plenitude of God in the eschatological sense. We experience epistemologically the fullness of God always in a "may-be" mode. Also, possibility as a dimension of perichoresis suggests that God in the future saturates creation with all possibilities that we can imagine (of course without contradicting what we have experienced in the Trinitarian economy of salvation).

We have also found the benefit of using temporal and spatial images of perichoresis. Even more, perichoresis—*peri-khora*—itself is a spatial image, in which we can maintain dialectically the notions of communion and otherness, closeness and distance, dynamic movement and static sitting-together. By maintaining such dialectic notions we can find the value accorded to freedom by the idea of perichoresis.

5

A Perichoretic Theology of Religions

Beyond Panikkar, D'Costa, and Heim

IN CHAPTERS 2 AND 3, I DISCUSSED THREE MODELS OF TRINITARIAN THEOLogy of religions proposed by Raimundo Panikkar, S. Mark Heim, and Gavin D'Costa. I also demonstrated that those models share at least two fundamental similarities. First, they all maintain the dialectic between universality and particularity rather than attempting to put an end to it. They exercise this dialectic in two parallel ways: through rejecting pluralistic theology insofar as it attempts to absolutize itself and to superimpose its truth on other particularities, *and* through arguments in support of the possibility of making universal truth-claims without abandoning the particularity of their own traditions. To do so, they make the Christian truth-claim based on the doctrine of the Trinity.

Second, they also respect the auto-description of other religions. They argue that a true theology of religions must be characterized by a willingness to understand other religions on their own terms. These two similarities can be summarized in two inseparable characteristics necessary to any robust Christian theology of religions: commitment to the Christian faith *and* openness to other religious truths.

While I am in basic agreement with the three theologians in defending these two characteristics, I have also criticized certain aspects of their models. I must remind the reader, however, that my critiques rest on two different levels: epistemological and theological. On the epistemological level, I disagree with Panikkar's flight from theoretical possibility and agree with the point emphasized by both D'Costa and Heim: any theology of religions must be supported by a particular theory. Regardless of my dissension from D'Costa's latest movements in an exclusivist direction, he is correct to warn us of the dangers of conceptualizing other religions within the Christian framework. From D'Costa's perspective, Heim's and Panikkar's constructive attempts to bring multiple religions into the Trinitarian framework are clearly unacceptable. Viewed from the non-absolutist perspective, however, Heim's and Panikkar's proposals are nonetheless commendable as two creative and imaginative ways of enfleshing the spirit of radical openness to other religions. Each shows its universal intent, yet does not lose its particular perspective.

This way of reading Heim and Panikkar is in line with my own proposal, which suggests a modest approach to theology of religions. In such an approach, any possible conceptualization is always guided by "an imaginative glimpse." This type of approach also allows us to construct a Trinitarian framework that embraces all religions by means of an internally complex structure, without demanding total confidence or certainty concerning its account or interpretation. Furthermore, its modesty is also obvious from the fact that the method of appropriation is not considered to be the *primary* way of dealing with other religions. Any attempt to accommodate multiple religions in a Trinitarian model is only *secondary* in importance, and symbolic in character. This is to say that the modest approach I develop warrants its universal openness and particular situatedness through the concept of perichoresis itself.

If this approach is acceptable, it can be seen not only as an alternative to Heim's and Panikkar's, but also as a contribution to the never-ending celebration of the richness of divine plenitude or excess. The idea, I believe, can still sustain a universal dimension. In this regard, Heim's orientational pluralism is helpful in emphasizing the universality of the Trinitarian faith. Yet, such a universal claim must also be non-absolutist and perspectival at the same time.

The perichoretic approach is non-absolutist in the sense that we have to pay respect to other religious traditions on their own terms. It is perspectival in that it starts from an explicitly Christian standpoint. One cannot make a neutral claim from a God's-eye perspective. In my personal context, my particular perspective has to guide me in talking about my faith, my attitude toward the religious other, and my personal perception of the whole of reality itself. At the same time, my personal perspective has not been made entirely explicit in this book. Yet, this does not mean that the project is non-perspectival. Although my social situatedness has influenced the proposal, my concern with the universal value of this project should be apparent. I will delve into this issue more deeply—especially in relation to the concept of personal and Christological hybridity—below.

Even though non-absolutist perspectivism can be found in Panikkar, Heim, and D'Costa, it is in Heim's orientational pluralism that this position receives its greatest support. Orientational pluralism provides a solid basis for maintaining the balance between particularistic and universalistic truth-claims. Treated alone, however, Heim's orientational pluralism is too static. It fails to provide a rich soil for building mutual interaction between different religious traditions. Thus, I have argued that Heim's orientational pluralism ought to be combined with Schrag's transversal rationality. The latter theory allows a more dynamic and relational communication among different traditions. According to this theory, the ultimate goal for any dialogue, including interreligious dialogue, is best expressed through Schrag's statement: "a convergence without coincidence, an interplay without synthesis, an appropriation without totalization, and a unification that allows for difference."[1]

What we need to attain this goal, I believe, is a theological category having within itself the capacity to embrace all reality and make room for all ultimacies promoted by all religious traditions. My thesis is that the concept of perichoresis best serves such a goal. It allows differences to converge into a complex reality without being conflated or unified into an overly simplistic theory.

Theologically, as I showed in chapter 3, I disagree most with D'Costa's crypto-exclusivist standpoint and find many insights in Panikkar's and Heim's models. Why then do I suggest perichoresis as the central category, instead of merely accepting Panikkar's cosmotheandric model of Heim's multiple religious ends model?

Panikkar's cosmotheandrism is similar to the idea of reality-perichoresis, in which the whole of reality—God and creation—are interrelated with each other. Panikkar often employs the term perichoresis to express cosmotheandric reality, using both interchangeably. Nonetheless, Panikkar tends to diminish the asymmetrical nature of perichoresis. His perichoresis is implausible for me because he believes that the divine *needs* the human and the cosmic. "There is no God without Man and the World. There is no Man without God and the World. There is no World without God and Man."[2] According to Panikkar, cosmotheandric reality is bigger than the divine, since God is part of it. Conversely, influenced by Moltmann's panentheism,

---

1. Schrag, *Resources*, 158–59.
2. Quoted in Raj, *New Hermeneutic*, 86; cf. Panikkar, *Dwelling Place*, 72.

A Perichoretic Theology of Religions

I understand reality-perichoresis as the result of person-perichoresis, in which the Trinitarian God—whose nature is love—gives others (creation) the possibility of participating within Godself. God, through God's love, determines and empties Godself in order for creation to exist and live within the divine life.

My second problem with Panikkar concerns his theological method, in which each person of the Trinity is appropriated to different religious traditions. Buddhism is the religion of the Father; Judaism, Christianity, and Islam are the religions of the Son; Hinduism is the religion of the Spirit. This method is problematic in light of the classical notion that the *ad extra* works of the Trinity are undivided (*opera trinitatis ad extra sunt indivisa*).

Nevertheless, apart from these two issues, Panikkar's grand vision of cosmotheandric reality is similar to my own understanding of reality-perichoresis. However, I suggest replacing the term "cosmotheandric" with Hodgson's "theo-cosmic-pneumatic," in which the cosmic—including humanity—is united in the Son. This term also expresses more clearly and consistently the relation between person-perichoresis and reality-perichoresis.

Mark Heim sees the problem with Panikkar's method of appropriation and follows the classical doctrine that the persons of the Trinity are undivided in their works *ad extra*. Yet he fails to give up the appropriation method. Undoubtedly, the method of appropriation is a powerful means by which to address the diversity of religions. Heim maintains the unity of the three persons and shifts the appropriation to the "dimensions of relation" of the Trinity. While this innovative approach is commendable, as has already been shown, I agree with Flett's critique that Heim's approach does not require the three persons.[3]

My proposal is to use the notion of perichoresis as the central category for theology of religions. Unlike Heim's model, however, this perichoresis-centered model does not consider the appropriation method the primary means of respecting people from other religious traditions. The danger of using the appropriation method in the interreligious context is that it can lead easily to the totalization of other religious *systems* and of *people* from other religious traditions. In allocating each member of the Trinity to different religions, theologians usually employ a very specific religious category such as "spirituality" (Panikkar) or "religious end" (Heim), and then attempt to link each of the Triune persons (Panikkar) or each of the dimensions in the Trinity (Heim) to a particular religion. It is by so doing that these religions are included within the Trinitarian framework. No matter how wide

---

3. Flett, "In the Name," 10.

the inclusion is, "what is included from a religion being engaged with, is not that religion *per se*, but a reinterpretation of that tradition in so much that which is included is now included within a different paradigm."[4] However helpful and promising the appropriation method is, there is always a danger of totalization of other religious systems.

Totalization can also occur toward people from other religious traditions. When a totalization of a religious system happens, the adherents of that particular religion are right to reject the appropriated version of their religion as the only picture available to them. In fact, the historical nature of world religions suggests that any religion must experience pluralization due to many factors. We cannot say, for instance, that the Islam that I discuss represents all of the Islamic schools or all Muslims throughout the world. Such generalizations do injustice not only to Islam as a religious system but also to each Muslim, who deals with her/his Muslim identity in light of her/his historical situatedness.

The application of perichoresis to multiple religions is also different from Heim's model. Heim focuses on the dimensions of the Trinity, one of which is perichoresis. In my model, perichoresis becomes the focus that has in itself multiple dimensions corresponding to different religious ultimacies. By employing the doctrine of perichoresis as the central category, and suggesting a different method of appropriation, I may be criticized in much the same way as I have criticized Heim. My reply to such a critique would be twofold. First, the term perichoresis here signifies the classical doctrine that has been closely identified with the Trinity. Thus, even though my suggestion that perichoresis be applied to the issue of religious diversity is unprecedented, I claim that such perichoresis is still grounded in the Christian tradition in which it arose and developed. Second, while it is true that I propose my own version of applying or appropriating the dimensions of the Trinitarian perichoresis to different religions, I am still open to other alternatives, such as those proposed by Panikkar and Heim (of course, while maintaining my critical distance from those proposals). The recognition of multiple models is possible precisely because we are faced with the complex reality of perichoresis arising out of the plenitude of God's surplus of grace toward creation. It must be acknowledged that one single model can hardly capture the depth of the riches of God's Triune life, even as we attempt to address the necessity of discerning the most plausible model.

My perichoretic model is also different from Heim's in that it perceives the relation between the divine and creation to be located not only

4. D'Costa, *Meeting of Religions*, 23.

A Perichoretic Theology of Religions

"in the end" but also "in the beginning" of creation. Moltmann's panentheism is of much help in demonstrating that the Trinity not only works *ad extra* in relation to the world but also, in the same time, *ad intra*, through the divine self-contraction that makes room for the whole universe to exist. While Heim concentrates on the religious ends, my model stresses the complex and multidimensional reality of perichoresis—or, more precisely, reality-perichoresis—in light of the continuation of God's economy in history. In this sense, we need to talk not only about multiple religious ends (as in Heim's model), but also about multiple religious beginnings. The idea of perichoresis, in combination with Moltmann's panentheistic *zimzum*, provides a basis for talking about both the beginning and end of all reality, including religious ultimacies.

Religions and Perichoretic Participation

One key, ever-recurring question in theology of religions concerns whether there is a deeper "sameness" under or beyond the diversity of religions, or "radical differences" among religions. Struggling with the same issue, Jeannine Fletcher points out that contemporary discourse in theology of religions has left us at an impasse between sameness and difference. Writing from the feminist perspective, she argues that, even in his proposal of multiple religious ends, Heim still employs "conceptual categories of 'the religions' as discrete wholes that can be set against the other for comparison."[5] Furthermore, she summarizes the problem of sameness and difference this way, "If all 'religions' are essentially the same, we cannot account for, appreciate, or learn from their differences. We miss the possibility for unfolding new affirmations about the overabundant mystery of God. If, on the other hand, each 'religion' is radically different, we lose the common ground necessary for real engagement. Again, we miss the possibility for unfolding new affirmation about God. The realization that neither total sameness nor radical difference works as the basis for real encounter with religious others underscores the failure in contemporary theologies of religious pluralism."[6]

Interestingly, Fletcher relates the issue of sameness and difference to "the possibility for unfolding affirmation about [the overabundant mystery of] God." She believes that the remedy for the impasse is to be found in "a new concept of identity . . . that might provide a framework for interreligious

---

5. Fletcher, *Monopoly*, 80.
6. Ibid., 81.

An Imaginative Glimpse

encounters that allows for conversation across difference without erasing particularity and distinctiveness."[7] Such a new concept of identity is that all human beings are hybrid. As much as I like her idea, which I incorporate into my own proposal, Fletcher's is too anthropocentric a concept. I will discuss further below the possibility of hybridity as a category that combines both the dialectic of the divine and human nature Jesus Christ in the Christian tradition and the multiplicity of particular contexts, in which one needs to engage seriously with that Christological dialectic. But, before discussing it, I need to explore the idea of perichoretic participation as the most important point of my proposal.

By making perichoresis the starting point of my theology of religions, I offer a different way of dealing with the issue of religious unity and difference. My argument is that the impasse of sameness and difference on the level of creatures can be answered satisfactorily if we relate it to the dialectic between unity and difference in the inner life of God. The idea of perichoresis maintains precisely such a dialectic within the scope of the divine communion. It is obvious that I do not approach the problem of "sameness and difference," but rather that of "unity and difference," in the Trinity. We must remember Moltmann's rejection of the notion of sameness applied to the Trinity. Although the Christian tradition in the West warrants us to talk about sameness in terms of substance, Moltmann argues that the unity of God cannot be found in the sameness of substance. Neither can the unity be found in the same divine subject, (cf Barth and Rahner). Neither approach—the same substance or the same subject—allows divine unity to be understood as "a *communicable* unity and as an *open, inviting unity, capable of integration.*"[8]

Perichoresis specifically refers to the unity of God, in which God is "a God *at one* with himself."[9] In other words, the one nature of God is nothing other than the perichoretic communion of the three persons.[10] From this perspective, perichoresis can answer the problem of unity and difference of multiple religions because of its ability to embrace creation without diminishing the diversity found in the world. In asserting the unity and difference within God's Triune life, perichoresis also highlights the way in which the whole of creation can participate freely in the perichoretic life of the Triune God. Reality-perichoresis, in short, is the logical implication

---

7. Ibid.
8. Moltmann, *Trinity*, 149–50.
9. Ibid., 150.
10. Fiddes, *Participating*, 77.

A Perichoretic Theology of Religions

of person-perichoresis. In adopting this perspective, I reject any argument that says that religions are simultaneously the same and different *because* the Triune God is also simultaneously the same and different. Such a direct "copying" is problematic, precisely because God and creation are radically different. The unity and difference within the Trinity, however, can shed light on the problem of sameness and difference of religions by utilizing the notion of perichoretic participation.

To be more precise, in perichoretic participation, the whole of creation, and all religions, participate in the Triune divine life. In saying this, I by no means superimpose the Christian narrative over other religions. Rather, this idea is consistent with my belief that any theology of religions must be simultaneously *perspectival, universal,* and *respectful* of other religions. Perichoresis, used in the context of theology of religions, is perspectival because it is certainly a Christian idea referring to the Christian understanding of the Triune God. It is universal in that it allows all reality to be embraced within the open communion of the Trinity. It respects other religions insofar as two requirements are fulfilled: the acknowledgment of the auto-descriptions of other religions *and* the emphasis on the freedom of people from other religious traditions to accept or reject God's invitation of salvation. The Trinity, in Vanhoozer's words, "far from being a *skandalon*, is rather the transcendental condition for interreligious dialogue, the ontological condition that permits us to take the other in all seriousness, without fear, and without violence."[11] While I have discussed the first two characteristics at length in the preceding chapters, the last characteristic needs deeper exploration.

I have so far argued that human beings and all creation participate in the space vacated by God's self-withdrawal. As Moltmann correctly points out, all acts of God are characteristically Trinitarian. God's self-withdrawal, which makes room for creation to exist, is also Trinitarian. Consequently, we must say that the vacated space resulting from such divine self-withdrawal takes place in the Triune communal life, in person-perichoresis.

Since there cannot be perichoresis—*peri-chora*—without *khora*, the vacated space, through which God creates everything, also takes place in *khora*. The vacated space, however, is not *khora* in its entirety. It is part of *khora*. For, if *khora* and the vacated space of creation are identical, we cannot but say that person-perichoresis (*peri-khora* of the Triune persons) is contained by the vacated space, and this idea would either lead to pantheism or make no theological sense at all. In other words, there must be more in *khora*, around which the three persons dance together. That part of *khora*,

11. Vanhoozer, "Trinity," 71.

An Imaginative Glimpse

which is not occupied by the vacated space of creation, remains to be the womb of mystery for all creatures. *Khora*, thus, is not God or against-God. It is the divine space, only through which the idea of perichoresis can make any sense. As Kearney says, *khora* is "neither identical with God nor incompatible with God but marks an open site where the divine may dwell and heal."[12] What concerns me now, however, is the dimension of *khora* as vacated space, out of which the universe is created and struggles for its final fulfillment. I will show in the next section that *khora* can also be seen as a dimension of perichoresis represented most fully by Buddhism, which I will discuss later.

The self-withdrawal, which results in the vacated space within God-self, implies God's willingness to give freedom to all created beings, so that God can have free relationships with them. Such free relationships between the Triune God and the elements of creation (reality-perichoresis) are the broadening of the loving communion among the three persons of the Trinity (person-perichoresis). Moltmann, once again, provides a helpful insight in connecting, through more spatial thinking, the inner freedom among the Triune persons and the freedom of creation. He maintains that all living beings have freedom only if there are free spaces. Ontologically those free spaces are located in the divine space. Perichoresis supplies the availability of the space, since in the perichoretic communion or the mutual indwelling, "every trinitarian Person is not merely *Person* but also *living space* for the two others. In perichoresis each Person makes himself 'inhabitable' for the two others, and prepares the wide space and the dwelling for the two others."[13]

If human freedom is ontologically linked to the free spaces, which are parts of the divine space given up by the Triune God in self-withdrawing and creating the universe, then whatever human beings decide with their freedom must take place in the perichoretic space, within the divine life. The freedom inherent in all human beings enables them to actualize their spiritual journeys to engage with what they perceive as the Ultimate. Thus, the reality of religious diversity demonstrates the multiplicity of religious experiences of the multiple ultimacies. Each religious experience can be an authentic engagement with its own ultimacy.

One of the fundamental meanings of having freedom in this perichoretic "milieu" is that human beings can freely say "No" to God's invitation. In this regard, Hans Urs von Balthasar suggests an illuminating insight. Describing the creature's No as the "wanting to be autonomous without acknowledging

---

12. Kearney, *Strangers*, 194.
13. Moltmann, *Experiences*, 318–19.

A Perichoretic Theology of Religions

its origin," he believes that the No of creation "must be located within the Son's all-embracing Yes to the Father, in the Spirit."[14] Balthasar's idea affirms what I have suggested so far: that the whole universe is created within the divine vacated space of God, and receives its freedom precisely by existing in that space. Balthasar continues, "Man's refusal was possible because of the trinitarian 'recklessness' of divine love, which, in its self-giving, observed no limits and had no regard for itself . . . within God's own self—for where else is the creature to be found?—and in the defenselessness of absolute love, God endures the refusal of this love; and, on the other hand, in the omnipotence of the same love, he cannot and will not suffer it."[15]

Thus, the possibility of creation to reject and say "no" to God exists in parallel with the superabundant love of the Triune God for creation; both are experienced in the vacated space within the perichoretic relation. Since the Son always becomes the mediator between God and the universe—meaning, the Son in the power of the Spirit always says "yes" to the Father, for the sake of the world—then creation can—and , it is to be hoped, will—say "yes" to God by accepting life as offered by the Son. This is to say that the "yes" and the "no" of creation are not wholly parallel. In Rahner's words, "every 'no' always derives the life which it has from a 'yes' because the 'no' always becomes intelligible only in light of the 'yes,' and not vice versa. Even the transcendental possibility of freedom's 'no' lives by that necessary 'yes.'"[16]

William Placher comes to a similar conclusion by saying that, "In the incarnation, the three show that there is always within God a space large enough for the whole world, and even all its sin: the Word's distance from the one he calls Father is so great that no one falls outside it, and the Spirit fills all that space with love."[17] The notion that "no one falls outside" perichoresis suggests that the creation's "no" occurs within the divine life, precisely because of the Triune "yes" to the world. For Placher, perichoresis implies *khora* as "a kind of space [that] lies within the triune God—a space potentially inclusive of the space of sinners and doubters—and yet this place is no dessert but a spiritual garden of mutual love and glorification."[18]

We might, however, extend Rahner's excellent comment by putting it in the context of religious diversity. In light of the multiple religious alternatives, I argue that the creation's answers to God are not simply binary, "yes"

14. Balthasar, *Theo-Drama*, 329.
15. Ibid.
16. Rahner, *Foundations*, 102.
17. Placher, *Triune God*, 155.
18. Ibid.

or "no." The Christian "yes" might present a "no" to other religions. Similarly, what Christians see as a "no" from other religions can be an authentic "yes" to God. This more complex range of answers, I believe, is still consistent with Rahner's overall understanding that freedom's "no" implicates the necessity of "yes." Moreover, the possibility of multiple "yeses"—which also implies the possibility of multiple "nos" from a particular perspective—reflects the superabundant excess of divine love and grace.[19]

Balthasar is correct to emphasize the fact that any answer to God is always done "within God's own self" and that it takes place "in a generous, Eucharistic availability that matches the limitless proportions of the divine nature," but I believe he is mistaken in saying that "the creature's No is merely a twisted knot within the Son's pouring-forth; it is left behind by the current of love."[20] This binary thinking generalizes all "no" answers as ones "left behind by the current of love." We need to imagine, on the contrary, that the excessive divine love is like a fountain flowing in many directions or currents.

To return to the metaphor of dance: the "no" answers from religious traditions may be seen as multiple dances inharmonious with the divine perichoretic dance. Yet, the creative fluidity and the dynamic possibility of the divine perichoresis, which allows all creation to participate in the divine dance, "consummates" those different dances into a much richer, more complex, and more beautiful dance. In the final dance—the eschatological consummation—each of those discordant dances must still be clearly recognizable, yet each is undanceable, so to speak, without being performed together with other dances, in the harmonious movements of the ultimate Dance. In this sense, perichoresis as the divine dance can be considered as a hybrid dance, in which the relation between the Triune God and creation (both the human and the cosmic) is fluid, dynamic, joyful, and full of possibility.

Both Placher and Balthasar locate the "withinness" of creation's perichoretic participation in the Son. I have also argued, using the metaphor of God's two hands, that the Son as *khora* is what Volf calls the "life-giving ambience of the Spirit." The Son is *he khora ton zonton*, the Container of the living.[21] Moreover, I will demonstrate below that we cannot appropri-

---

19. To be sure, we have to give space for what Rahner calls "a radical, subjective, resolute and definitive 'no' to God," or radical "mystery of evil," which is beyond the scope of this discussion. See Rahner, *Foundations*, 102–3.

20. Balthasar, *Theo-Drama*, 329–30.

21. Manoussakis informs about this statement inscribed in the monastery of *Khora*

A Perichoretic Theology of Religions

ate the Son as the principle of differentiation, nor the Spirit as the principle of unity. Rather, what I suggest is that we find both principles dialectically maintained within each of these members of the Trinity, and that the cooperative and perichoretic work of the Son and the Spirit creates a more dynamic relationship between difference and unity. It is in such a complex Christic-pneumatic relation (or cosmic-pneumatic relation, if *cosmos* is seen as existing in the Son) that the multiplicity of "yeses" or "noes" take place. It is also in such a complex relation that all "noes" from non-Christian religions become simultaneously "yeses," precisely through the "Yes" of the Son to the Father.[22] At the same time, although affirmed by the Son's "Yes," the "yeses" of other religions must be seen as different from the Christian "yes." They are different because each one refers to a different dimension of perichoretic participation. Such a dialetical idea is the consequence of the Triune God creating the world and giving all creatures freedom.

The central idea of my overall project may be succinctly stated as follows: There are multiple religious participations in reality-perichoresis. On the one hand, I cannot but employ particularly Christian languages (Trinity, perichoresis, or even participation) to express my perspectival standpoint with regard to the problem of religious diversity. On the other hand, each of the perichoretic participations is authentic on its own terms. In other words, to say that all religious traditions partake in reality-perichoresis is already to use a Christian language. It must also be clear by now that the multiple perichoretic participations of religions, from the Christian perspective, occur through the two hands of God, the Son and the Spirit. The Son is the ambience or container of creation, while the Spirit is the life-giving power that enables creation to participate in the divine life, in and through the Son. Nonetheless, at the same time, such Christian language and perspective does not preclude the multiple traditions from demonstrating their uniqueness and particularities insofar as their participations in the different dimensions of perichoresis are consistent with their own auto-descriptions.

In this study, I have also demonstrated some fundamental characteristics of perichoresis. First, perichoresis basically points to the unity of all reality, which can be referred to as reality-perichoresis or theo-cosmic-pneumatic reality. Second, perichoresis also opens the possibility for creation to

---

in Istanbul; see Manoussakis, *God after Metaphysics*, 92; cf. Ousterhout, *Architecture*, 74. Christ, according to Manoussakis, is "par excellence the *khora* that receives both humanity and creation in their entirety, but with no confusion, in His incarnate person." Manoussakis, *God after Metaphysics*, 92.

22. Fiddes, *Participating*, 289.

An Imaginative Glimpse

participate within *khora*, the vacated space within Godself. Third, perichoresis suggests personal relationship among the Triune persons, as well as between the divine and the created. Fourth, perichoresis is fundamentally dynamic, and fluid, since it reflects the divine excess (plenitude, surplus, or superabundance), which opens up open-ended possibilities. Christians can claim *all* of these characteristics of perichoresis as a unity. Yet, it is also true that a particular characteristic becomes a single dimension that is best represented by a particular religious tradition. Moreover, when taken alone, such a particular perichoretic dimension might be more profoundly expressed or engaged with in other religion than in Christianity.

Three important notes need to be emphasized here. First, the conclusion that the fullness of perichoretic participation exists in the Christian tradition, while other religions partake in such participation in a more partial way, is unavoidable.[23] Second, this position does not necessarily entail a "superior" attitude. It rather extends an invitation to embrace otherness from within a particular perspective, i.e., the Christian belief in the Triune God. Third, consequently, Christians must also be open to any invitation from other religions, which offers a possibility to embrace systems other than their own. According to this view, Christians should welcome engagement with members of other religions who are willing to engage with them, even though such interaction means that Christian ultimacy may then become a partial dimension of another religion's universal framework.

We must be aware of the trap of the neutralism, often arising as a problem in pluralistic theologies, that seems to do justice to every religious tradition, yet hides an absolute norm that excludes consideration of other religious traditions on their own terms. The willingness to be embraced by others requires both a kenotic humility and a decision to let others be themselves. I will explore this idea through the metaphor of embrace in the last section of this chapter.

---

23. The fullness of Christian participation cannot be found in any particular Christian tradition, although the term "participation" itself is much closer to the Eastern tradition. Each tradition within Christianity might emphasize a particular dimension of perichoresis. For instance, the idea of unity of reality finds its basis in the Eastern tradition more than any other tradition. The mystical tradition emphasizes the absence of God similar to *khora* as no-place reality. The Western tradition puts much emphasis on personal and communal relations between the divine and the human. Finally, the struggle of liberation and humanization in certain strands of atheism echoes Third-World theologies.

Appropriating Perichoresis: An Imaginative Glimpse

I believe there can and must be more characteristics of perichoresis than those discussed here, which I have to leave for future investigation. The limited observations above, however, are sufficient to support the conclusion that perichoresis is the most plausible way of dealing with the issue of religious diversity. It allows us to maintain both commitment to the Christian faith in the Triune God and openness to other religious traditions. Although I believe that what I have thus far suggested is sufficient for emphasizing the importance of perichoresis for theology of religions, it will be challenging and interesting to see if we can move further, and appropriate the Trinitarian perichoresis for use with multiple religious traditions. In this section, I discuss such a possibility.

The appropriation method I employ is not intended as a fixed or precise description of the locations of religions in the perichoretic reality. Rather, it arises out of the recognition that any attempt to elucidate our engagement with the divine as the "revealed mystery" must be the result of human imagination, and will never be exhaustive. In short, the method points to what I have previously called "an imaginative glimpse" of the perichoretic appropriation of religions. The importance of imagination here is central. I agree with Mayra Rivera, who, following Gayatri Spivak, correctly states that "Theology cannot encompass the divine Other and yet, divine transcendence 'must be thought and must be thought through imagining.'"[24]

The term "glimpse" that I use implies two limitations of my proposal. First, I cannot claim absolute certainty concerning my own proposal. I can only see "the others" (both the divine Other and the religious other) from my limited perspective or insofar as they have revealed parts of themselves to me. They certainly relate to me (so that I am able to touch them), yet their beyond-ness always transcends me (so that I am unable to grasp them fully).[25] Second, my proposal can only hope to glimpse the perichoretic reality to come. Here, what I offer is a present foretaste of the fullness in the future, as St. Paul testifies in 1 Corinthians 13:12, "For now we see in a mirror, dimly, but then we will see face to face. Now I know only in part; then I will know fully, even as I have been fully known."

---

24. Rivera, *Touch of Transcendence*, 128.

25. This is the main thesis of Rivera, *Touch of Transcendence*. In this work, Rivera tries to interpret God's transcendence not as extra-cosmic or vertical but as relational or planetary.

An Imaginative Glimpse

Given these two limitations, I have to acknowledge that my proposal, or any other proposal, will always be tentative and inchoate, and that my suggestion must always be "vulnerable to correction," as Neville frequently says about the nature of any theological enterprise.[26] It is also from the same perspective that I treat other appropriation methods such as Panikkar's and Heim's as different alternatives that, in the end, can enrich each other.

The imaginative glimpse in the perichoretic theology of religions suggests that perichoresis (both as person-perichoresis and reality-perichoresis, through their dynamic relationship), has multiple dimensions, each of which corresponds to one or more different religious traditions. A particular dimension linked to a specific religion might also be found in other religious tradition, yet in a more undeveloped way. Since perichoresis is a specifically Christian notion, it is unavoidable that Christians might claim the fullest (or, perhaps, ultimate) understanding of the notion. When this is the case, other religions' systematic proposal will be considered penultimate. This does not mean, however, that Christians have adequately given their attention to multiple dimensions of perichoresis. It will be obvious later that some dimensions have not received enough consideration by Christians, while other religious people have strongly emphasized those dimensions.

Moreover, other religions might also present a similar claim to fullness or ultimacy when they find what Panikkar calls "homeomorphic equivalence" of perichoresis in their own religious systems that perform equivalent functions. In such a case, it would make sense if they argued for the decisiveness of their proposals compared to the Christian perichoresis. It is also possible that certain particular dimensions of perichoresis are equally important for two or more religious traditions. The religions that focus on those dimensions might compete with each other, but they might also be willing to put their different ultimacies into fruitful dialogue.

First Dimension: Unity of Reality

The first dimension of perichoresis is the unity of reality. It points to the unitive element of perichoresis, in which all reality, both divine and non-divine, are unified without diminishing each other. I find that the idea of non-dual unity in the Advaita tradition of Hinduism expresses this dimension to its fullest extent. The unity of all reality occurs because Atman is Brahman and Brahman is Atman. Many Christian theologians who work in

---

26. Neville, *Scope and Truth*, 105–9.

A Perichoretic Theology of Religions

Christian-Hindu dialogue suggest a direct appropriation of each person of the Trinity to the three different moments of Brahman-Atman.[27] According to this perspective, the Father refers to nirguna Brahman (Brahman without attributed qualities), the Son points to saguna Brahman (Brahman with attributed quality), and the Spirit corresponds to Atman. Similarly, a parallel can also be drawn between the Trinity in Christianity and in *saccidānanda* in Hinduism: the Father as *sat*, the Son as *cit*, and the Spirit as *ānanda*.

Although this is a compelling way of thinking, I suggest a revision employing the difference between person-perichoresis and reality-perichoresis, or in LaCugna's terms, between *theologia* and *oikonomia*. On the one hand, person-perichoresis or *theologia* refers to the mystery of the Triune God, which is ineffable yet always "the mystery of God *with us*."[28] In response to Advaita tradition, we might say that person-perichoresis or *theologia* as a unity resembles nirguna Brahman. Moreover, combined with the idea of the two hands of God, occurring in reality-perichoresis or *oikonomia*, I propose to follow what been said by Panikkar, Griffiths or Brück that the Son refers to saguna Brahman and the Spirit to Atman. There is always a relation between person-perichoresis and reality perichoresis, or between *theologia* and *oikonomia*, in which both make up the unity of reality characterized by non-duality.

This proposal, of course, needs deeper exploration. However, some advantages are obvious.[29] First, on the one hand, the proposal enables me to avoid the danger of monism in which all reality is seen as a singular entity called Brahman, since nirguna Brahman still refers to person-perichoresis. On the other hand, in considering the question of person-perichoresis, we can still say that the Father is the source or ground of all being, not in a direct

---

27. Brück, *Unity of Reality*; Griffiths, *Return*; Panikkar, *Religious Experience*.

28. LaCugna, *God for Us*, 224, italics mine.

29. The problem with my approach, however, is that it might not be a satisfying answer to the question of the one and the many. If the Nevillean perspective is employed here, one might reject my position by saying that nirguna Brahman is supposed to refer to the indeterminate One, while the Trinity points to God who determines Godself in the creating act. Since I adopt Moltmann's basic idea, that the one nature of God is nothing other than the perichoretic communion of the three Persons, my position cannot be used to explain the move from the indeterminate One to the many. This, I believe, is also one of some weaknesses in Moltmann's account. The best I can offer here is that my Trinitarian position (symbolized as "the Three") is the bridge between "the One and the Many," in which the ineffable mystery of the One can be found in the Father, in the inner or immanent relation of the Trinity (person-perichoresis). The broader issue of "the One, the Three, and the Many" obviously needs to be explored in future work.

manner, but through the Son and with the power of the Spirit. The mediating process of the Son and the Spirit, however, occurs in reality-perichoresis.

Second Dimension: Khora

Khora is the second dimension of perichoresis.[30] Without *khora* there is no perichoresis (*peri-khora*). The image of dance perfectly relates perichoresis to *khora*, since the dance takes place only in the space of *khora*. In this project, I have argued that *khora* refers to the space of the creation, vacated by the Triune divine through the act of self-contraction. It is the space around which the divine and creation dance harmoniously. *Khora* can thus be seen simultaneously as God's acts of limiting Godself and of embracing the world. From Moltmann's panentheistic point of view, both images suggest that *khora* exists within God's inner life, reflecting the freedom of creation as God's gift and relationality between God and creation. Here, paradoxically, God transcends the vacated space to the extent that it is possible that the created beings dwelling in the space have no direct relation with God.

On the other hand, from the Christian perspective of perichoresis, we can say that the divine remains involved in the vacated space without diminishing the freedom of creation. Here, the Spirit of God permeates all created reality. Alternatively, we can say that God dwells immanently in the vacated space through the power of the Spirit. The presence and act of the Spirit in *khora* can be illustrated by the analogy of air seeping into a porous sponge—an unseen presence.

I believe that *khora*, the dimension of the absence of God, is best represented both by Buddhist emptiness and some strands of atheism. My proposal is therefore different from both Panikkar's and Heim's. While Panikkar connects Buddhism to the first person of the Trinity by identifying it with the silence of the Father, Heim identifies Buddhism (as well as Advaita Hinduism) with the dimension of impersonal relations within the Trinity. More specifically, Heim utilizes, although not extensively, two images that are central in my model: perichoresis as the mutual-indwelling of the three persons of the Trinity *and* God's self-contraction. He suggests that the basic emptiness in Buddhism (and the total immanence in Hinduism) result from

---

30. Despite my indebtedness to Kearney's understanding of *khora*, I avoid a more philosophical analysis of *khora*. Please consult Charles P. Bigger's and John Sallis' philosophical works; see Bigger, *Chora*; Sallis, *Chorology*.

A Perichoretic Theology of Religions

the divine inner relation, "by which the divine persons indwell each other and make way for the others to indwell them."[31]

Moreover, God's self-contraction or withdrawal, for Heim, also implies emptiness as a "purposeful absence or a divine secret, in which God shields us from the blinding divine presence."[32] The centrality of *khora* as a dimension of perichoresis, explicit in these two images, is already present in Heim's model. Nor are these the only approaches in Christian-Buddhist dialogue with regard to the issue of ultimate reality. Robert Neville engages in a more comparative mode by correlating the classic contrasts of emptiness-form or nirvana-samsara *and* creation *ex nihilo*.[33] Another option is suggested by Nishida Kitarō, who compares the problem of knowledge in the Platonic *chora* and the Japanesse *basho*.[34] Finally, Masao Abe employs *kenosis* as the fundamental category for comparing emptiness and the Christian idea of the Triune God.[35]

My approach is different from all of these. By using *khora* as a dimension of perichoresis I suggest that Christians can now understand the Buddhist notion of emptiness more clearly. Even more, *khora* is the "space" within Godself, yet outside Godself in the same time, in which the authentic emptiness desired by Buddhism can take place more fully. In *khora* we find the dialectic between place and no-place,[36] and it is precisely the second aspect of *khora*—as no-place—to which the Buddhist emptiness corresponds. Klaus Held explicates clearly the idea of *khora* as emptiness by stating, "As this happening, the *chora* is objectively no different from that emptiness which is the world itself. Since complete inconspicuousness makes up the essence of this emptiness, it does not lend itself to any sort of comprehension. The absolutely inconceivable is appropriately designated as nothingness. This concept also plays a significant role in Western thought. Yet it is only in the East-Asian tradition that nothingness has been treated as that space-giving emptiness which is no mere lack of filling and is nothing other than the being of the world itself."[37]

Held's idea of *khora* as "space-giving emptiness" is similar to the Buddhist contrast between emptiness and form or nirvana and samsara. Neville

---

31. Heim, *Depth of the Riches*, 185.
32. Ibid., 189.
33. Neville, *Behind the Masks*, 85–106.
34. Yusa, *Zen and Philosophy*, 202–4.
35. Cobb and Ives, *Emptying God*.
36. Kearney, *Strangers*, 204.
37. Held, "World," 158.

succinctly summarizes the idea by saying, "[I]n the strange identity between emptiness and form, and nirvana and samsara, the latter terms, form and samsara, can be described in their own language, where the former terms are described by virtue of their relation to the others: emptiness is emptiness of form, and nirvana is blowing out the flame of samsara. Furthermore, despite the identity alleged by Mahayana Buddhism in each case, emptiness and nirvana are the more fundamental truths, and form and samsara by themselves are derivative and illusory without reference to emptiness and samsara."[38]

Neville's understanding that Buddhist form and samsara are contingent upon on emptiness and nirvana is clearly similar to Held's idea of *khora* as space-giving emptiness.

We can also see the relation between *khora* and Buddhist emptiness from the perspective of *kenosis*.[39] Moltmann is correct in showing that *kenosis* is appropriate not only for the Son, but also for all of three persons of the Triune God.[40] In my understanding, *khora* is the space vacated by God within Godself, a product of the divine self-limitation or self-emptying. While the centrality of incarnation as *kenosis* is always predominant, I agree with Moltmann that *kenosis* can also be seen in the Triune act of creating the world (*creatio ex nihilo*), after God's act of vacating Godself (*vacatio ex Deo*). In this sense, the classical idea that the world is created in and through the Son once again comes to the fore. Even more, it is safe to say that the Son *is* the product of creation in the triadic pattern of "source-product-creative act"[41] or "producer-product-producing."[42]

While Buddhism reflects one aspect of *khora*, the no-place, some strands of atheism emphasize the other aspect: *khora* as place of the world and humanity. Unlike Buddhists who make emptiness their ultimate goal

---

38. Neville, *Behind the Masks*, 100. Neville goes further by proposing that the contrast between emptiness and form, or nirvana and samsara, can be reinterpreted in terms of creation *ex nihilo*; see Neville, *Behind the Masks*, 100–101.

39. There are at least two compiled works that focus on Masao Abe's reflection on the Christian *kenosis* in light of the Buddhist emptiness; Cobb and Ives, *Emptying God*; Ives, *Divine Emptiness*.

40. I have demonstrated in the previous chapter that creation is the emptying act of the Triune God: Father, Son, and Spirit. Distinguishing between the incarnation of the Logos and the inhabitation of the Spirit, Moltmann argues that we must talk about the kenosis of the Spirit in relation to the kenosis of the Logos. He maintains, "If God commits himself to his limited creation, and if he himself dwells in it as 'the giver of life', this presupposes a self-limitation, a self-humiliation and a self-surrender of the Spirit." Moltmann, *God in Creation*, 102.

41. Neville, *Tao and the Daimon*, 51–55; Neville, *Behind the Masks*, 16–17.

42. Cunningham, *Trinitarian Theology*, 57–58.

A Perichoretic Theology of Religions

some atheists strive toward full human autonomy, either personally or communally, or worldly well-being, without reference to any divine or transcendental being. From my perichoretic perspective, this vision must also be considered authentic and real, although it is "severed from the living Trinity."[43]

Third Dimension: Personal Relation

Generally, all Abrahamaic religions conceive of human and cosmic engagement with the divine in the terms of personal relationship. Here, I agree with both Panikkar and Heim that the divine is encountered in personalistic or iconic mode. However, I agree more with Heim in seeing the divine as a common "I" or a single "Thou" than with Panikkar, who attempts to limit such an encounter to the second person of the Trinity, that is, the Word. The classical dictum that the external works of the Trinity are undivided (*opera trinitatis ad extra sunt indivisa*) becomes the central principle. Heim's idea, moreover, is consistent with my perichoretic model, in which the mutual interiority of the Triune persons makes it possible for creation to approach and to be approached by the divine in a singular mode.

Islam and Judaism best represent this dimension. Both religious traditions see God as the transcendent Being, who communicates Godself either through God's iconic expression in the Quran (Islam) or through God's covenant with the believers (Judaism). However, for Christians, this approach is shadowed by a shortcoming, especially if we remember Moltmann's criticisms of the traditional views of the Trinity either as a Supreme Substance or as an Absolute Subject. Both views, according to Moltmann, have reduced Trinitarianism into a mere monotheism. This need not to be the case, if we understand that the singular "I" or "Thou" is nothing but the result of the human panoramic overview of the perichoretic union of the Triune persons. This panoramic overview of the divine as a singular person is acceptable insofar as the divine transcendence is emphasized and to the extent that the economic, immanent, or salvific acts of God are experienced by creation in a more iconic mode.

In this sense, Christians can still retain their faith in the Triune God, who eternally enters the perichoretic union, while respecting Jewish or Islamic radical monotheism. Christians can claim that a closer engagement

---

43. Panikkar, *Religious Experience*, 78.

An Imaginative Glimpse

with the divine, as exemplified by the Christian faith, must result in the divine and perichoretic union of the three persons.

Fourth Dimension: The Possible

Living in a country such as Indonesia, with a countless number of ethnic and local religions, I have often felt troubled by the little attention paid by scholars in religious or theological studies to these religious traditions.[44] This lack of interest in local practices and beliefs is apparent in other countries all over the world.[45] More often than not, we scholars of religion concentrate on the "great" or "world" religions such as Christianity, Islam, Judaism, Buddhist, Hinduism, etc. There are only six official religions recognized by the Indonesian government: Islam, Protestantism, Catholicism, Hinduism, Buddhism, and Confucianism. Oddly, those who do not subscribe to any of these six official religions, although they follow local religions, are treated in one of three ways: some might be considered *belum beragama* ("do not yet have a religion");[46] others might be classified as belonging to *aliran kebatinan*, ("mystical systems," understood by the government as cultural rather than religious practices and beliefs);[47] and still others are labeled as belonging to "Hindu" sects,[48] even though they are not Hindu. In short, these local religions are not respected on their own terms.

There are thousands of local religions compared to the few world religions we are accustomed to discussing, although the quantity of adherents of each of these local religions is small. There are also other "major" religions, such as Confucianism, Taoism, and Jainism, which I do not include in my appropriation model. The question is whether the religions, large and small, neglected by my study reflect real dimension(s) of reality-perichoresis? It is difficult to answer this question with complete certainty. As I have argued, there cannot be absolute certainty regarding the participatory roles of even

---

44. With more than 18,300 islands, Indonesia has over 300 ethnic groups; each has its own *adat* (ancestral customs) with its religious dimensions. Some of these may be considered "local religions."

45. I found an interesting article, written by an Indonesian theologian, Andreas A. Yewangoe, about the Trinity in the context of local religions; see Yewangoe, "Trinity." Yewangoe does not provide any proposal as to how to make a constructive Trinitarian theology in the context of local religions. However, he provides interesting insights that need to be considered in future work.

46. Kipp and Rodgers, *Indonesian Religions*, 21–25.

47. Mulder, *Mysticism*.

48. Persoon, "Religion," 145.

the great world traditions in reality-perichoresis. The best I can do with regard to this question is to employ the imaginative glimpse rooted in my attempts to respect their auto-descriptions and my particular belief in the Trinitarian faith.

In the case of local religions, the level of uncertainty is even higher. Although we might learn from anthropologists or religious historians focused on specific groups of people, the diversity of local religions across the world is so great that it is difficult to have an accurate and comprehensive picture of those religions. Nonetheless, not despite but because of a limited understanding, the *possible* as a dimension of perichoresis comes to the fore when conceptualizing local traditions. As I have argued in chapter 4, I attempt to reinterpret Kearney's idea by shifting the possible from the core of divinity, as Kearney has done, to one among many dimensions of perichoresis. The idea of the possible as a dimension of perichoresis suggests that in the eschatological consummation, God appears as a surprising God, since God is more than what we or our traditions can comprehend. The superabundant grace of God is always excessive. Through our basic belief that God embraces everything in and through the Son, by the life-giving power of the Spirit, we are enabled to say that the local religions also partake in reality-perichoresis. This perspective, while still requiring us to engage both dialogically and critically with the local religions, simultaneously offers a kind of cosmic confidence or cosmic trust[49] that ultimately results in our amicable acceptance of their possible places within reality-perichoresis.

The Two Hands of God Revisited

Of the three theologians under discussion, D'Costa stands alone in using the Irenaean theory of the Son and the Spirit as the two hands of God. Compared to Panikkar and Heim, D'Costa has taken the best route to "even out" the Son and the Spirit. Panikkar, through his separation between the cosmic Christ and the historical Jesus, has harshly criticized the Western primacy of the *logos* over the Spirit. Yet, he goes too far by reversing the Western model and insisting that an authentic pluralism does not belong to *logos*; rather, it belongs to *mythos* and *pneuma*. Heim stands at the other pole, giving very

---

49. These are Panikkar's terms to refer to an attitude in pluralism, which "permits a polar and tension-filled coexistence of *ultimate* human convictions, cosmologies, and religions. It neither eliminates nor absolutizes evil or error." Panikkar, *Dwelling Place*, 147. However, I use his term loosely, pointing to our basic attitude toward the unknown others within the conviction of a larger space of embrace of reality-perichoresis.

little attention to the Spirit, especially in his argument that the Trinity is always Christocentric. Although D'Costa's adoption of the Irenaean two hands of God is commendable, he does not elaborate it to its fullest extent, especially because he does not relate it directly to the doctrine of perichoresis.

What I offer here is not a revision of Irenaeus' or D'Costa's theory of the two hands of God. Rather, I simply affirm the value of this theory and interpret it in light of my perichoretic model. The importance of this section is that it provides intermediate principles between my perichoretic theology of religions and its ethical implications. A careful reading would lead to a question of the practicability of my model. It is also true that the plausibility of a theoretical model is, at the end, testable only when it empowers us to engage with others in a more ethical manner. By reinterpreting the notion of God's two hands, I will be able to construct a bridge between my theologically abstract model and the ethical necessity of the theology of religions.

Amos Yong strongly argues that there is a close affinity between the doctrine of perichoresis and the Irenaean two hands of God.[50] Even more, the development of the doctrine of perichoresis is dependent on two aspects of the Irenaean two hands model: "that which envisions the interdependence and mutuality of the two hands, and that which emphasizes the unity of the two hands with the Father."[51] In the following pages, I explore the two hands in the light of both the perichoretic idea and the issue commonly found in any theology of religions: particularity and universality. Unlike D'Costa, I will argue that the notions of particularity and universality can be found equally in each of the two hands and, moreover, that, when joined together, both hands can even more brightly illuminate the richness of perichoresis for theology of religions.

The Hybrid Christ

Any Christian theology of religions must address what is known as the "scandal of particularity"; that is, that God makes Godself known through the particular person of Jesus Christ, through whom salvation is offered to the world. The issue thus addresses the dialectic between God's universal salvific will and Jesus Christ's particular saving work. Of the three theologians whom I have discussed, D'Costa is the one who maintains that the scandalous particularity of Christ is the only norm available to everyone, no matter

---

50. Yong, *Spirit-Word-Community*, 53–56.
51. Ibid., 53.

A Perichoretic Theology of Religions

what her or his religion is. Of course, he makes his argument more sophisticated by relating the particular and historical Jesus to the universality of Logos, the universal work of Spirit, and even to the universal dimension of the church. On the other side, we have Panikkar, who has been accused as having severed the relation between the cosmic Christ and the historical Jesus. For Panikkar, the cosmic Christ is the symbol of the cosmotheandric reality, which is not necessarily related to the historical Jesus. Heim seems to have tried to bridge the gap between Panikkar and D'Costa and, therefore, also between the second person of the Trinity and the historical Jesus. Despite its success, Heim's attempt is also problematic. He goes too far in his attempt to universalize the meaning of the resurrected Jesus: in his theory, Christ becomes the reconciler of multiple religious paths and, consequently, multiple religious ends. The path that Heim takes is unavoidable because of his understanding of *sin*—which is overcome by Christ's resurrection—as standing between humans and all religious ends.

My perichoresis-based proposal is twofold, each of which has two dimensions expressing the dialectic of universality and particularity. First, we need to adopt a vaguer definition of the human condition that revises Christian notions of sin. With such a vague definition, each religion can explore—in a more comparative manner—its own particular concepts of human condition. With a vague idea of the human condition, multiple particular descriptions of human condition become possible and clearer—as do the destructive burdens attached to the human, religious (sin, samsara, etc.) or non-religious (injustice, gender bias, racism, etc.).

Second, with regard to the place of Christ, I argue that perichoresis allows me to emphasize the Son, the second person of the Trinity, through whom all are created and with whom the Spirit makes it possible for creation to participate in the perichoretic divine dance. In the participation of all creation in the divine dance, person-perichoresis is broadened to reality-perichoresis or theo-cosmic-pneumatic reality. This particularly Christian perspective of the person of Christ, however, needs to be redefined in such a way that neither exclusively identifies it with the historical Jesus nor diminishes its relationship to the historical Jesus. In other words, what we need is the possibility of having multiple and hybridized images of Jesus Christ.

The notion of the hybridized Jesus has been popularized by the Asian feminist Kwok Pui-lan, using the postcolonial lens.[52] Her central question is: "How is it possible for the formerly colonized, oppressed, subjugated subaltern to transform the symbol of Christ—a symbol that has been used to

---

52. Kwok, *Postcolonial Imagination*.

An Imaginative Glimpse

justify colonization and domination—into a symbol that affirms life, dignity, and freedom?"[53] To answer this question Kwok employs the hybrid concept, which is popular among postcolonial and feminist thinkers, arguing that even in the Christian tradition the concept of Jesus/Christ is already highly hybridized and pluralistic. She writes,

> The space between Jesus and Christ is unsettling and fluid, resisting easy categorization and closure. It is "the contact zone" or "borderline" between the human and the divine, the one and the many, the historical and the cosmological, the Jewish and the Hellenistic, the prophetic and the sacramental, the God of the conquerors and the God of the meek and the lowly. Jesus' question "Who do you say that I am?" is an invitation for every Christian and local faith community to infuse that contact zone with new meanings, insights, and possibilities.[54]

Obviously, Kwok's targets of criticism are both those who try to insist on purifying the doctrine of Jesus Christ and those who attempt to recover the historical Jesus in the interests of historical or scientific positivism. In both cases, "the space between Jesus and Christ is fixed."[55] Thus, in contrast to "the quest of the historical Jesus," Kwok suggest "the quest of the hybridized Jesus."[56] Furthermore, she discusses five examples of how the images of hybridized Jesus/Christ have been proposed by people from marginalized communities: The Black Christ, the Corn Mother, the Feminine Shakti, the Theological Transvestite, and Jesus as Bi/Christ.

In reading those images carefully, we have a strong impression that Kwok's foci are sexism, political injustice, and racism. All of these, however, are centered on the attempt to relate the Christian understanding of Jesus/Christ to the problem of identity, especially as this problem has affected those who have been victimized throughout history. Any hybrid image of Jesus/Christ, Kwok insists, maintains fluidity, allows imaginative diversification, and provides culturally, politically, and religiously liberating resources for confronting oppressive structures.

Kwok's concept of the hybrid Jesus/Christ is highly commendable in its ability to reinforce her postcolonial agenda. Theologically, the proposal is also helpful in stressing the importance of local traditions for constructing contextual and liberating Christologies in more fluid and creative ways.

53. Ibid., 168.
54. Ibid., 171.
55. Ibid.
56. Ibid., 170.

A Perichoretic Theology of Religions

Unfortunately, Kwok does not see the significance of her own proposal in terms of interreligious encounter. When talking about the issue of religious difference, in the very chapter that follows her discussion of hybrid concepts of Jesus/Christ, Kwok does not connect the two subjects. Her concern is rather how to place gender "within the wider intrareligious and interreligious network of cultural and religious relations."[57] Thus, the hybrid images of Jesus/Christ that we expect to emerge must be constructed with greater interreligious sensitivity.

Kwok's proposal of the hybrid Jesus/Christ is particularly helpful for my own project. In the discourse of interreligious encounter, the historical Jesus and the Christ of faith are almost always identified so much that the space between both is fixed and their fluid relationship is diminished. By allowing the multiple images of hybrid Jesus/Christ to emerge, I believe we can have a non-absolutist Christology that could enrich, rather than weaken, the interreligious discourse. This Christology must at all times consider both the historical Jesus (without objectifying her/him in a positivist mode) and the Christ of faith (without purifying her/him in an ideological mode). The creative and imaginative attempts to construct multiple images of hybrid Jesus/Christ still need to be conducted in conversation with classical or "ecumenical" hybrid image of Jesus/Christ, as expressed in the historical Jesus and the Christ of faith.

My project leans very heavily on the idea of the cosmic Christ, which begins with the Son as the second person of the Trinity. In this sense, on the one hand, my affinity with Panikkar is evident. Yet, by engaging with the construction of hybrid images of Jesus/Christ, I try to fill the gap left by Panikkar, which consists of a severe discontinuity between the Logos and the historical Jesus. On the other hand, my position also reflects a critical distance from D'Costa, who seems to presume the identification of Jesus and Christ as taught by Catholic dogma. Heim's position is more complex in that he understands Jesus Christ as the reconciler of multiple religious ends. The problem with Heim, however, is that he moves further by universalizing and applying the homogenous image of Christ—based on his homogenously Christian image of sin—to those multiple religious ends. What he lacks here is, therefore, multiple images of (hybrid) Jesus/Christ corresponding to multiple religious ends.

Through equally emphasizing the cosmic role of the Son within the theo-cosmic-pneumatic reality (or, reality-perichoresis), and the necessity of constructing multiple images of hybrid Jesus/Christ through as many

---

57. Ibid., 207.

An Imaginative Glimpse

particular encounters with other religious traditions as possible, I argue that we can maintain the dialectic of the universality and particularity of Jesus Christ. The universality of the Son, through and in whom all reality is created, meets the particularity of the historical Jesus, resulting in the endless possibility of hybrid images of Jesus/Christ. The manifold hybridized images of Jesus/Christ, in turn, enrich the theological meaning of human participations in the Triune life, and contribute to the final or eschatological dance of reality-perichoresis. Despite its limitedly speculative nature, I believe my proposal can shed light on our search of a robust theology of religions.

The images of hybridized Jesus/Christ therefore become a third category standing dynamically between the cosmic Christ and the historical Jesus. If the idea of cosmic Christ indicates, or in some sense refers to, the divine grace that embraces all created reality, and the historical Jesus points to the historical particularity of incarnated grace, then multiple images of the hybridized Jesus/Christ create many in-between spaces, in which a thin yet rich notion of God-creation conciliation is creatively preserved in conversations with non-Christian mediatory paths.[58]

The Transversal Spirit

It is obvious from the Christological discussion above that the idea of hybrid Jesus/Christ reflects the complex relation between universality and particularity. In this section, I argue that a similar complexity can also be expected in our discussion of the Spirit. In the Spirit we also see the dialectic between universality and particularity, though in a different operation from that of the Son.

It is commonly argued that the Spirit operates universally by unifying all reality, while the differentiating role is found in the Son.[59] This idea is only partially true, since we also find, especially in the Eastern tradition, another concept where the cosmic Son plays a unifying role, while the Spirit plays a differentiating role. It is safer to say, therefore, that both hands of

---

58. Although not using the typically postcolonial term "hybrid," many Third-World theologians offer a similar idea through their contextual Christology; cf. Sugirtharajah, *Asian Faces*.

59. This typically Western idea is represented, for example, by Pannenberg. For a brief discussion of Pannenberg's idea on this matter consult Wegter-McNelly, "Entanglement," 58–63. He summarizes Pannenberg's idea by saying, "According to Pannenberg, the work of the spirit is closely related to the work of the Son, though different in character. Whereas the Son is the principle of distinction, the Spirit is the principle of fellowship and participation" Wegter-McNelly, "Entanglement," 62.

A Perichoretic Theology of Religions

God, the Son and the Spirit, work simultaneously in differentiating and unifying all reality in their interaction with the Triune God. When related to the problem of religious diversity, we may say that both the Son and the Spirit demonstrate, though in different manner, the dialectic of universality and particularity.

It is true, however, to say that the Spirit's universal dimension occurs when the Spirit unifies all reality in the consummation of the world, when God becomes all in all. But, this unifying work does not by any means diminish the particularity of each religious tradition. The problem is that each religion has its claim of universality, while each also makes such a claim from a particular perspective. I believe that the Spirit works differently from the Son in that the Spirit maintains the multiplicity of the universal claims of religions.

We have seen that the idea of hybrid images of Jesus/Christ does not undermine the universal character of religions, precisely because this idea links the cosmic Christ and the historical particularity of Jesus tightly together. Amos Yong is correct in saying that pneumatology is "the key to overcoming the dualism between Christological particularity and the cosmic Christ."[60] However, he also says that the dualism is overcome by the Spirit so much that "the either/or of particularity/universality dissolves."[61] To say that the disjunctive either/or of particularity/universality is dissolved does not mean, however, that the dialectic nature of particularity and universality is dissolved as well. On the contrary, both characteristics are maintained creatively through a conjunctive logic of both/and. We cannot emphasize the universality of the Son without, at the same time, respecting the particularity of Jesus.

There is another way of seeing the particular role of the Spirit in relation to other religions. Not only does the Spirit sustain Christian salvation centered on the dialectic between the universality of the Son and the particularity of the historical Jesus, but she also sustains the dialectic of particularity/universality of other religions' paths through her transversal activity. In chapter 3, I discussed Calvin Schrag's idea of transversal rationality as a necessary conjoiner of Heim's orientational pluralism. Transversality, Schrag argues, offers a third way between "the Scylla of a hegemonic and ahistorical universalism and the Charybdis of a lawless, self-effacing particularism and enervated historicism."[62] Transversal rationality is promising because it en-

---

60. Yong, *Beyond the Impasse*, 47.
61. Ibid.
62. Schrag, *Resources*, 9.

An Imaginative Glimpse

ables us to recognize the universal scope of each religion, in such a way that there may be multiple *uni*-versals (hence, pluriversal). It operates through "a diagonal movement across the group, acknowledging the otherness and integrity of each, while making the requisite accommodations and adjustment along the way."[63]

Theologically speaking, the transversal movement can be imagined as the work of the Spirit. The Spirit sustains all of the religious universals, nurtures their own developments, and finally consummates them in the eschatological and perichoretic participation of all creation in the Triune God. Such activities of the Spirit, however, occur without encroaching on their freedom. There are two particular ways in which the Spirit's transversal activities can be perceived.

First, the Spirit sustains the space inhabited by creation and fills it with the power of life necessary for creation to move forward to the consummation of the future. The space that was once vacated through God's self-limitation must be characterized by otherness and differentiation, since the vacated space itself reflects God's willingness to make "the other" come to be. Also, since the space was vacated through God's free love, it must also reflect and be guided by the freedom of creation. Thus, the first way the Spirit works transversally is through the sustenance of the spatial creation characterized by life and freedom. This is a diagonal activity in which the vertical transcendence of God and the horizontal immanence of God meet.

Moreover, the third person of the Trinity also works diagonally or transversally in bringing together, through creative conversations, the freedom of all creation by virtue of their existence as created beings, as recognized in non-Christian traditions, *and* the freedom offered freely by the Son, the incarnated grace. Here, the possibility of multiple images of the hybridized Jesus/Christ re-emerges to the fore. While Christians can argue faithfully that the freedom in Christ is the perfected freedom, the Spirit still preserves the values of freedom as recognized by non-Christians. This is so because freedom always arises out of the divine surplus and culminates in the ultimate participation of creation in the divine dance. To abandon the freedoms recognized in non-Christians is to reject the reality that the ultimate dance is complex, rich and hybridized.

The second dimension of the transversal activity of the Spirit is to bring together all religious universals into an authentic dialogue. Since each universal claim is warranted by the freedom inherent in creation, there must be a "membrane" or "boundary" surrounding each universal claim that

63. Schrag, *Self after Postmodernity*, 132.

A Perichoretic Theology of Religions

separates one religion from all others, and that sustains this otherness. Such a "membrane," of course, also functions in maintaining the distinction between God and creation. However, those membranes are also porous, so that relationships with both other religions and God are made possible, and without destroying the identity of the membranes. The construction of a particular image of hybrid Jesus/Christ is possible when a particular Christian person or community has a genuine conversation with a non-Christian person or community, in which the membrane of each participant is both maintained and traversed so that a common space is created. It is the Spirit who demonstrates the power of traversing religious membranes, creating such common space as the result of interreligious dialogue.

Jesus Christ, in all his particularity, cannot break through other religious membranes to occupy the cores of other religions to the extent that we can say that the particular Christ is also found in other religions. Rather, the images of hybridized Jesus/Christ are always found in the common spaces, created through the power of the traversing of the Spirit, located in between Christianity and other religions. Of course, it is possible, as occurs in *syncretism*, that the membranes of two religions overlap. But, in such a case, what we have is a new religious entity. It is also possible that a common space may include the cores of two or more religions; in this case, we have *multiple religious belongings*. In most cases, however, the common space does not diminish the core of each religion. Rather, the persons involved in common space dialogue stand at the border of their religious membrane, ready to meet people from other traditions. It is at the border of the religious membrane that Christ and other religious paths are hybridized. All this is made possible through the power of the Spirit, who traverses the religious membranes and invites all people to engage with a rich and enriching experience. In short, this second dimension of the Spirit points to dialogue, love, and solidarity. The goal of a Spirit-fuelled, dynamic religious encounter echoes Schrag's ideals of transversality: "a convergence without coincidence, an interplay without synthesis, an appropriation without totalization, and a unification that allows for difference."[64]

Before concluding this section, another note regarding the works of the Spirit is in order. To imagine the transversal or traversing power of the Spirit does not mean having a clear and fixed vision of what will happen with the final perichoretic dance that involves other religions: instead, there is a vague picture of the ultimate dance in the perfected reality-perichoresis. There are many possibilities for what kind of perichoretic reality it is. This

64. Schrag, *Resources*, 158–59.

insight is consistent with Kearney's God who may be or the possible God. Interestingly, Kearney distinguishes between two different meanings of the Spirit's *dunamis*, power and possibility, and subscribes to the latter.[65] "Resisting all modes of causal determinism," he insists, the divine possibility (*dunamis theou*) "constantly surprises us."[66] Thus, every time I refer to the "power" of the Spirit in the preceding pages, it would also be illuminating to read them in Kearney's perspective of *dunamis* as the possibilizing power of the Spirit.

To conclude, in this section I have reflected imaginatively on the classical idea of God's two hands—the Son and the Spirit—by employing the ideas of the hybrid Jesus/Christ and the transversal Spirit. I believe I have succeeded in showing the difference, mutuality, and interdependence of the Son and the Spirit in the light of perichoretic communion among, and the perichoretic participation of creation in, the Triune God. Since I believe that reality-perichoresis is not only an eschatological reality that will be perfected in the eschatological consummation in the future, but has also been present since the beginning of time, I argue that perichoretic participation must also be experienced historically, *hic et nunc*. I have also argued that the two hands of God, the Son and the Spirit, who relate God to the world, operate both universally and particularly. Although by way of the appropriation method we can say that each hand has different activities, we can still maintain that the Triune persons work in togetherness, and undividedly. All of the Triune persons work in complex movements of dance: embracing creatures, yet letting them exist in their freedom; and finally orchestrating all dances into the final, ultimate, and hybrid dance.

The perichoretic theology of religions suggested here is perfectly compatible with this fundamental image, as it maintains the particularity and universality of religions at the same time. All religions, on the one hand, are respected on their own terms, and their universal claims are recognized. On the other hand, as a Christian, I still can retain my universal as well as particular belief in the Triune God. Moreover, this model has the tremendous advantage of enabling us to preserve these two dimensions even until "the end"; that is, when all realities perfectly participate in the divine dance and God becomes all in all. This is possible since reality-perichoresis, which is rooted in person-perichoresis, is fundamentally a multidimensional and complex reality.

---

65. Kearney, *God Who May Be*, 80–83.
66. Ibid., 81.

Embracing, Rather than Including, Others
Toward an Interreligious Ethics of Perichoresis

An Epilogue

In chapter 4 I demonstrated the necessity of supplementing orientational pluralism with transversal rationality. While the former works on the epistemological level, the latter is helpful in our praxial and communicative process. I have also shown that Heim's Trinitarian inclusivism, along with its attempt to utilize Rescher's perspectivism, is consistent with the direction of transversality, even though it is still a journey that goes only "halfway," as can be expected from any constructive theology.

If, however, we try to apply our constructive model to the praxis of interreligious dialogue, then it is necessary to think in a transversal way about the universality of our model. In this regard, I need to remind the reader of my rejection of the typology of exclusivism, inclusivism, and pluralism. I have demonstrated that the shortcomings of this typology far outweigh its advantages. Here, I need to highlight another ethical problem it presents, this time from the perspective of transversal praxis.

It is clear that, for Heim, only two final options exist for any theology of religions: exclusivism or inclusivism. He chooses the latter after revising it through his "more pluralistic hypothesis." D'Costa goes further by saying that every tradition-specific position is by nature exclusivist. D'Costa's position is problematic when we subscribe to the principles provided by the transversal communicative praxis. The dynamism of this theory suggests that unification has to be achieved "in such a manner that it is able to critique, articulate, and disclose [different systems] without achieving a coincidence with any particular form of discourse, thought, or action."[1] From this point of view, we may ask whether Heim's inclusivism can lead him not into the ideal "convergence" that Schrag hopes for, but into a "coincidence" with a particular form of belief, which in this case is the Christian Trinity. As should be clear from the preceding chapter, I believe it is acceptable to employ an inclusivist model and its universal implications when we talk on a metaphysical level, insofar as it reflects a version of the lateral universal. Yet, an inclusivist model is problematic when applied to dialogical praxis. The issue centers on the question of whether others are *willing* to be included in a construct other than their own that is theologically strange to them. In his critique of Heim's inclusivism D'Costa has rightly raised the question of whether it is legitimate to preserve or include the Advaitic belief that negates the category of "relation" in the Trinitarian relational framework.[2] This act of inclusion, along with the universal intent inherent in Heim's inclusivism, results in an ordering of multiple religious ends in such a way that non-Christian ends are considered penultimate, in contrast to the Christian ultimate end. From the perspective of Schrag's transversal rationality, this inclusion can be easily seen as an attempt at achieving convergence "via a vertically ordered and hegemonic decision-making arrangement that simply subordinates the lower to the higher."[3]

A spatial image may be helpful here to clarify the problem. The language of exclusion or inclusion presumes a circle with a static center around which we decide what should be excluded or included. The fact that in Christianity the center—the Trinity—is plural does not make the problem disappear. It is only softened, if not concealed. The center itself does not result from a transversal communication; rather, it is decided by one party. Miroslav Volf, in his *Exclusion and Embrace*, has made important points concerning this issue. He argues that inclusion and exclusion are, in fact, not two contradicting acts. Rather, exclusion is a result of inclusion. "The undeniable progress of inclusion fed on the persistent practice of exclusion."[4] In other words,

1. Schrag, *Resources*, 158.

2. We have also seen that the same question can be raised with regard to D'Costa's idea of the work of Spirit in other religions in such a way that "the inchoate reality of the Kingdom" is present in other religions, or even concerning Panikkar's appropriation of Buddhism as the religion of the Father (the first "person" of the Christian Trinity).

3. Schrag, *Self after Postmodernity*, 129–32.

4. Volf, *Exclusion*, 60.

through the act of inclusion one excludes the very identity of the others by absorbing them within one's own walls. Thus, the act of inclusion creates a reality where there are no longer boundaries, and in such a situation the act of exclusion appears. "A constant pursuit of inclusion places one before the impossible choice between a chaos without boundaries and oppression with them."[5]

In contrast to the acts of inclusion and exclusion, I rather suggest the dynamic image of "embrace" proposed by Volf. He develops his "theology of embrace" from within the context of the conflict in his country, Croatia. Volf argues that there are four acts of embracing:[6] 1. Opening the arms; 2. Waiting; 3. Closing the arms (by both parties); 4. Opening the arms again. What is interesting for me here is his usage of spatial symbolism. By opening the arms (act 1), "I have *created space* in myself for the other to come in and . . . I have made a movement out of myself so as to enter space created by the other."[7] Also, opening the arms is a symbol of invitation. The second act, waiting, occurs when I "halted at *the boundary* of the other."[8] The peak of this embrace (act 3) is the reciprocal closing of the arms by both parties. Is not closing the arms presuming a destruction of the centers? Volf says no. "In an embrace the identity of the self is both preserved and transformed, and the alterity of the other is both affirmed as alterity and partly received into the ever changing identity of the self."[9] The final act is opening the arms again, since embrace does not make "two bodies one." The final act is of great importance, since each party releases her or his previously embraced companions and lets them be themselves.

Of course, Volf develops his theology of embrace more deeply than I can present here. Nonetheless, the four acts in the drama of embrace described briefly above best illustrate the transversal communication supplied by transversal rationality. Moreover, it does not close the door to possible transformation as the result of dialogue. The transformation expected in such a dialogical embrace is what Schrag calls "convergence without coincidence."

Any constructive theology with an inclusivist character is plausible only on the theoretical level. Once we enter a concretely dialogical encounter with others, such a theory needs to be replaced by transversal views critical of any attempt at inclusion. In place of such theoretical "inclusion," I suggest

5. Ibid., 63–64.
6. Ibid., 140–47.
7. Ibid., 141, italics mine.
8. Ibid., italics mine.
9. Ibid., 143.

An Imaginative Glimpse

a praxial "embrace" that encourages unconditional offering and gift of self and respect for others. In short, I believe that the perichoretic *theology* of religions can and should be transformed into the perichoretic *embrace* of religions.

Bibliography

Balthasar, Hans Urs von. *Cosmic Liturgy: The Universe according to Maximus the Confessor.* San Francisco: Ignatius, 2003.

———. *Theo-Drama: Theological Dramatic Theory, Vol. IV: the Action.* San Francisco: Ignatius, 1988.

Barnes, Michael. "Theology of Religions." In *The Blackwell Companion to Christian Spirituality*, edited by Arthur G. Holder, 401–16. Oxford: Blackwell, 2005.

Barth, Karl. *Church Dogmatics, Vol. I.*1. Translated by G. T. Thomson. Edinburgh: T. & T. Clark, 1936.

———. *Church Dogmatics, Vol. III.*2. Translated by G. T. Thomson. Edinburgh: T. & T. Clark, 1960.

Beeley, Christopher A. "Divine Causality and the Monarchy of God the Father in Gregory of Nazianzus." *Harvard Theological Review* 100 (2007) 199–214.

Bigger, Charles P. *Between Chora and the Good: Metaphor's Metaphysical Neighborhood.* New York: Fordham University Press, 2005.

Boersma, Hans. "The Feet of God: In Stomping Boots or Dancing Shoes? The Trinity as Answer to Violence." In *Living in the Lamblight: Christianity and Contemporary Challenges to the Gospel*, edited by Hans Boersma, 67–96. Vancouver: Regent College, 2001.

Boff, Leonardo. *Trinity and Society.* Maryknoll, NY: Orbis, 1988.

———. "Trinity." In *Systematic Theology: Perspectives from Liberation Theology*, edited by Jon Sobrino and Ignacio Ellacuría, 75–89. Maryknoll, NY: Orbis, 1996.

Brück, Michael von. *The Unity of Reality: God, God-Experience and Meditation in the Hindu-Christian Dialogue.* Mahwah, NJ: Paulist, 1991.

Butin, Philip Walker. *The Trinity.* Louisville, KY: Geneva, 2001.

Butler, Michael. "Hypostatic Union and Monotheletism: The Dyothelite Christology of St. Maximus the Confessor." PhD diss., Fordham University, 1993.

Buxton, Graham. *The Trinity, Creation and Pastoral Ministry: Imaging the Perichoretic God.* Milton Keynes, UK: Paternoster, 2005.

Cenkner, William. "Interreligious Exploration of Triadid Reality: The Panikkar Project." *Dialogue & Alliance* 4 (1990) 71–85.

Cobb, John B. "Beyond 'Pluralism.'" In *Christian Uniqueness Reconsidered: The Myth of a Pluralistic Theology of Religions*, edited by Gavin D'Costa, 81–95. Maryknoll, NY: Orbis, 1990.

Cobb, John B., Jr. "Some Whiteheadian Assumptions about Religion and Pluralism." In *Deep Religious Pluralism*, edited by David R. Griffin, 243–62. Louisville, KY: Westminster John Knox, 2005.

———. *Transforming Christianity and the World: A Way beyond Absolutism and Relativism.* Edited by Paul F. Knitter. Maryknoll, NY: Orbis, 1999.

Bibliography

Cobb, John B., and Christopher Ives, editors. *The Emptying God: A Buddhist-Jewish-Christian Conversation*. Maryknoll, NY: Orbis, 1990.

Cornille, Catherine. *Many Mansions? Multiple Religious Belonging and Christian Identity*. Maryknoll, NY: Orbis, 2002.

Cousins, Ewert H. *Christ of the 21st Century*. Rockport, MA: Element, 1992.

———. "Panikkar's Advaitic Trinitarianism." In *The Intercultural Challenge of Raimon Panikkar*, edited by Joseph Prabhu, 119–30. Maryknoll, NY: Orbis, 1996.

Crisp, Oliver D. *Divinity and Humanity: The Incarnation Reconsidered*. Cambridge: Cambridge University Press, 2007.

Crosswhite, James. *The Rhetoric of Reason: Writing and the Attractions of Argument*. Madison: University of Wisconsin Press, 1996.

Cunningham, David S. *These Three Are One: The Practice of Trinitarian Theology*. Malden, MA: Blackwell, 1998.

Davis, Stephen T. "Perichoretic Monotheism: A Defense of a Social Theory of the Trinity." In *The Trinity: East/West Dialogue*, edited by Melville Y. Stewart, 35–52. Dordrecht: Kluwer, 2003.

D'Costa, Gavin. "Christ, the Trinity, and Religious Plurality." In *Christian Uniqueness Reconsidered: The Myth of a Pluralistic Theology of Religions*, edited by Gavin D'Costa, 16–29. Maryknoll, NY: Orbis, 1990.

———. *John Hick's Theology of Religions: A Critical Evaluation*. Lanham, MD: University Press of America, 1987.

———. *The Meeting of Religions and the Trinity*. Maryknoll, NY: Orbis, 2000.

———. "Preface." In *Christian Uniqueness Reconsidered: The Myth of a Pluralistic Theology of Religions*, edited by Gavin D'Costa, vii–xxii. Maryknoll, NY: Orbis, 1990.

———. Review of *The Depth of the Riches: A Trinitarian Theology of Religious Ends*, by S. Mark Heim. *Modern Theology* 18 (2002) 137–39.

———. "Theology of Religions." In *The Modern Theologians: An Introduction to Christian Theology since 1918*, edited by David Ford, 626–44. Oxford: Blackwell, 2005.

———. *Theology and Religious Pluralism: The Challenge of Other Religions*. Oxford: Blackwell, 1986.

———. "Towards a Trinitarian Theology of Religions." In *A Universal Faith? Peoples, Cultures, Religions, and the Christ: Essays in Honor of Prof. Dr. Frank De Graeve*, edited by Catherine Cornille and V. Neckebrouck, 139–54. Louvain: Peeters, 1992.

———. "Trinitarian Différance and World Religions: Postmodernity and the 'Other.'" In *Faith and Praxis in a Postmodern Age*, edited by Ursula King, 28–46. London: Cassell, 1998.

D'Costa, Gavin, editor. *Christian Uniqueness Reconsidered: The Myth of a Pluralistic Theology of Religions*. Maryknoll, NY: Orbis, 1990.

D'Sa, Francis X. "The Notion of God." In *The Intercultural Challenge of Raimon Panikkar*, edited by Joseph Prabhu, 25–45. Maryknoll, NY: Orbis, 1996.

Duck, Ruth C., and Patricia Wilson-Kastner. *Praising God: The Trinity in Christian Worship*. Louisville, KY: Westminster John Knox, 1999.

Edwards, Denis. *The God of Evolution: A Trinitarian Theology*. New York: Paulist, 1999.

———. *Jesus the Wisdom of God: An Ecological Theology: Ecology and Justice*. Maryknoll, NY: Orbis, 1995.

Egan, John P. "Toward Trinitarian Perichoresis: Saint Gregory the Theologian, *Oration* 31.14." *The Greek Theological Review* 39 (1994) 83–93.

Feder, Jens. *Fractals*. New York: Plenum, 1988.

Fiddes, Paul S. *Participating in God: A Pastoral Doctrine of the Trinity*. Louisville, KY: Westminster John Knox, 2000.
Fletcher, Jeannine Hill. *Monopoly on Salvation? A Feminist Approach to Religious Pluralism*. New York: Continuum, 2005.
Flett, John G. "In the Name of the Father, the Son and the Holy Spirit: A Critical Reflection on the Trinitarian Theologies of Religion of S. Mark Heim and Gavin D'Costa." *International Jornal of Systematic Theology* 10 (2007) 73–90.
Ford, Lewis S. *The Lure of God: A Biblical Background for Process Theism*. Philadelphia: Fortress, 1978.
———. *Transforming Process Theism*. Albany, NY: State University of New York Press, 2000.
Fredericks, James L. Review of *The Meeting of Religions and the Trinity*, by Gavin D'Costa. *Modern Theology* 18 (2002) 297–99.
Fredericks, James L. *Faith among Faiths: Christian Theology and Non-Christian Religions*. New York: Paulist, 1999.
Grenz, Stanley J. *Rediscovering the Triune God: The Trinity in Contemporary Theology*. Minneapolis: Fortress, 2004.
Griffin, David R. "Religious Pluralism: Generic, Identist, and Deep." In *Deep Religious Pluralism*, edited by David R. Griffin, 3–38. Louisville, KY: Westminster John Knox, 2005.
Griffiths, Bede. *Return to the Center*. Springfield, IL: Templegate, 1977.
Groppe, Elizabeth T. "Catherine Mowry LaCugna's Contribution to Trinitarian Theology." *Theological Studies* 63 (2002) 730–63.
Gunton, Colin E. *The Doctrine of Creation: Essays in Dogmatics, History and Philosophy*. Edinburgh: T. & T. Clark, 1997.
Harrison, Verna. "Perichoresis in the Greek Fathers." *St. Vladimir's Theological Quarterly* 35 (1991) 53–65.
Heim, S. Mark. *The Depth of the Riches: A Trinitarian Theology of Religious Ends*. Grand Rapids: Eerdmans, 2001.
———. "The Depth of the Riches: Trinity and Religious Ends." In *Theology and the Religions: A Dialogue*, edited by Viggo Mortensen, 387–402. Grand Rapids: Eerdmans, 2003.
———. "Orientational Pluralism in Religion." *Faith and philosophy* 13 (1996) 201–15.
———. "The Pluralistic Hypothesis, Realism and Post-Eschatology." *Religious Studies* 28 (1992) 207–19.
———. *Salvations: Truth and Difference in Religion*. Maryknoll, NY: Orbis, 1995.
Held, Klaus. "World, Emptiness, Nothingness: A Phenomenological Approach to the Religious Tradition of Japan." *Human studies* 20 (1997) 153–67.
Hick, John. *An Interpretation of Religion: Human Responses to the Transcendent*. New Haven: Yale University Press, 1989.
Hodgson, Peter Crafts. *Winds of the Spirit: A Constructive Christian Theology*. Louisville, KY: Westminster/John Knox, 1994.
Hunt, Anne. *Trinity: Nexus of the Mysteries of Christian Faith*. Maryknoll, NY: Orbis, 2005.
Huyssteen, Wentzel van. *The Shaping of Rationality: Toward Interdisciplinarity in Theology and Science*. Grand Rapids: Eerdmans, 1999.
Irenaeus. *Five Books of S. Irenaeus: Bishop of Lyons*. Translated by John Keble. Oxford: Parker, 1872.

Bibliography

Ives, Christopher. *Divine Emptiness and Historical Fullness: A Buddhist-Jewish-Christian Conversation with Masao Abe*. Valley Forge, PA: Trinity, 1995.

James, Robison B. *Tillich and World Religions: Encountering Other Faiths Today*. Macon, GA: Mercer University Press, 2003.

Jantzen, Grace. "Human Diversity and Salvation in Christ." *Religious Studies* 20 (1984) 579–92.

John of Damascus, "Exposition of the Orthodox Faith." Translated by S. D. F. Salmond. In *Nicene and Post-Nicene Fathers*. Second Series, Volume IX—Hilary Poitiers, John of Damascus. Edited by Philip Schaff and Henry Wallace. New York: Cosimo, 2007.

John Paul II. *On the Permanent Validity of the Church's Missionary Mandate (Redemptoris Missio)*, 1990. Online: http://www.vatican.va/holy_father/john_paul_ii/encyclicals/documents/hf_jp-ii_enc_07121990_redemptoris-missio_en.html.

Johnson, Elizabeth A. *She Who Is: The Mystery of God in Feminist Theological Discourse*. New York: Crossroad, 1992.

Johnson, Keith E. "A 'Trinitarian' Theology of Religions? An Augustinian Assessment of Several Recent Proposals." PhD diss., Duke University, 2007.

Kaplan, Stephen. *Different Paths, Different Summits: A Model for Religious Pluralism*. Lanham, MD: Rowman & Littlefield, 2002.

Kärkkäinen, Veli-Matti. *An Introduction to the Theology of Religions: Biblical, Historical, and Contemporary Perspectives*. Downers Grove, IL: InterVarsity, 2003.

———. *Trinity and Religious Pluralism: The Doctrine of the Trinity in Christian Theology of Religions*. Aldershot, UK: Ashgate, 2004.

———. *The Trinity: Global Perspectives*. Louisville, KY: Westminster John Knox, 2007.

Kearney, Richard. *The God Who May Be: A Hermeneutics of Religion*. Bloomington, IN: Indiana University Press, 2001.

———. "Philosophizing the Gift: A Discussion between Richard Kearney and Mark Manolopoulos." In *The Hermeneutics of Charity: Interpretation, Selfhood, and Postmodern Fatih: Studies in Honor of James H. Olthuis*, edited by James K. A. Smith and Henry I. Venema, 52–72. Grand Rapids: Brazos, 2004.

———. *Strangers, Gods, and Monsters: Interpreting Otherness*. London: Routledge, 2003.

Keller, Catherine. *Face of the Deep: A Theology of Becoming*. London: Routledge, 2003.

Kiblinger, Kristin B. *Buddhist Inclusivism: Attitudes towards Religious Others*. Aldershot, UK: Ashgate, 2005.

Kilby, Karen. "Perichoresis and Projection: Problems with Social Doctrines of the Trinity." *New Blackfriars* 81 (2000) 432–45.

Kipp, Rita Smith, and Susan Rodgers, editors. *Indonesian Religions in Transition*. Tucson, AZ: University of Arizona Press, 1987.

Knitter, Paul F. "Cosmic Confidence or Preferential Option?" In *The Intercultural Challenge of Raimon Panikkar*, edited by Joseph Prabhu, 177–91. Maryknoll, NY: Orbis, 1996.

———. *One Earth, Many Religions: Multifaith Dialogue and Global Responsibility*. Maryknoll, NY: Orbis, 1995.

———. *Introducing Theologies of Religions*. Maryknoll, NY: Orbis, 2002.

Knitter, Paul F., and John Hick, editors. *The Myth of Christian Uniqueness: Toward a Pluralistic Theology of Religions*. Maryknoll, NY: Orbis, 1987.

Komulainen, Jyri. *An Emerging Cosmotheandric Religion? Raimon Panikkar's Pluralistic Theology of Religions*. Leiden: Brill, 2005.

Kwok, Pui-lan. *Postcolonial Imagination and Feminist Theology*. Louisville, KY: Westminster John Knox, 2005.

Bibliography

LaCugna, Catherine M. *God for Us: The Trinity and Christian Life*. San Francisco: HarperSanFrancisco, 1993.
Larson, Gerald J. "Contra Pluralism." In *The Intercultural Challenge of Raimon Panikkar*, edited by Joseph Prabhu, 71–87. Maryknoll, NY: Orbis, 1996.
Lawler, Michael G. "Perichoresis: New Theological Wine in an Old Theological Wineskin." *Horizons* 22 (1995) 49–66.
Lee, Jung Young. *The Trinity in Asian Perspective*. Nashville: Abingdon, 1996.
Leftow, Brian. "Anti Social Trinitarianism." In *The Trinity: An Interdisciplinary Symposium on the Trinity*, edited by Stephen T. Davis, Daniel Kendall and Gerald O'Collins, 203–49. New York: Oxford University Press, 1999.
Lindbeck, George A. *The Nature of Doctrine: Religion and Theology in a Postliberal Age*. Philadelphia: Westminster, 1984.
MacIntyre, Alasdair C. *After Virtue: A Study in Moral Theory*. Notre Dame, IN: University of Notre Dame Press, 1981.
———. *Three Rival Versions of Moral Enquiry: Encyclopedia, Genealogy, and Tradition: Being Gifford Lectures Delivered in the University of Edinburgh in 1988*. Notre Dame, IN: University of Notre Dame Press, 1990.
———. *Whose Justice? Which Rationality?* Notre Dame, IN: University of Notre Dame Press, 1988.
MacPherson, Camilia Gangesingh. *A Critical Reading of the Development of Raimon Panikkar's Thought on the Trinity*. Lanham, MD: University Press of America, 1996.
Manoussakis, John Panteleimon. *God after Metaphysics: A Theological Aesthetic*. Bloomington, IN: Indiana University Press, 2007.
McDougall, Joy Ann. *Pilgrimage of Love: Moltmann on the Trinity and Christian Life*. Reflection and Theory in the Study of Religion. Oxford: Oxford University Press, 2005.
McGaughey, Douglas R. *Strangers and Pilgrims: On the Role of Aporiai in Theology*. Berlin: de Gruyter, 1997.
Medley, Mark S. *Imago Trinitatis: Toward a Relational Understanding of Becoming Human*. Lanham, MD: University Press of America, 2002.
Merleau-Ponty, Maurice. "From Mauss to Claude Lévi-Strauss." In *Signs*, 114–25. Evanston, IL: Northwestern University Press, 1964.
Migliore, Daniel L. *Faith Seeking Understanding: An Introduction to Christian Theology*. Grand Rapids: Eerdmans, 2004.
Milbank, John. "The End of Dialogue." In *Christian Uniqueness Reconsidered: The Myth of a Pluralistic Theology of Religions*, edited by Gavin D'Costa, 174–91. Maryknoll, NY: Orbis, 1990.
Miyahira, Nozomu. *Towards a Theology of the Concord of God: A Japanese Perspective on the Trinity*. Carlisle, UK: Paternoster, 2000.
Moltmann, Jürgen. *A Broad Place: An Autobiography*. Minneapolis: Fortress, 2008.
———. *The Coming of God: Christian Eschatology*. Minneapolis: Fortress, 1996.
———. *The Crucified God: The Cross of Christ as the Foundation and Criticism of Christian Theology*. London: SCM, 1974.
———. *Experiences in Theology: Ways and Forms of Christian Theology*. Minneapolis: Fortress, 2000.
———. *God in Creation: A New Theology of Creation and the Spirit of God*. Minneapolis: Fortress, 1993.

Bibliography

———. "God's Kenosis in the Creation and Consummation of the World." In *The Work of Love: Creation as Kenosis*, edited by J. C. Polkinghorne, 137–51. Grand Rapids: Eerdmans, 2001.

———. *In the End—the Beginning: The Life of Hope*. Minneapolis: Fortress, 2004.

———. "Perichoresis: An Old Magic Word for a New Trinitarian Theology." In *Trinity, Community, and Power: Mapping Trajectories in Wesleyan Theology*, edited by M. Douglas Meeks, 111–25. Nashville, TN: Kingswood, 2000.

———. *The Spirit of Life: A Universal Affirmation*. Minneapolis: Fortress, 1992.

———. *The Trinity and the Kingdom: The Doctrine of God*. Minneapolis: Fortress, 1993.

———. *The Way of Jesus Christ: Christology in Messianic Dimensions*. Minneapolis: Fortress, 1993.

Mulder, Niels. *Mysticism in Java: Ideology in Indonesia*. Yogyakarta, Indonesia: Penerbit Kanisius, 2005.

Neville, Robert C. *Behind the Masks of God: An Essay toward Comparative Theology*. Albany, NY: State University of New York Press, 1991.

———. *God the Creator: On the Transcendence and Presence of God*. Albany, NY: State University of New York Press, 1992.

———. *On the Scope and Truth of Theology: Theology as Symbolic Engagement*. London: T. & T. Clark, 2006.

———. *The Tao and the Daimon: Segments of a Religious Inquiry*. Albany, NY: State University of New York Press, 1982.

———. "Toward a Theology of World Religions: The Existential Threats." In *The Stranger's Religion: Fascination and Fear*, edited by Anna Lännström, 113–30. Notre Dame, IN: University of Notre Dame Press, 2004.

Neville, Robert C., editor. *The Human Condition*. Albany, NY: State University of New York Press, 2001.

Newbigin, Lesslie. *The Gospel in a Pluralist Society*. Grand Rapids: Eerdmans, 1989.

O'Leary, Joseph S. "Questions to and from a Tradition in Disarray." In *After God: Richard Kearney and the Religious Turn in Continental Philosophy*, edited by John P. Manoussakis, 185–207. New York: Fordham University Press, 2006.

Oliver, Harold H. *Metaphysics, Theology, and Self: Relational Essays*. Macon, GA: Mercer University Press, 2006.

Otto, Randall E. "The Use and Abuse of Perichoresis in Recent Theology." *Scottish Journal of Theology* 54 (2001) 366–84.

Ousterhout, Robert G. *The Architecture of the Kariye Camii in Istanbul*. Washington, DC: Dumbarton Oaks Research Library and Collection, 1987.

Panikkar, Raimundo. *Blessed Simplicity: The Monk as Universal Archetype*. New York: Seabury, 1982.

———. *Christophany: The Fullness of Man*. Maryknoll, NY: Orbis, 2004.

———. "Cosmic Evolution, Human History and Trinitarian Life." *The Teilhard Review* 25 (1990) 61–71.

———. *The Cosmotheandric Experience: Emerging Religious Consciousness*. Maryknoll, NY: Orbis, 1993.

———. *Cultural Disarmament: The Way to Peace*. Louisville, KY: Westminster John Knox, 1995.

———. *A Dwelling Place for Wisdom*. Louisville, KY: Westminster/John Knox, 1993.

———. "Eruption of Truth: An Interview with Raimon Panikkar. Interview by Henri Tincq." *Christian Century* 117 (2000) 834–36.

———. *The Experience of God: Icons of the Mystery*. Minneapolis: Fortress, 2006.
———. *The Intrareligious Dialogue*. New York: Paulist, 1978.
———. *Invisible Harmony: Essays on Contemplation and Responsibility*. Minneapolis: Fortress, 1995.
———. "The Jordan, the Tiber, and the Ganges: Three Kairological Moments of Christic Self-Consciousness." In *The Myth of Christian Uniqueness: Toward a Pluralistic Theology of Religions*, edited by Paul F. Knitter and John Hick, 89–116. Maryknoll, NY: Orbis, 1987.
———. "The Meaning of Christ's Name in the Universal Economy of Salvation." In *Service and Salvation*, edited by Joseph Pathrapankal, 125–218. Bangalore: Theological Publications, 1973.
———. "The Mysticism of Jesus the Christ." In *Mysticism in Shaivism and Christianity*, edited by Bettina Bäumer, 73–173. New Delhi: Printworld, 1997.
———. "Reader's Response." *International Bulletin of Missionary Research* 13 (1989) 80.
———. *The Rhythm of Being: The Gifford Lectures*. Maryknoll, NY: Orbis, 2009.
———. "A Self-Critical Dialogue." In *The Intercultural Challenge of Raimon Panikkar*, edited by Joseph Prabhu, 227–91. Maryknoll, NY: Orbis, 1996.
———. *The Silence of God: The Answer of the Buddha*. Maryknoll, NY: Orbis, 1989.
———. "Toward an Ecumenical Theandric Spirituality." *Journal of Ecumenical Studies* 5 (1968) 507–34.
———. *The Trinity and the Religious Experience of Man: Icon-Person-Mystery*. New York: Orbis, 1973.
———. *The Trinity and World Religions: Icon-Person-Mystery*. Madras: The Christian Institute for the Study of Religion and Society, 1970.
———. *The Unknown Christ of Hinduism: Towards an Ecumenical Christophany*. Maryknoll, NY: Orbis, 1981.
Pannenberg, Wolfhart. *Systematic Theology, Vol. 2*. Grand Rapids: Eerdmans, 1994.
Parks, Miles Robert. "A Trinitarianism of Interreligious Engagement: The Thought of Raimon Panikkar and Its Contribution to Christian Theology of Religions." Ph.D. diss., Boston University, 2001.
Paul VI. *Declaration on the Relation of the Church to Non-Christian Religions (Nostra Aetate)*, 1965. No pages. Online: http://www.vatican.va/archive/hist_councils/ii_vatican_council/documents/vat-ii_decl_19651028_nostra-aetate_en.html.
Paul VI. *Dogmatic Constitution on the Church (Lumen Gentium)*, 1964. No pages. Online: http://www.vatican.va/archive/hist_councils/ii_vatican_council/documents/vat-ii_const_19641121_lumen-gentium_en.html.
Paul VI. *Pastoral Constitution on the Church in the Modern Word (Gaudium Et Spes)*, 1965. No pages. Online: http://www.vatican.va/archive/hist_councils/ii_vatican_council/documents/vat-ii_cons_19651207_gaudium-et-spes_en.html.
Perry, Tim S. Radical Difference: A Defence of Hendrik Kraemer's Theology of Religions. Waterloo, ON: Wilfrid Laurier University Press, 2001.
Persoon, Gerard A. "Religion and Ethnic Identity of the Mentawaians on Siberut (West Sumatra)." In *Hinduism in Modern Indonesia: A Minority Religion between Local, National, and Global Interests*, edited by Martin Ramstedt, 144–59. London: RoutledgeCurzon, 2004.
Peters, Ted. *God as Trinity: Relationality and Temporality in Divine Life*. Louisville, KY: Westminster/John Knox, 1993.

Bibliography

Placher, William C. *The Triune God: An Essay in Postliberal Theology*. Louisville, KY: Westminster John Knox, 2007.

Polanyi, Michael. *Personal Knowledge: Towards a Post-Critical Philosophy*, Gifford Lectures. Chicago: University of Chicago Press, 1964.

Prestige, Leonard G. *God in Patristic Thought*. London: SPCK, 1956.

Race, Alan. *Christians and Religious Pluralism: Patterns in the Christian Theology of Religions*. Maryknoll, NY: Orbis, 1983.

Rahner, Karl. *Theological Investigations, Vol. 1*. London: Darton, Longman & Todd, 1965.

———. *The Trinity*. New York: Herder & Herder, 1970.

———. *Foundations of Christian Faith: An Introduction to the Idea of Christianity*. New York: Seabury, 1978.

Raj, Anthony S. *A New Hermeneutic of Reality: Raimon Panikkar's Cosmotheandric Vision*. Bern: Lang, 1998.

Rescher, Nicholas. *The Strife of Systems: An Essay on the Grounds and Implications of Philosophical Diversity*. Pittsburgh, PA: University of Pittsburgh Press, 1985.

Rivera, Mayra. *The Touch of Transcendence: A Postcolonial Theology of God*. Louisville, KY: Westminster John Knox, 2007.

Rundell, John. "Imaginings, Narratives, and Otherness: On Diacritical Hermeneutics." In *Traversing the Imaginary: Richard Kearney and the Postmodern Challenge*, edited by Peter Gratton and John P. Manoussakis, 103–16. Evanston, IL: Northwestern University Press, 2007.

Saarinen, Risto. "After Rescher: Pluralism as Preferentialism." In *Theology and the Religions: A Dialogue*, edited by Viggo Mortensen, 409–13. Grand Rapids: Eerdmans, 2003.

Sallis, John. *Chorology: On Beginning in Plato's Timaeus*. Studies in Continental Thought. Bloomington, IN: Indiana University Press, 1999.

Schmidt-Leukel, Perry. "Exclusivism, Inclusivism, Pluralism: The Tripolar Typology—Clarified and Reaffirmed." In *The Myth of Religious Superiority: Multifaith Explorations of Religious Pluralism*, edited by Paul F. Knitter Knitter, 13–27. Maryknoll, NY: Orbis, 2005.

Schrag, Calvin O. *Convergence amidst Difference: Philosophical Conversations across National Boundaries*. New York: State University of New York Press, 2004.

———. *The Resources of Rationality: A Response to the Postmodern Challenge*. Bloomington, IN: Indiana University Press, 1992.

———. *The Self after Postmodernity*. New Haven, CT: Yale University Press, 1997.

Smart, Ninian, and Steven Konstantine. *Christian Systematic Theology in a World Context*. Minneapolis: Fortress, 1991.

Stewart, Angus. *John of Damascus and the Perichoresis*. No pages. Online: http://www.cprf.co.uk/articles/covenant4.htm.

Stout, Jeffrey. *Democracy and Tradition*, New Forum Books. Princeton, NJ: Princeton University Press, 2004.

———. *Ethics after Babel: The Languages of Morals and Their Discontents*. Princeton, NJ: Princeton University Press, 2001.

Stramara, Daniel F. "Gregory of Nyssa's Terminology for Trinitarian Perichoresis." *Vigiliae Christianae* 52 (1998) 257–63.

Sugirtharajah, Rasiah S., editor. *Asian Faces of Jesus*. Maryknoll, NY: Orbis, 1993.

Tanner, Kathryn. *Jesus, Humanity and the Trinity: A Brief Systematic Theology*. Edinburgh: T. & T. Clark, 2001.

Thomas, Owen C. "Religious Plurality and Contemporary Philosophy: A Critical Survey." *The Harvard Theological Review* 87 (1994) 197–213.
Törönen, Melchisedec. *Union and Distinction in the Thought of St. Maximus the Confessor.* Oxford: Oxford University Press, 2007.
Torrance, Thomas F. *The Christian Doctrine of God: One Being Three Persons.* Edinburgh: T. & T. Clark, 1996.
Twombly, Charles C. "Perichoresis and Personhood in the Thought of John of Damascus." PhD diss., Emory University, 1992.
Vanhoozer, Kevin J. "Does the Trinity Belong in a Theology of Religions? On Angling in the Rubicon and the 'Identity' of God." In *The Trinity in a Pluralistic Age: Theological Essays on Culture and Religion*, edited by Kevin J. Vanhoozer, 41–71. Grand Rapids: Eerdmans, 1997.
Vidu, Adonis. "Lindbeck's Scheme-Content Distinction: A Critique of the Dualism between Orders of Language." *Journal for the Study of Religions and Ideologies* 9 (2004) 110–23.
Vishnevskaya, Elena. "Divinization as Perichoretic Embrace in Maximus the Confessor." In *Partakers of the Divine Nature: The History and Development of Deification in the Christian Traditions*, edited by Michael J. Christensen and Jeffery A. Wittung, 132–45. Madison, Teaneck, NJ: Fairleigh Dickinson University Press, 2007.
Volf, Miroslav. *After Our Likeness: The Church as the Image of the Trinity.* Grand Rapids: Eerdmans, 1998.
―――. *Exclusion and Embrace: A Theological Exploration of Identity, Otherness, and Reconciliation.* Nashville, TN: Abingdon, 1996.
―――. "'The Trinity Is Our Social Programme': The Doctrine of the Trinity and the Shape of Social Engagement." In *The Doctrine of God and Theological Ethics*, edited by Michael C. Banner and Alan J. Torrance, 105–24. London: T. & T. Clark, 2006.
Wegter-McNelly, Kirk. "Natural Evil in a Divinely Entangled World." In *Physics and Cosmology, Vol. 1: Scientific Perspectives on the Problem of Natural Evil*, edited by Nancey Murphy, Robert J. Russell and William R. Stoeger, 219–56. Vatican City State & Berkeley, CA: Vatican Observatory Publications & Center for Theology and the Natural Sciences, 2007.
―――. "The World, Entanglement, and God: Quantum Theory and the Christian Doctrine of Creation." PhD diss., Graduate Theological Union, 2003.
Westphal, Merold. "Hermeneutics and the God of Promise." In *After God: Richard Kearney and the Religious Turn in Continental Philosophy*, edited by John P. Manoussakis, 78–93. New York: Fordham University Press, 2006.
Williams, Rowan. "Trinity and Pluralism." In *Christian Uniqueness Reconsidered: The Myth of a Pluralistic Theology of Religions*, edited by Gavin D'Costa, 3–15. Maryknoll, NY: Orbis, 1990.
Wilson-Kastner, Patricia. *Faith, Feminism, and the Christ.* Philadelphia: Fortress, 1983.
Wolfson, Harry A. *The Philosophy of the Church Fathers: Faith, Trinity, Incarnation, Vol. I.* Rev. ed. Cambridge: Harvard University Press, 1970.
Yewangoe, Andreas A. "The Trinity in the Context of Tribal Religion." *Studies in Interreligious Dialogue* 13 (2003) 86–105.
Yong, Amos. *Beyond the Impasse: Toward a Pneumatological Theology of Religions.* Grand Rapids: Baker Academic, 2003.
―――. *Spirit-Word-Community: Theological Hermeneutics in Trinitarian Perspective.* Aldershot, UK: Ashgate, 2002.

Bibliography

Yusa, Michiko. *Zen and Philosophy: An Intellectual Biography of Nishida Kitarō*. Honolulu: University of Hawai'i Press, 2002.

Zizioulas, John. *Being as Communion: Studies in Personhood and the Church*. Crestwood, NY: St. Vladimir's Seminary Press, 1985.

Index

Abe, Masao, 169–70
Absolutism, 13, 59–60, 62–63, 76, 101, 152
Aliran kebatinan, 172
Anacyclesis, 110
Apophatism, 26, 53
Aposkatastasis, 86
Appropriation, 2, 7, 25, 28, 54, 56–57, 65, 89–90, 100–101, 153, 155–56, 165–67, 172, 182, 184
Aquinas, Thomas, 38, 110
Atheism, 54, 64, 129, 164, 168, 170–71
Augustine, 25, 52, 54, 56, 109, 118

Balthasar, Hans Urs von, 112, 114, 160, 161–62
Barnes, Michael, 20
Barth Karl, 4, 87, 92, 115–17, 158
Boff, Leonardo, 4, 130–32, 134, 137, 150
Bohm's holographic model, 4, 56, 71
Brahman-Atman, 22–23, 27, 30, 53, 166–67
Brück, Michael von, 167
Buddhism, 13, 26–27, 29, 32, 48, 53–54, 60, 63, 74, 82, 86, 89, 96–97, 100, 155, 160, 168–70, 172, 184
Butler, Michael, 112–13
Buxton, Graham, 132
Buxton, Graham, 4, 132

Caputo, John D., 147
Christophany, 24, 98
Circum-incedere. See *Circumincessio*

Circumincessio, 1, 14, 17, 96, 110–11
Circumincessio, 1, 14, 25, 17, 96, 110
Circum-in-sedere. See *Circuminsessio*
Circuminsessio, 1, 110, 129
Cobb, John, 4, 56, 75–76, 169–70
Cohn-Sherbok, Dan, 29, 30, 32
Coinherence, 1, 68, 99–100, 107–8, 130
Communicatio idiomatum, 105, 107
Communion-in-difference, 56, 92, 100
Comparative theology, 11, 44, 102, 169, 175
Confucianism, 172
Cousins, Ewert H., 18, 26, 27, 64, 82
Creatio continua, 24
Creatio ex inferno, 121
Creatio ex nihilo, 120–21, 170
Crisp, Oliver, 1, 111
Crosswhite, James, 80
Cusanus, Nicolaus, 145

D'Costa, Gavin, 2–3, 5–6, 8–12, 28–44, 52, 57–59, 61, 63–70, 74–75, 82–84, 86, 88, 90–91, 95, 98–99, 101–2, 144, 152–54, 156, 173–75, 177, 183–84; Auto-description of religions, 63, 67, 70, 152; Critique of pluralism, 29–32; Inchoate reality of the Kingdom, 41, 44, 66, 99, 184; Move from inclusivism to exclusivism, 33–38, 44; Relation with Karl Rahner, 33, 41, 61, 83–84; Silence toward other religions, 39, 44, 65–66, 86;

197

Index

D'Costa, Gavin (*cont.*)
  Tradition-specific position, 29, 30–32, 36–37, 42, 44, 61, 64, 70, 75, 183; Two hands of God, 28, 34–35, 40, 61, 90, 163, 173–74
D'Sa, Francis X., 16
Dance of the Trinity, 1, 95, 139–42, 146–48, 151, 159, 162, 168, 175, 178, 180–82
Davis, Stephen T., 5
Deification. See *Theosis*
Derrida, Jacques, 147
Dialectic between particularity and universality, 1, 7–9, 33–34, 40, 48, 58–59, 40, 152, 174–75, 178–79
Dialectic between Son and the Spirit, 28, 35, 61, 163
DiNoia, Joseph A., 44
Divinization. See *Theosis*
Dupuis, Jacques, 5, 28, 41

Ecclesial-perichoresis, 99
Edwards, Denis, 4
Embrace, 43, 102, 128, 132, 139, 143, 150, 153, 168, 173, 178, 182–83, 185
Enlightenment, 29, 35, 46, 61
Eschatology, 7, 34, 41, 43, 65–67, 83–84, 86, 99, 103, 117, 119, 126, 128, 139, 143–46, 150–51, 162, 173, 178, 180, 182
Excess, 5, 83–84, 86, 133, 143, 147, 151, 153, 156, 161–62, 164, 173, 180
Exclusivism. See Race's typology
Exitus-reditus, 142, 151

Fedorov, Nicholas, 4, 132, 138–39
Feminist perspective, 4, 121, 157, 175–76
Fletcher, Jeannine H., 157–58
Flett, John G., 85, 92, 100–101, 155

Ford, Lewis S., 144
Foundationalism, 35, 77
Fredericks, James L., 44, 65–66, 102

Gaudium et Spes, 40, 42
God who may be, *see* possible God
God's-eye perspective, 49–50, 62
Gratia non tollit naturam, sed perficit, 38
Gregory Nazianzus, 10, 104–6, 108–9
Gregory of Nyssa, 109–10
Griffiths, Bede, 167
Gunton, Colin E., 121–23

He khora ton zonton, 162
Heim, S. Mark, 2–3, 5–6, 8–10, 12, 26, 44–59, 61–70, 73–76, 78–80, 82–86, 88–95, 99–103, 152–57, 166, 168–69, 171, 173, 175, 177, 179, 183–84; Communion as the third dimension, 52, 55–56, 62, 85–86, 92, 94, 99–100; Critique of pluralism, 45–48; Impersonal relation as the first dimension, 52–55, 92, 99–100, 168; Multiple religious ends, 5, 10, 44–45, 50–57, 62–63, 66–68, 75, 78–79, 85–86, 91–94, 154–55, 157, 166, 175, 177, 184; Personal relation as the second dimension, 52, 54–55, 92, 100, 171; Pluralistic inclusivism or inclusivist pluralism, 48, 50–52, 62, 68–69; Rescher's orientational pluralism, 8, 46, 48–51, 57, 62–63, 67, 70–71, 73–76, 78, 84, 153–54, 179, 183
Held, Klaus, 169–70
Hick, John, 4, 8, 29–33, 46–47, 49, 51, 61, 67, 69
Hilary Poitiers, 109

Index

Hinduism, 13, 18, 20–21, 26–27, 29–30, 32, 46, 53, 60, 63–64, 69, 74, 82, 86, 89, 100, 102, 155, 166–68, 172
Hodgson, Peter C., 98, 148, 155
Hunt, Anne, 1, 4
Huyssteen, Wentzel van, 77
Hybridity, 154, 158, 162, 174–82
Hypostatic union, 1, 104–14, 132–33, 149

Identist pluralism, 4
Immanent and economic Trinity, 7, 17, 41, 56, 80–83, 85–86, 117, 131, 133–34, 139, 141–44, 151, 167, 171
incarnatio continua, 24
Incarnation, 1, 25, 30, 39–40, 106, 109, 112–13, 119, 121–26, 128, 133, 145, 150, 161, 163, 170, 178, 180
Inclusivism. *See* Race's typology
Indonesia, 11, 172
Inner life of the Triune God, 1, 4–5, 14, 17, 25, 43, 53, 95–96, 100, 109, 116–20, 124, 128–30, 132, 134–37, 141, 144, 146, 150, 158, 160, 167–69
Irenaeus, 28, 34, 61, 90, 148, 173–74
Islam, 26, 30, 38, 55, 64, 89, 107, 155–56, 171–72

Jainism, 172
Jantzen, Grace, 55
John of Damascus, 10, 104, 106–9, 114, 127
John Paul II, 39, 40, 66, 91
Johnson, Elizabeth, 4, 140, 141
Johnson, Keith E., 82
Judaism, 26, 29–30, 38, 64, 89, 119, 122, 155, 171–72, 176

Kabbalist tradition, 119–20, 150
Kantianism, 30, 31, 54

Kaplan, Stephen, 4, 56, 71–73
Kärkkäinen, Velli-Matti, 2, 4, 27–28, 40, 43, 60, 65, 68, 82, 84, 95, 142–43
Kearney, Richard, 6–7, 9–10, 139, 144–49, 160, 168–69, 173, 182
Keller, Catherine, 121
Kenosis and emptiness, 23, 53–54, 121–22, 124–25, 144, 164, 168–70
Khora, 6, 9, 121, 123–24, 146–48, 159–64, 168–70
Kilby, Karen, 134–36, 139, 150
Kingdom of God, 41, 44, 66, 83, 134, 136, 138, 146, 184
Kitarō, Nishida, 169
Knitter, Paul F., 3–4, 8, 11, 16, 29–33, 41, 44–47, 49, 51, 61, 67, 69
Knitter's typology, 3, 44
Komulainen, Jyri, 3, 8, 16, 97
Konstantine, Steven, 52–54, 91
Kwok Pui-lan, 175–77

LaCugna, Catherine, 1, 4, 81, 87, 111, 131, 134, 139–43, 145, 161, 167
Lama, Dalai, 29, 32, 65
Larson, Gerald J., 59–60
Latin Trinity, 4, 5, 141
Lawler, Michael G., 105
Lee, Jung Young, 11
Leftow, Brian, 5
Lévi-Strauss, Claude, 7
Lindbeck, George A., 44, 135
Local religions, 172–73
Logos, 26, 35, 40–41, 59–60, 71, 77, 82, 90–91, 113, 123, 170, 173, 175, 177
Lumen Gentium, 38, 40
Luria, Isaac, 119–20, 150

Index

MacIntyre, Alasdair, 29, 31, 35–36, 61, 63–65
MacPherson, Camilia G.m 17, 27, 86
Manoussakis, John P., 162–63
Maximus the Confessor, 10, 24, 104–5, 111–14, 132
McDougall, Joy Ann, 118–19, 125, 137, 139, 150
McGaughey, Douglas R., 135
Merleau-Ponty, Maurice, 78–80
Metachôrêsis, 112
Migliore, Daniel L., 115
Milbank, John, 29, 35–36, 61, 63–65
Moltmann, Jürgen, 4, 6–7, 9–10, 104, 110, 115–34, 137–38, 140, 144–46, 149–51, 154, 157–60, 167–68, 170–71
Monotheism, 5, 18, 54, 71, 115–16, 127, 130, 171
Multiple religious belongings, 64, 181
Mutual indwelling, 1, 43, 53, 82, 84, 98–99, 104–51, 160, 168–70
Mythos and *pneuma*, 59, 60, 71, 173

Nature-perichoresis, 1, 104, 105–7, 110–11, 113–14, 132–33, 149
Neville, Robert C., 11, 94, 120, 136, 166–67, 169–70
Newbigin, Lesslie, 80
Nirguna-saguna Brahman, 167
Nirvana, 26, 53, 169–70
Nostra Aetate, 38–39

O'Leary, Joseph S., 145
Oikonomia and *theologia*, 134, 139, 141–43, 151, 167
Oliver, Harold H., 150
Omnium gatherum, 150
Open Trinity, 6–7, 125, 150
Opera trinitatis ad extra sunt indivisa, 28, 52, 54, 155, 171
Origen, 86

Otto, Randall E., 114, 132–33

Panentheism, 117, 119, 121, 128–29, 150, 154, 157, 168
Panikkar, Raimundo 2, 5–6, 8–28, 41, 44, 52, 54, 57–60, 62–66, 69–75, 81–84, 86, 88–102, 140, 148, 152–6, 166–68, 171, 173, 175, 177, 184;
Advaita, 18–22, 25–26, 53, 60, 68, 94, 184; Cosmic confidence, 71, 73, 173;
Cosmotheadrism, 5, 12–13, 16–19, 22, 25, 27, 60, 81, 82, 86, 92, 94–98, 101, 148, 154–55, 175; Homeomorphic equivalents, 18, 19, 166; Iconolatry, 19–22, 26, 54, 171; Individual vs. person, 88;
Karmamārga, jnānamārga, and *bhaktimārga*, 20–22, 46;
Metaphor of window, 14, 60, 74; Personalism, 21–22, 26, 89, 90; Perspectivism, 14–15, 19, 74; *Pratītyasamutpāda*, 96–97; Radical Trinity, 16–17, 28, 81–82, 84, 86, 96; Three forms of spirituality, 19–27, 96, 155; Transcendence vs. immanence, 20–24, 89, 94; Version of pluralism, 13–16, 26–27, 58–60, 62–64, 69, 71–73
Panikkar, Raimundo, 2, 5–6, 8–28, 41, 44, 52, 54, 57–60, 62–66, 69–75, 81–84, 86, 88–102, 140, 148, 152–56, 166–68, 171, 173, 175, 177, 184
Pannenberg, Wolfhart, 119, 122–23, 126, 178
Pantheism, 18, 119, 129, 159
Parallelism, 69
Parks, Miles R., 60–61

Participation, 1, 6, 9, 24, 33, 43, 86, 92, 96–99, 102–4, 112–15, 117, 125, 127, 132, 137–39, 148–51, 157–59, 162–64, 172, 175, 178, 180, 182
Particularism, 75, 77–78, 154, 179
Person vs. individual, 87–88, 91, 104
Personal relation and religions, 6, 52, 55, 89, 168, 171
Person-in-communion, 92, 104
Person-in-relation, 87
Person-perichoresis, 1, 6, 17, 43, 82, 96–98, 104, 106, 108–11, 114, 125–29, 132–33, 137, 139–41, 148–49, 155, 159–60, 166–67, 175, 182
Peters, Ted, 4, 81, 87–88, 134–39, 143, 150–51
Plenitude. See Excess
Pluralism. See Race's typology
Polanyi, Michael, 80
Possible God, 6–7, 9–10, 139, 143–49, 172–73, 179, 182
Postcolonialism, 175–76, 178
Postliberalism, 3, 134–35
Postmodernity, 63, 65, 77–80, 88, 180, 184
Post-pluralism, 3–4, 8, 11, 58, 63, 70
Preparatio evangelica, 38, 40–42
Prestige, Leonard G., 108, 110
Process thought, 56, 76, 144
Pseudo-Cyril of Alexandria, 10, 104, 106–8

Quaternitas, 24, 89, 127

Race, Alan, 2–3, 32, 44, 69,
Race's typology, 2–2, 12, 32–34, 44, 50, 52, 59, 61, 66, 69–70, 72, 183
Radhakrishnan, 29, 32
Rahner, Karl, 4, 33, 41, 61, 83–84, 87, 115–16, 131, 141, 158, 161–62

Rahner's Rule, 33, 83, 116, 143, 161
Reality-based model of the immanent-economic Trinity, 86, 94, 101
Reality-perichoresis, 1, 5–6, 17, 82, 84, 96–99, 109, 111–15, 125–29, 132–33, 143–44, 148–51, 154–55, 157–58, 160, 163, 166–68, 172–73, 175, 177–78, 181–82
Redemptoris Missio, 39–42, 66
Relativism, 13, 33, 35, 59, 74–77, 101
Relativity, 13–15, 81–82, 96–97
Resurrection of Christ, 39, 43, 93, 130, 175
Revelation, 23–24, 26, 35–36, 41, 53, 83–84, 111–13, 118, 131, 165
Rivera, Mayra, 165

Salvation-history, 45, 51, 55, 83–84, 86
Salvation-history-based model of the immanent-economic Trinity, 86
Samsara, 169–70, 175
Schmidt-Leukel, Perry, 2–3
Schrag, Calvin O., 77–80, 154, 179–81, 184–85
Self-contraction. See Zimzum
Self-limitation. See Zimzum
Self-witdrawal. See Zimzum
Shekinah, 120, 124–25, 128, 150
Sin, 56, 93–94, 139, 161, 175, 177
Smart, Ninian, 52–54, 91
Smith, Wilfred C., 46–49, 51, 61, 67, 69
Social Trinity, 4–5, 91–92, 115, 126, 130–32, 134–39, 150–51
Society-perichoresis, 130, 132–33, 137, 139, 149–51
Spivak, Gayatri, 165
Stewart, Angus, 106
Stout, Jeffrey, 7, 64

Index

Summus pontifex, 24
Śūnyatā, 26
Superabundance of God. *See* Excess
Surplus. *See* Excess

Taoism, 23, 54, 172
Theo-cosmic-pneumatic, 98, 148, 155, 163, 175, 177
Theological bricolage, 7, 58, 101
Theosis, 105–7, 112, 132, 149
Törönen, Melchisedec, 112–13
Transversality, 8, 58, 70, 73, 77–80, 154, 178–85, 183
Trinity is our social program, 4, 132, 137–39
Tritheism, 4, 82, 87, 108, 115–16, 126, 150
Two hands of God, 28, 34–35, 40, 61, 90, 148, 162–63, 167, 173–74, 178, 182

Unity of reality, 5–6, 164, 166–67
Unity-in-difference, 108, 112
Unity-in-distinction, 56

Vacatio ex Deo, 121, 123–24, 159–61, 164, 168, 170, 180
Vanhoozer, Kevin J., 159
Vatican II, 29, 37, 39, 65–66
Vedanta, 18, 53
Vestigium Trinitatis, 82, 131
Volf, Miroslav, 4, 132–3, 137–39, 143, 148–51, 162, 184–85

Wegter-McNelly, Kirk, 121, 126, 178
Westphal, Merold, 145
Whitehead, Alfred N., 4, 56, 144

Yewangoe, Andreas A., 172
Yong, Amos, 5, 28, 95, 174, 179

Zimzum, 53, 100, 117–24, 128–29, 150, 157, 159–60, 168–70, 180
Zizioulas, John, 91–92

www.ingramcontent.com/pod-product-compliance
Lightning Source LLC
Chambersburg PA
CBHW070324230426
43663CB00011B/2208